Finding Faith
in the
Biblical God

Table of Contents

Introduction

What comes to mind when you hear "The United States of America"? The important keyword is "United." What does it mean? One definition posted on the internet from Oxford Languages is, "joined together politically, for a common purpose, or by common feelings."[1] Is that what you think of when you hear the term "The United States"? In 2020, this does not seem to be the case.

There is little agreement of what the problems of our country are, let alone the solutions. Consider the term "global warming." Is it a serious problem or a temporary cycle? Some people argue that it is a severe problem that should be addressed immediately. Others believe that despite current melting glaciers, the world has experienced several hot and cold cycles over millions of years. Therefore, the problem is not as dire as it seems.

We have seen mass shootings by lone gunmen in recent years that is unmatched in our nations history. The Las Vegas shooting in 2017 resulted in 59 killed and more than 500 injured. Is lack of gun control a problem? Some argue that guns are a problem. Others argue that they are not the problem, "Guns don't shoot people," "People shoot people." We have a people problem, not a gun control problem.

Do we have an illegal immigration problem? How many illegals are there? According to factcheck.org, regarding immigration, they write, "The Pew Research Center estimates the number at 10.7

---

[1] *united.* (n.d.). Lexico.Com. https://www.lexico.com/en/definition/united

million in 2016.[2] However, they also write, "… a study by researchers at Yale University and the Massachusetts Institute of Technology estimated that the illegal immigration population was much higher: an average 22.1 million for 2016."[3] Which is the correct number?

We had a Presidential election in 2016 that was very unusual. Several polls projected that the Democratic contender Hillary Clinton would win by about 3% right up to the actual election. But as it turned out, the Republican contender Donald Trump won. The Democrats cried foul; "Donald Trump only won as a result of his relationship with the Russian government." Therefore, congress initiated a Special Counsel investigation headed up by Robert Mueller. After a lengthy and detailed investigation, the results showed that Donald Trump was not guilty of collusion; however, they found "irregularities."

Primarily Democrats wanted a "deeper dive" into the irregularities specified by the Special Counsel investigation. These produced further accusations. Meanwhile, the President believed that the former Democratic Vice President Joe Biden might have applied political pressure to the Ukrainians for his son's financial gain. Therefore, he tried to get the Ukrainians to investigate. The Democrats' charged that President Trump had used his office's authority illegally to pressure the investigation of the former Vice President. The Democrat-controlled House of Representatives impeached the President, but the Republican-held Senate disagreed. The President proudly and confidently proclaimed his innocence of wrongdoing. Democrats were furious. As a result, we saw the House's Democratic-led Speaker rip up the President's State of the Union speech on national television in February 2020.

---

[2] Robertson, L. (2019, June 7). *Illegal Immigration Statistics*. FactCheck.Org. https://www.factcheck.org/2018/06/illegal-immigration-statistics/

[3] Ibid

Push…, pushback…, push harder…, pushback harder. Going into the November 2020 election, the political divide was at a fever pitch.

In 2020, we also experienced a pandemic that caused the worst unemployment since the great depression beginning in 1929 and lasting through 1939. Everyone agreed that the pandemic's origin was in Wuhan, China, but the dispute was how it happened. Was it planned? Was it an experiment that had gone awry? Why didn't China notify the United States sooner? When did U.S. officials learn about it, and could they have done more to control it? Again, there was significant disagreement. Returning to the political divide, Democrats claimed that the President knew about it and should have done something sooner. However, the President said that he immediately stopped all flights from China from coming into the country as soon as he knew about it. He accused the Democrats of not taking the pandemic seriously, and many of them making fun of him when he stopped the flights. We saw "accuse and confront" by both sides, followed by "deny and make counterclaims."

There was also great turmoil as the nation dealt with the murder of a black man, George Floyd, on May 25th, 2020. One of the arresting police officers was charged with 2nd-degree manslaughter after keeping his knee on Floyd's neck for 8 minutes and 46 seconds as he laid face down and handcuffed. The public outcry of police injustice resulted in violent protests across the country, demands for police reform, and demand for defunding police departments in some cities.

Floyd had originally been charged for passing a counterfeit $20 bill. The idea that a black man should lose his life for such a minor offense screamed racial injustice. In addition to racial injustice, two points were abundantly clear. White men don't understand what it is like to live in a black man's community and culture. Similarly, blacks do not know how difficult it is for police officers to maintain law and order.

These are just a few examples of the many high profile arguments, confrontations, and injustices we have seen during the last several years. As we continue to watch news media and listen to others speak about issues, our opinions and emotions grow. Human nature causes us to be swayed by both news sources and the views of people we trust. Conversely, if we don't trust news sources because we believe they are biased or are trying to push an agenda, we usually dig in our heals and move in the opposite direction.

We are supposed to be united, "joined together politically, for a common purpose, or by common feelings." But we presently don't see much of this in our country. Instead, we see great divisiveness. A friend said he is losing faith in humanity. Our easy and immediate access to vast sources of information (sound, flawed, real, and made up) is intensifying the problem. We all need to step back and take a breath (if it's possible).

Our most essential differences appear to be over politics and racism. I agree that at the practical, everyday, surface level, these are huge issues. However, there is a more fundamental, underlying problem. It lies deep within our soul. It involves how we should treat people. How do we get people to understand and respect our fellow citizens? How should we take care of others? How do we get people to believe that:

> **"We hold these truths to be self-evident, that all men are created equal, that they are endowed by their Creator with certain unalienable Rights, that among these are Life, Liberty and the Pursuit of Happiness."**

Unfortunately, our thinking has become skewed. We have lost our compass. Many no longer consider that all men are created equal by a loving God.

Mike Huckabee, a former governor of Arkansas and presidential candidate, recently talked about the racial protests:

"One thing that I would hope people start realizing. This is not a political divide, this is a spiritual divide. This isn't so much a skin problem, it is a sin problem. It's a problem when people think they are better than others. If you have cops who don't believe their authority is limited to the law and you have a guy who puts his knee on the guy's neck and kills him, that's a sin problem," Huckabee said.

Huckabee explained that the 'Ultimate government of the United States is not the federal, state, and local level institutions, it is self-governance.'"[4]

Huckabee is just one of many people who believe that our society's problems live within the attitude and control of each individual. Along the same line, Martin Luther King Jr. occasionally spoke about the brokenness of humanity. He said in his August 11th, 1957 sermon "Conquering Self-Centeredness"[5]:

"An individual has not begun to live until he can rise above the narrow horizons of his particular individualistic concerns to the broader concerns of all humanity. And this is one of the big problems of life, that so many people never quite get to the point of rising above self. And so they end up the tragic victims

---

[4] Nelson, J. (2020, June 3). *Mike Huckabee rips Mayor de Blasio for comments about National Guard: His ignorance is stunning.* Fox News. https://www.foxnews.com/media/mike-huckabee-rips-mayor-de-blasio-for-comments-about-natl-guard-his-ignorance-is-stunning

[5] *Conquering Self-Centeredness, Sermon Delivered at Dexter Avenue Baptist Church.* (2020, September 18). The Martin Luther King, Jr., Research and Education Institute. https://kinginstitute.stanford.edu/king-papers/documents/conquering-self-centeredness-sermon-delivered-dexter-avenue-baptist-church

of self-centeredness. They end up the victims of distorted and disrupted personality."

The problem in the United States is not just skin color. It is not just a problem of politics. People at all government and private business levels, and all colors, and all diverse backgrounds have been affected. We all have a sin problem. We all have a self-centeredness problem. We filter our concept of right and wrong, justice and injustice, good and evil people through the lens of a sinful nature, and a self-centered viewpoint. No one is excluded; we are all inclined to be self-centered, self-righteous, and self-governing. Worse yet, the inclinations make us think we have the correct perspective and a pretty good idea of how to fix things. If people would only ______ . Depending on individual experiences, everyone has their solution.

Because the real problem is that of being a human, the solution can not be conventional to resolve the specific issues. We can create new laws and hire other police to try to fix the problem, but this is only a temporary fix. Similarly, we can elect a new President, new Congressmen, and Senators. We can elect new mayors, governors, and judges, but this does not guarantee things will get any better. This kind of solution is only temporary. It skirts around the real issue.

Is there a way to fix the sin problem? Not entirely, but we can make significant progress. For the many who acknowledge that there is a God, they believe that the answer is to pray. Pray that God gives us peace; pray that God gives calmness to the police; pray that the police recognize the humanity of all individuals and treat everyone with respect; pray that there can be understanding and respect of all humans; pray that all potential perpetrators of crime stop and think about their consequences before they take action. We can pray for so many things, and the Almighty God, who is loving, will answer our prayers.

Oh, how I wish this were true. I believe in God, and I believe in the power of God, but I don't believe that He will answer such prayers. Many of us claim we make prayers to the Almighty, but what kind of prayers do we make? I have observed that most people ask God to take control of events, other people, and situations. We want His intervention to bring our country together. But when we look at all the turmoil that goes on in our society, we would have to conclude there is not much evidence that He answers these types of requests.

Part of our problem is that we ask for the wrong things, but another part of the problem is that we don't even understand the God to which we pray. Many people claim to believe in God, but only 56% of the people in our country claim to believe in the Biblical God.[6] Therefore, this statistic's converse is that 44% of the people in this country don't believe in the Biblical God. As a nation, we will not make significant progress in becoming united until these percentages are much higher. In the meantime, everyone will go about reacting to situations as they feel like it. They will not submit themselves to the power of the Spiritual, Biblical God.

Let's assume you do not entirely agree with me, but you are willing to trust me a little bit. Therefore, you dust off your Bible and begin reading. You read the first five chapters(books), which covers about 250 pages. You reflect on specific excerpts such as where:
- God floods all the earth killing all people except Noah and his family (Genesis 6, 7).
- God destroys Sodom and Gomorrah (Genesis 19).
- God requires sin offerings for unintentional sins (Leviticus 1-7).
- God demands death for anyone working on the Sabbath (Exodus 31:5).

---

[6] Research Center Religion and Public Life, "When Americans Say They Believe in God, What Do They Mean?," https://www.pewforum.org/2018/04/25/when-americans-say-they-believe-in-god-what-do-they-mean/04-25-18_beliefingod-00-01/ (Pew April 23, 2018)

• God gave a plague that killed people because they complained
  about the food He provided (Numbers 11:1, 32-34).

You think to yourself, "My parents and ministers have told me that
God is a loving Deity. I don't see it! He is harsh, demanding,
punishing, and homophobic. Furthermore, you reflect on how He
favored and made promises to the man named Abraham and
claimed that through him, He would bless the entire world. He tells
his descendants to avoid the people group called Gentiles. You
have been told you are a Gentile; therefore, you conclude, "This
God is a racist. He is not for me!"

You express your thoughts to a friend who calls himself a
Christian, and he tells you, "You started reading in the wrong
place. You should have started reading about Jesus in the Gospels."

You respond with an appropriate question, "Where is that at?"

Your friend politely tells you, "It is about two-thirds back in the
Bible."

Now you are really confused. "What?! Who writes a book where
you need to skip about the first 1400 pages?"

Your friend responds with, "Just trust me."

Like many people, because you call him a "friend," you reluctantly
begin reading "Matthew." As you read, you have a range of
thoughts. The fact that Jesus was born without the aid of a human
father sounds pretty farfetched. Jesus performs many miracles, the
first of which He turns water into wine. Why would He do this?
How much did the world benefit from this miracle? Secondly, you
thought drinking a lot of wine was a sin!

Still thinking about what was written in Matthew, you continue
cogitating. "I am not sure that reading about Jesus is much better
than reading about God. He emphasizes that we must still obey the

same restrictive laws that were mentioned in the first five "chapters" of the Bible. Furthermore, He adds to them. He said that if we in as much as call someone a "fool," then we are in danger of going to hell! You have heard enough about hell that you know it is a place where evil people are supposed to spend eternity. Likewise, married people who have affairs, divorce, or even look at a naked person are also in danger of going to hell! You thought that Jesus was supposed to show love and forgiveness?!

Furthermore, Jesus is just as much a racist as God. He, too, spends all of His time ministering to Jews and avoids Gentiles. Not only is this His action, but He also teaches this same concept to His disciples. How can we overcome racism in our country by believing in God, when He and His Son are portrayed in the Bible as racists?

You go back to your friend and express your concerns. He tells you that the Bible is not as it seems. There is another guy by the name of Paul, who gives us the real scoop. He tells us that we aren't made acceptable to God by obeying His commandments or doing what Jesus told us. God really does love us and forgive us. We shouldn't be racists, but in fact, Jesus tells Paul to spend his life ministering to Gentiles.

Your reaction is: "Are you kidding me? What a bizarre story. Who would ever dream up such a boatload of crap?"

Your friend is offended. "No, really! I know this sounds strange, but when you believe in Jesus, He sends the Holy Ghost to come and live in you, and God gives you the power to overcome bad habits, the power to speak in a strange language, and the power to heal. All you need to do is to have faith!"

This sounds too outlandish to be believable. So you ask this person you once called a friend one final question. "What proves that I have faith?"

Your friend's face turns red and says, "Well… You have to get dunked in a pool (baptized), start going to church every Sunday, take communion (which means you drink Jesus' blood), and give 10% of your money to the church."

When people tell stories like this, we should be greatly surprised that as many as 56% of U.S. adults actually believe in the Biblical God. But we shouldn't be surprised when atheists state that people who believe in the Bible are fools and idiots. On the surface, they are the ones who appear more intelligent.

However, for those who persist in their investigation of God and continue to study their Bible, they find that God reveals much more about His character and His will than what is projected in the Old Testament.

Likewise, those who persist in learning about Jesus discover that He was *not* put on earth just to reiterate how we should follow God's laws and demonstrate perfect behavior. He is more than a prophet, more than a perfect man, and more than the Son of God. He is the Savior of the world.

Many churches emphasize various sections of the Bible; however, many leaders also stretch and distort what it means to be a Christian. Consequently, many people never learn the Biblical God's real character, His will, or what He has provided for us. However, here is one indisputable fact: God knows you, and He wants you to know Him at a deep, transformational level. He wants to affect your relationship with Him and others.

Because God is omnipotent, no one can completely know Him or explain Him. However, His Word, the Bible, was divinely provided so we can continually study and learn about Him.

Concerning how our faith in Him affects how we interact with others, here are a couple of things to consider. The Bible claims that all humans came from two people, Adam and Eve. Therefore, we are all brothers and sisters, regardless of our various shades of skin color. The Biblical God does not intend for us to hate our own flesh and blood, but He allows it.

God did not make us Republicans, Democrats, Libertarians, or Independents. These are ideologies we have decided to accept. He allows us to have individualistic political views, but He wants us to love Him first and, secondly, love one another. According to Jesus, these are the first and second greatest commandments. There should be no room for hatred. All other preferences, ideologies, and values should be secondary to these two commandments.

For someone who definitely doesn't believe that understanding and having faith in the Biblical God is the answer to our society's woes, then put this book down. Reading it would be a waste of time. However, if you are open to the idea that understanding and believing the Biblical God could somehow be transformational..., although you might have some reservations…, then you will want to continue reading.

Here is a spoiler alert; we all live in a physical world, and we all have physical attributes, but our Creator has provided a spiritual life. The more we understand and believe Him, the more our spirits are driven by His Spirit and less by our physical desires. How does this work? That's the rest of the story…

CHAPTER

1 Where Is Your Scotoma?

There was a time when large companies invested a relatively significant amount of money in their employees. They would do this by hiring a consultant to come in and put on a seminar. The sessions would last for several days and would cover a variety of subjects. The intent was to get employees to think differently about problems, think differently about possible solutions, and help them communicate with other employees. A company whose employees understand their mission statement well and can relate it to their job becomes a valuable asset to the company and its customers. At least that is what my supervisor said.

I remember one of those seminars I attended, and the consultant began the session with a simple question, "Where is your scotoma?" I can't remember what company put on the seminar or even the decade I attended, but the question and reaction of those around me were memorable. The unfamiliar word, "scotoma" drew many puzzled looks (myself included). I didn't even know I had a scotoma. If this was another name for a dog or a cat, I didn't have one. Therefore, I didn't lose it. Other people equally confused would start looking on the floor like they dropped something. I know one guy felt around his belly button, either thinking a scotoma was another name for a belly button, or he just dropped a pretzel crumb down his shirt and was feeling for it.

As it turns out, we were all wrong. According to the Merriam-Webster dictionary, a scotoma is defined as, "a spot in the visual field in which vision is absent or deficient."[7] We might experience a temporary scotoma by trying to view a solar eclipse. Of course, our seminar leader was not talking about actual visual blindness, but instead, blindness caused by a lack of experience or sometimes caused by too much experience in the wrong things. He stated that we sometimes do the same thing over and over to the point that we can't see any other (better) way of solving a task.

In one of my jobs many years ago, I was given the task of maintaining our manager group's capital spending. I had a technical assistant to help with this endeavor. She was a kind, elderly lady named Janet, who wore her hair in a bun. She had been performing this task for years. She spent a considerable amount of time every month, looking at each project individually and manually adding up the numbers. There were more than a hundred projects, each one printed on a separate piece of paper. I envisioned a large oak tree being chopped down every year.

I could not stop the printing of the individual project papers, but I was able to convince someone in the data processing department to generate a summary report. He was glad to do it.

I thought when I told Janet that she no longer had to spend days preparing the report, she would be elated. As it turned out, I was greatly mistaken. She said she had to continue compiling the manual report. To her, I was just some young snotty-nosed kid who didn't know anything. An elderly manager she had trusted started the report, and she wasn't going to stop it just because I said so. When I explained I had all the information I needed, she still wouldn't stop. She wasn't sure what the last manager did with the report she prepared, but she was confident it was still necessary. Besides, the computer-generated report never exactly matched her

---

[7] *scotoma.* (1828). The Merriam-Webster.Com Dictionary. https://www.merriam-webster.com/dictionary/scotoma

manual information. It was close, but she was convinced her manually added total was the correct number. (It must have been the computer that made a mistake).

We know how these things happen; we see it over and over. People are shown how to do something. They find their importance in doing a job well done, especially if no one else knows how to do it. Therefore, they can't find a better way to do it themselves. I am no genius, but even I could see there was a better way.

My seminar instructor gave a pretty good example of a mental scotoma. He displayed on a screen the following sentence:

FINISHED FILES ARE THE RESULT OF YEARS OF SCIENTIFIC STUDY COMBINED WITH THE EXPERIENCE OF MANY YEARS.

# of F's ______

The instructor did not flash the sentence on the screen and give us only 10 or 15 seconds to answer, but he left it up there for several minutes. The simple task was to count the number of "F's" in the sentence. If you have not seen this before, then try it now. See how many you count. Write the number in the blank space provided. Several people in our class counted two or three "F's." There were a few people who counted up to five "F's," but no-one counted the correct number of six "F's."

You say,' Six "F's," Come on; you must be dreaming! There are not six 'F's' there.'

The leader explained, "Oh, but there are. Don't forget the 'F's' in the three words 'OF.' He explained that we often overlook them because we usually learn to spell phonetically and because the "F's" sound like "V's," we miss them.

The instructor said he couldn't overemphasize the effect of scotomas. They not only keep us from seeing and solving problems, but they affect our lives in ways we don't realize. We accept behaviors and lifestyles because of our many experiences. One person believes that a person of a particular ethnic or racial background is honest and reliable while another person professes "absolutely not." Believe it or not, we often learn prejudices in subtle and sometimes not subtle ways, and they stick with us for years.

Rightly or wrongly, scotomas affect our trust of people. In a social setting after a training class, I was told by a fellow student that he didn't believe he could trust me. I don't think he would have confessed this other than he was holding his fourth beer in his hand. But his reason for not trusting me was because I was too quiet in class. I wasn't overtly expressing my opinion, as he did. Apparently, there were experiences in his past, which affected his view of who can and can not be trusted.

A co-worker and a friend, who was also in the class, was surprised by his comments. He had not seen me as overtly critical of others. Of course, he knew me and believed I could be trusted. But the life lessons from the classmate who did not know me kept him from seeing me as my friend did. It had taken him only a couple of days to form an opinion of me.

Based on our trust of people causes us to filter information as primarily true or false. We believe some people and not others. All through life, we develop friendships and rivalries. We form partisan biases; in favor of some and against others. Scotomas often keep us from seeing people and situations as they exist. Therefore, we often develop skewed racial, political, and religious views.

We all have difficulty seeing objects that are portrayed differently than the usual way we look at them, therefore, we miss them.

Likewise, when we see or hear concepts that are different than what our experiences have led us to believe, then we have a difficult time accepting them. Those things we have heard over and over again incorrectly instills in us skewed viewpoints.

A concept we don't hear much about these days is the term "brainwashed." It was a popular term used in the 1950s and '60s, but it isn't near as popular today. The Merriam-Webster definition is, "a forcible indoctrination to induce someone to give up basic political, social, or religious beliefs and attitudes and to accept contrasting regimented ideas." This is the fear of many people today in that social media is so widely used; we have become easy targets to being brainwashed. Political statements are made in some form of media, and the "facts" are relayed. "Oh, those statements weren't true? I thought they were." Worse yet, we might hear someone say, "Don't tell me I'm wrong. I read something on Facebook that contradicts what you just said." What is the truth? How biased are the various forms of media?

Brainwashing is defined as a "forcible indoctrination." That is, there is an agenda. Someone is deliberately trying to influence another person through deception. But how often are we brainwashed without an intent to deceive? When it comes to religious matters, have we been deceived by religious leaders? Is it deliberate, or has it just happened over the years by well-intending people?

How Have Your "Religious" Views Affected Your Opinion of God?

The only way we can make sense of this world is to use deductive reasoning. Here is a fundamental algebra problem. Given variables:

$$A = B$$
$$B = C$$

Therefore, by deductive reasoning: A must equal C

But we must be cautious when studying the Bible that we don't use inductive reasoning. Inductive reasoning starts with observation and then moves towards generalizations and theories.

For example, a person might say that Jesus healed many, many people (despite their sins). Therefore, inductive reasoning might lead a person to believe that God never holds people accountable for their sins because of His Grace. Everybody is going to heaven.

Someone else might conclude that because Jesus is the Son of God, and He healed many sinful people, then God wants to heal us also. Therefore, if we pray to God, it would be unusual for God not to heal us.

Someone else may read in the Bible that God greatly favored his people financially and gave them land. Therefore, God wants prosperity for those who believe in Him and try to follow His commands. Conversely, He will punish those who break His laws.

None of these conclusions are correct, but it is hard to keep someone from believing what they want to think.

Most people believe that "religion" involves not only our Spiritual life but also physical life. In fact, most people think that there is a strong relationship between their physical life and God. A Pew research survey, determined that: "Nearly eight-in-ten U.S. adults think God or a higher power has protected them, and two-thirds say the Almighty has rewarded them. Half of the adults believe God determines what happens to them most or all of the time."[8] I find these statistics interesting. Most people don't arrive at such

---

[8] Research Center Religion and Public Life, "When Americans Say They Believe in God, What Do They Mean?," https://www.pewforum.org/2018/04/25/when-americans-say-they-believe-in-god-what-do-they-mean/04-25-18_beliefingod-00-01/ (Pew April 23, 2018)

conclusions based on a single event. It probably took selective readings, conversations with others, religious teachings, thinking about beating the odds of danger, etc. to arrive at such conclusions.

In summary, 80% of the study people believe that God has protected them, but only 56% believe it is the God of the Bible. My inductive conclusion is that many people believe the God of the Bible is too judgmental to be that loving.

I understand this belief. At one time, I held this view myself. When we read the book of Leviticus, God lays out rigorous punishment for not obeying His laws. Likewise, when we read other books of the Old Testament, we see where God harshly punished people who did not follow his commands. In some cases, these were God's favorite people! They did not obey Him, and they suffered consequences. How does this religious view of God affect people's opinions of everyday life events?

Thirty-plus years ago, my mom had an accident. She was visiting my brother and his family (including their small dog). They wanted to keep the dog contained, so they put a piece of plexiglass in the doorway to the kitchen. The transparent plastic was short enough to walk over but tall enough to keep this small Lhasa Apsos out of the living room. My mom tripped over the plexiglass and went down with a crashing thud. She wasn't walking towards the carpeted side but she landed on the hard kitchen floor. My mom, a woman of faith, was in a great deal of pain, and I remember her saying, "Why did God want me to fall? I don't remember doing anything wrong."

I was puzzled by my mom's comment. What made her think her accident was an act of God's punishment? Furthermore, I believe if God were punishing her, he would have made it clear why. Think about this! As a parent, if you punished your child, wouldn't you make it clear why?

"Johnnie, Come here! You are getting a severe spanking!"

Johnnie responds, "But why, dad? What did I do?"

But you don't answer him; instead, you simply say, "bend over."

After a few incidents of this, Johnny would become scared to death, if not psychotic.

This type of discipline is not what we expect from a parent or God.

Many of us have watched a news report where a tornado strikes an area. One family's house is decimated while another family's home is barely damaged. The reporter interviews the family whose house was still standing. The owner says, "I feel so fortunate. God was watching over us." Their comment sounds reasonable, and as an observer, we might think, "Yes. As a believer in God, he protected you."

However, we don't see on TV that the unbeliever's houses in the neighborhood were also untouched. How do we rationalize this? Do we assume that God protected them all because of the belief of one person? My assessment of this event is that sometimes believers and unbelievers are both fortunate.

We like to think that needy and deserving people only win lotteries, but this isn't the case. Criminals win lotteries too. And sometimes good people win lotteries and are later killed. Did God have a hand in these incidents? Again, good and bad events happen to both deserving and undeserving people.

While I don't doubt God's ability to punish and bless people, do we have to try to explain everything that happens from a perspective of our personal view of Him? Can't we assume that God's plan of free will is also responsible for many of the bad and good things that happen to us?

I don't want to be misleading and disregard Bible scripture. Yes, there were times God blessed and punished people in the Old Testament. For example, He blessed Abraham and His covenant people. He helped them win wars and parted the Red sea when being chased by Pharaoh's army. He gave His people the land of "milk and honey," a land that was so plentiful that they had to transport the huge native grapes on a poll. But then He punished the same people and left them in the desert for 40 years because they wouldn't believe Him. So yes, according to the Bible, God has blessed and punished many people.

In today's times, we find ourselves asking, "Why do so many bad things happen?" Small children die at birth or a young age. People of all ages are experiencing more cancer, freak medical diseases, cases of Alzheimer's, people going crazy in shooting sprees, etc. Where is God, while all these bad things are happening? Is it that our hearts are so cold that God has chosen to punish us?

I remember shortly after the attack on the New York twin towers on 9/11/2001, the Reverend Jerry Falwell and Pat Robertson made the following statements:

> Mr. Falwell said: "The abortionists have got to bear some burden for this because God will not be mocked. And when we destroy 40 million little innocent babies, we make God mad. I really believe that the pagans, and the abortionists, and the feminists, and the gays and the lesbians who are actively trying to make that an alternative lifestyle, the ACLU, People for the American Way, all of them who have tried to secularize America, I point the finger in their face and say, 'You helped this happen.' "
>
> To which Mr. Robertson said: "I totally concur, and the problem is we have adopted that agenda at the highest levels of our government."[9]

If Mr. Falwell and Mr. Robertson are correct, then certainly they wouldn't want to have the perpetrators punished. After all, with

------

[9] *Falwell: blame abortionists, feminists and gays.* (2017, June 24). The Guardian. https://www.theguardian.com/world/2001/sep/19/september11.usa9

their logic, weren't those who launched the attack on the twin towers, the pentagon, and flight 93, the plane that went down in Shanksville, Pennsylvania merely doing what God told them to do? It wasn't their will; it was the will of God. Really?

Granted, it may seem like God is punishing us. After all, we regularly see in the TV sitcoms and on the news a barrage of programming antithetical to God's commandments. We see great political turmoil, divisiveness, road rage, public shootings, and anger in general; much more than what we have seen in our country's history. Many people are getting divorced. Many more people are declaring themselves as "LGBT." (Don't take my statement about people declaring themselves as LGBT as a personal prejudice; it's God's commandments against such a lifestyle, not mine.) Many women are having abortions, and yet loving husbands and wives are having problems with infertility. Are we sure our behavior has caused God's wrath?

So here are some thought-provoking contradictions to consider. God allowed Adolph Hitler to kill 6 million Jews in World War II. He didn't stop these horrible atrocities. Why? I don't have a clue. I am sure he could have intervened but didn't. Conversely…, was our society's actions leading up to the tragedy on 9/11/2001 (supposedly caused by God) worse than what Hitler had done? Do we think our actions brought the intervention of God one day, but yet He allowed Hitler's torturing and murdering to go on for years without reprisal? Yes, Hitler eventually met his Waterloo, but God could have stopped it or prevented it in the first place.

Many people believe in pre-destiny. They believe that God controls when we are born, and when we die. They might even use Bible verses to back up their claim.

> …even the very hairs of your head are all numbered. -
> Matthew 10:30

For he chose us in him before the creation of the world to be holy and blameless in his sight.- Ephesians 1:4

And while this concept of pre-destiny sounds reasonable, don't we have some control also? There are many events that seem like they do not happen by the will of God. For example, nearly two million people in the United States of various backgrounds and ages get cancer every year. Hundreds of people all from different walks of life suddenly die in airplane crashes, tens of thousands of people die in wars and pandemics. Should we attribute all these events to God? I can't believe that a loving God would predestine all these tragedies.

Our entire life, we formulate an opinion about who God is and what he is like. Some of these opinions are grounded in nature, but most are crafted from parents, religious leaders, friends, and school academia. To a much lesser degree, opinions are formed by an objective study of the Bible. Consequently, these are explanations why there are so many people who believe in a Life Force/God without believing in a Biblical God. Most of them are looking for a reason for the creation of our beautiful, self-sustaining, diverse earth and can't rationalize any other explanation other than a Higher Power.

Our amazing earth gives evidence that God created it; however, the Biblical God did much more than create our planet. He also provided the Savior. Unfortunately, what happens to many people when they read the Bible, their eyes glaze over. They become so infatuated with the miracles and other astounding events that they miss the significant aspects of the Spiritual world.

Jesus said, "God is Spirit, and his worshipers must worship in Spirit and in truth." These words sound impressive, but what the heck does it mean? It is not easy to explain, but hopefully, by the time you finish this book, you'll better understand who the God of the Bible really is. What does He want for you, and how much does He really provide both physically and spiritually.

CHAPTER
2 The Jesus, Peter, Paul Conundrum

I remember a minister say something I found to be genuinely remarkable. He said that the Bible was shallow enough for babies to walk in, yet it was deep enough for elephants to drown. That's quite a statement, and which sounds impossible. How can a small baby walk in a shallow pool, and yet a large elephant will drown? Ironically, the older I get, the more I have found this statement to be true.

When I first attended church and listened to ministers preach, I got many baby walk teachings. This is not to say the preaching was necessarily that simple, although much of it was. The problem was that I didn't have enough smarts to recognize the "elephant drown" philosophy. However, as I have grown older and studied my Bible more, I have found much deeper things. It is only then that I have been amazed and astounded by this book. How could I have missed so many things in the past? I know it seems impossible, but I can read a page of the Bible repeatedly, and one day, I find it says something I never saw before. How does this happen?

Let me be clear; there are still many chapters and verses I don't hold a firm grasp. Do I thoroughly understand the book of Revelation? No. Do I know how God created the earth in 7 days and that the planet, according to the Bible, is less than 10 thousand years old. Yet scientists have performed carbon dating to say that dinosaurs lived a million years ago? No, I can't explain that either. Perhaps, a "day" was much longer. But in the grand scheme of things, maybe we couldn't understand it, so God tried to simplify it using the term seven days. Who knows?

I study my Bible every day, and I hope to continue as long as I live. Notice I did not say "I read it" every day, but "I study it" every day. There is a difference. I compare verses. I contemplate what various verses say, as well as what they don't say. I consider the historical context.

I don't claim to be a quick learner; however, I happened to run across a teacher who has explained many verses of scripture that contradicts several teachings I have learned from previous churches I attended. Why is this? Why were his views so different?

I discovered that several concepts I had learned in the past had gaping holes in them. I found this new teacher knows his Bible inside and out, upside down, and backward and forward. He continually says he is not a theologian. That in itself adds credibility to my statement that I don't know much. How much can I know if my teacher isn't even a theologian?

My teacher's name is …, wait a minute; if I tell you his name, then the first thing you are going to do is Google him, and if you run across a person who "dislikes" him or thinks he is a crackpot, then you will put this book down and never read it. However, if you Google me, you won't find much of anything, at least as of now. Therefore, I won't tell you who my teacher is. However, I will tell you that he often says things like, "Don't take my word for anything. It doesn't make a difference what I say, or someone else says. Instead, search the Bible for yourself and see if you can find something that contradicts what I am saying." Or he will make a statement of a belief commonly taught in churches and say, "That isn't true. You can't find Bible scripture to support that view." Or he will say, "Some people think this scripture means such and such," and then he will take 30 minutes going through several other scriptures to show that there are much deeper things implied from what sometimes appears as simple scripture.

There is one thing I have learned; if we read the Old Testament by itself, we get one picture of God. If we read the Old Testament and the Gospels, we will get another perspective of God. If we read only the letters of the Apostle Paul, we will get yet another picture of God. Much of our concept of God is also related to our frame of reference. What were we taught when we were growing up…, and

I don't mean just about God and the Bible. What did we learn about love, discipline, obeying laws, and obeying those in authority while growing up? All of these things either helps us or hinders us from understanding the entire Biblical God.

It should not be a surprise that so many people have difficulty understanding the Bible. I have heard people argue, "An eye for an eye, and a tooth for a tooth." Then someone else says that this concept is no longer valid. Jesus superseded the original idea; we are now to love one another and not argue with our enemies. Ironically, some of the lessons taught by Jesus and many of the concepts taught by the Apostle Paul are contradictory, or at least they don't seem to be the same. We will tackle some of these concepts in the next several chapters. However, if you read and understand what Paul has written, his teachings give us a deeper meaning to what Jesus said and did. Now don't get your feathers ruffled; I am not saying that Paul knew more than Jesus. I am merely saying that Jesus drew a rough sketch of God's plan for salvation in crayon. Paul was instructed by Jesus to make the picture a Picasso, completing it with fine details.

Many people believe in various aspects of the Bible, but many people don't accept it as all true. The Jews believe most of the Old Testament. They believe in Moses, crossing the Red Sea, the 40 years in the desert, etc. But the Orthodox Jews do not believe that Jesus was the Messiah.

Muslims also believe in parts of the Old Testament, and they believe that Jesus was born of the Virgin Mary. They believe in much of the 4 Gospels (the Injil/Injeel), but they think that these books were altered from the original text. They definitely don't believe that Jesus was the Son of God nor that he was crucified on the cross; instead, he was "taken up," similar to Enoch, the father of Methuselah.

Then there are the Christians. Some believe in the creation of the earth as described in Genesis, while others are much more skeptical. Some don't believe in the great flood covering the whole world. Some don't accept that God parted the Red Sea waters and that the Jews walked across on dry ground. Many groups of people have their individual concept of God.

While all these various beliefs fall in contention, some believe the whole kit and caboodle, from beginning to end. And while the people who believe it all are relatively few, many more people claim to believe it all but still have their niche religious beliefs. What must we do to have eternal life? Do we need to be baptized? Was Jesus unquestionably the Son of God? Was Jesus really resurrected? Will gays and homosexuals be excluded from eternal life? Are we saved by Grace? Is there a limit to the amount of sin we can commit, and God will be like the soup Nazi, "Enough is enough. No eternal life for you." While the answer to these questions has the most consequences, we have other concerns that affect our daily lives. Is Jesus the incarnate God? Can we pray to God and expect Him to heal our cancer without any doctor intervention? Are we allowed to work on the Sabbath? Is it wrong to have a blood transfusion? Are we expected to tithe, and will God bless us greatly when we do? Can we pray the dead out of purgatory and into heaven? Is there such a thing as an unforgivable sin?

We ask all these questions in the name of religiosity, and various denominations have answers. Ironically, the answers are quite different among different groups, even though the source of the answers is supposed to be the Bible.

One of the reasons why the answers to such questions vary so widely is because you can find scripture that contradicts other scripture. Most notably and most controversial are the teachings of the Apostle Paul. He said several things that were in opposition to what Jesus taught, and consequently, Paul acquired many opponents. Some clergy flatly reject the books written by him. And if they exclude the books most scholars believe he wrote; then they would exclude about 40% of the text in the New Testament!

Why I Wrote This Book

The primary reason I wrote this book is because of my dad. He lived to be 98 years old. Pretty good, eh? To live to such an old age, then we might conclude that God significantly blessed him. Right?

He grew up in a Baptist church and then eventually became a Methodist. He told me his parents were both very "religious" people. I asked him, "What does 'very religious' mean?" He said that their church was very strict. They did not believe in playing cards or dancing. Furthermore, sex was only for procreating.

Right away, his comments surprised me. Where did they get these ideas? I don't recall reading in the Bible that we shouldn't play cards or dance. I don't even know if they had playing cards back then. And God's favored King David danced before the Lord (2 Samuel 6:14,16). Therefore, from the little bit he told me, it doesn't seem that my grandparent's instruction was Biblically based.

And the idea that married couples should have sex only for procreation is another non-Biblical concept. According to information I have read, the thought crept into Christianity by early Catholic teachers. Conversely, the Apostle Paul wrote that husbands and wives should abstain from sexual relations only during times set aside for prayer and fasting (1 Corinthians 7:3-5). Therefore, his view was that husbands and wives would be having sex for more than just making babies.

My dad's comments about the things my grandparents believed made me wonder about all the things the ministers taught them. I wanted to know more about the essentials of their beliefs. What were the main aspects of their faith? What did they believe about God's love and Grace? What did they believe about Jesus? He didn't know. What did my dad believe? He said he believed the Gospels and many other things in the Old Testament. Did he believe the epistles of Paul? No! Was that because he attended a church that did not preach about Paul? I don't know, and that could've been part of the reason. But the explanation he gave was that it was because of an experience he had while he was a technician working for the phone company. What? How could his job at the phone company affect whether he believed in the writings of Paul? Sometimes I am astounded how that we (not just my dad) take a few unrelated experiences and made a theology from it…, but the truth of the matter is that this is real life! These things really happen!

So here is the explanation:

My dad had to perform some work on a telephone circuit, therefore, he monitored it to see if anyone was talking. During his tenure, this was a common practice. The technicians are not to continually listen to conversations but only check to see when they can do their work. (It is frowned upon to cut off a conversation while it is active.) He checked several times, but it was a lengthy conversation. It just so happened that he recognized the voice of the person on the call. It was the pastor of a large church. After a short while, my dad understood that the pastor was having an affair with one of the parishioners. (Ok, so maybe he listened to more than he should have. Who can resist a good juicy story?) It was that event that had a big impact on him. How could a man of God do such a thing?

Another newsworthy event that had an effect on him was the scandal of Catholic priests having sex with underage children. Initially, he thought it was perhaps a false accusation. But when the John Jay report was issued in 2004, he discovered that the problem was much more significant than people originally thought. During a 52 year period beginning in 1950, there were 10,667 allegations made against 4,392 clergies.[10] His concern was one of shock, "How could these religious leaders commit such horrendous acts?"

---

[10] Wikipedia contributors. (2019, September 23). *John Jay Report.* Wikipedia. https://en.wikipedia.org/wiki/John_Jay_Report

Therefore, because of these incidents, he lost faith in all pastors, ministers, and priests. And because the Apostle Paul was an "enlightened minister," he was nothing more than another failed human. How could he be trusted when some of the verses he wrote did not align with what Jesus said? My dad certainly wasn't going to trust any new theology taught by Paul.

If a book of the Bible quoted a prophet from the Old Testament or Jesus, then my dad would believe it. However, if it was an epistle of Paul's, then it was unreliable. I talked to dad several times about this issue, showing how the former Saul (whose name was changed to Paul) became a believer and changed his attitude 100%. I showed him how a man named Ananias did not want to go to Saul to give him his sight back after being blinded because Saul was persecuting those who believed in Jesus. Ananias only went because Jesus Himself commissioned him to go. But it did not make a difference to my dad; he didn't accept that this Saul/Paul fellow had really changed all that much. To him, he could not trust Paul! His attitude troubled me greatly. And I don't think my dad understood the ramifications of his beliefs. If he didn't believe what Paul said, then in my mind, he was a lost man.

I was confused and perplexed. Why wouldn't dad listen to me? He was the man who instructed me my entire life, well past my adolescence. We had many good discussions over the years, talking about the problems of various people we knew, laws in society, injustices in society, etc. We had many philosophical debates, and we had agreed on many concepts. But when it came to our views of the Bible, our beliefs were vastly different. How could his opinions and mine be so far apart? In his forties, he had been a regular attendee at his Methodist church. No, he was more than just an attendee; he had been an usher, a finance committee member, and a church elder.

I know some children have feuds with their parents and are estranged from them, but this was not our family situation. I lived only about 20 miles from my parents. I saw them almost every birthday and holiday (including Father's Day and Mother's Day).

When my parents were in their early 90s, they could no longer take care of themselves, and they had to move into an assisted living facility. As my brother and I cleaned out their house, we found a closet full of books authored by Robert Schuller, a televangelist and founder of the Crystal Cathedral, a large church in Orange County, California. We also found several books written by renowned author and minister Norman Vincent Peale. Peale was also the founder of Guideposts magazine, a non-profit spiritual publication. (In case you were wondering, there were plenty of those magazines in the closet as well.) I know my mom read the books and magazines, but did my dad? Or did he read them and didn't connect with the message? Or did the messages focus only on the things Jesus said? My brother and I were too focused on cleaning out the hordes of stuff for me to read any of the books and magazines. But in hindsight, I find myself wondering what was in these "spiritual" publications. Were they Biblical teachings? I don't know; they could have been.

All I know is that my dad did not believe in the writings of the Apostle Paul. Consequently, he missed out on the greatest blessings of God. First, and most importantly, I believed it affected his salvation. Paul gave specific details about how we are saved. Because my dad didn't believe him, he was eternally lost. Secondly, any prayers he made were ineffective. He had asked God to intervene in his life, but he never asked for anything of a spiritual nature. The word "Spirit" was an abstract concept in his mind. I am not sure he ever believed in the Spirit. Consequently, after my mom had passed away, he had lost all joy. He had nothing to live for. He had no real hope of ever seeing her again. He had no joy nor peace. He didn't value relationships.

Unfortunately, my dad appeared to have fallen into the footsteps of his parents; they were religious people. But did they really understand what was in the Bible? Did they appreciate the Grace of God? Did they have a relationship with God? I don't think so. I grieve over this, but I don't know what else I could have done; I wanted him to read what was in the Bible. To read it and not believe it is one thing, but to have your mind closed to certain parts without ever reading it is something else.

My dad was like many other people in that his view of God was like a stern earthly father. He is the God who gave the Ten Commandments, and he expects his children to abide by them. If they don't, then they must pay the consequences. His thought was, "If people are sincere and try to obey but slip up occasionally, then God will forgive them." This was his big picture of God.

It's not too surprising that my dad believed as he did. Like all of us, he was a mixture of life experiences. He knew that when his earthly father gave him rules to follow, he had better follow them. He knew what his parents thought about God. But it just wasn't what his parents thought that gave him his view of God. He had gone to church, and he learned first hand what the minister taught. Finally, he had seen the award-winning Cecil B. DeMille movie "THE TEN COMMANDMENTS" and it reinforced in great detail and living color the things he learned in church.

I want to do whatever I can to help anyone who believes as my dad had; that a failure to believe Paul's epistles has severe and extenuating consequences. He failed to understand the bigger picture of God's plan. He was blinded and was unable to see the Biblical God.

The Problem with Paul

There are many things in the Bible that people question. "Did God create the universe in seven days? Did a snake deceive Eve? Was the entire story about Noah and the Ark true? Did the Jews cross the Red Sea on dry ground?" I can understand why people might have these questions. But when we question the Apostle Paul's doctrines, this is a concern at a higher level. Paul gave us his

Gospel message. It was only specified by him. It is the doctrine that clearly states what we must believe to have eternal life.

Perhaps the reason why many ministers don't like to preach about Paul is that several of the things he said are contrary to what Jesus professed. They were different from what Peter said also. If you are anything like me, you might be skeptical of this statement. We will review some of these controversial subjects in a few pages but analyze this Bible scripture for a moment:

> 11 My brothers and sisters, some from Chloe's household have informed me that there are quarrels among you.
> 12 What I mean is this: One of you says, "I follow Paul"; another, "I follow Apollos"; another, "I follow Cephas [Peter]"; still another, "I follow Christ." - 1 Corinthians 1:11,12

Why would Paul make such a statement if everyone was teaching the same thing? He wouldn't. There would not have been quarrels if conceptually they were all teaching the same thing.

This is quite a surprise to many people. Ministers and pastors do not talk a lot about these differences. Instead, they usually tell us just the opposite. "All biblical scripture is in perfect harmony." At a depth of the ankles of babes, this is not true. We will look at some significant differences. However, at a depth of the neckline of the elephant, I believe this is true. So what I am saying is that we need to go deep to see the harmony.

Just like many religions, there is a misunderstanding of many doctrines. Sometimes there just needs to be a clarification. However, there are other times when there are some major differences. That happens to be the case between those things taught by Jesus, Paul, and Peter.

Sometimes there just needs to be a clarification. However, there are other times when there are some significant differences. That happens to be the case between those things taught by Jesus, Paul, and Peter.

I find it interesting that so many people choose to ignore the different theologies taught by these three individuals. There are reasons for the differences, but some of your thoughts about Christianity may very well change when the differences are explained. I know it did for me. It challenged me to question the religious doctrine I had been taught in my twenties. It helped to clarify what was really important in the Bible. It helped me understand why Jesus said what he did and why Paul's explanations were different from anything else anyone else taught in his time.

Returning to one of the comments my dad made about ministers, I find I must agree on one point. Some ministers use a few Bible verses and make a sermon out of them. It may be legitimate to do this! But then if you read one verse in one place and you read something contradictory somewhere else, then what do you do with that? How do you know which is more accurate? Why don't they agree? Therefore, we must have an explanation for the apparent discrepancies. We need to see several Bible verses that confirm and complement an overarching concept. The more times we see confirming verses, the better we can depend on their reliability. For this reason, I have chosen to include lots of Bible verses in this book. And when I say a lot of verses, *I mean many, many verses*. In fact, you probably won't find another book containing so much scripture other than the Bible itself. But if a person is going to find the Biblical God, they must see a lot of Bible scripture. Elucidation must come from the Word of God Himself.

There is another reason for the vast quantity of Bible verses. Groups of them confirm a particular point. The sum of the collection of verses are used to challenge previously held mindsets.

I have chosen to quote the NIV version of the Bible unless otherwise noted. I have found this version to be easier to understand compared to the King James Version.

For most chapter titles, I provide a question. These questions are intended to get you to think about what you believe at a deep level.

Try to determine your answer before continuing. Think about the reason for your belief. Is it because of something a parent or relative told you? Is it because of what your minister or pastor taught in church? Is it because of one or more Bible verses that you can recall? Resume reading only after you have a somewhat firm answer in your mind.

I have grappled with some Biblical questions for many years. If I have struggled with controversial church doctrine, then chances are many other people have too. I have presented some of the major issues that affect not only our salvation, but also our daily walk with God. Without realizing it, our relationship with God should affect every other relationship we have or hope to have. This includes interactions with our mate, our children, neighbors, people with whom we work, and total strangers.

Many people find this concept hard to believe. They say they know many people who go to church, but they are anything but loving and forgiving. Their relationships are no better than anyone else's. Therefore, I am going to present a challenge. Personal change only occurs when our mind, mindset, belief, faith, and attitude change. Thus, every time you read one of these words as quoted from the Bible, either use a highlighter or underline the Bible verse.

With this guideline, let's begin.

CHAPTER

3 Are We Saved by Believing Jesus Is the Son of God?

T he most essential doctrine in the whole Bible concerns Jesus. To obtain eternal life, we need to have a correct view of who Jesus is, what He did, and why He said what He said. Indeed, Jesus was more than what many people claim. He was more than just a prophet, more than only a fine speaker who spoke about Godly love. He was more than a good man, and He was more than a man who knew Old Testament scripture inside and out. No, His claim was something much more significant. He claimed that He was the Messiah, the Savior, the Son of God. During His time on earth, He did much to prove it to the masses living in and around Israel, but the only people who really recognized it were a relatively small number of Jews.

However, after Matthew, Mark, Luke, and John wrote their Gospels, and they were circulated, many more people came to recognize that Jesus was more than what many people initially believed. Even today, many acknowledge that He is, in fact, the Son of God. Obviously, this is not to say that everyone believes, but only that there are many more people throughout the world who believe that Jesus is who He claimed to be.

The question that is important today is not whether Jesus was a great man or whether He was all He and the disciples claimed Him to be. Instead, the question is whether it is good enough to accept and acknowledge that Jesus is the Messiah, the Son of God? Stated more definitely, If we believe that Jesus is the Messiah, the Son of the Living God, will we be saved, that is, ultimately go to heaven?

Several Bible verses make it appear so. For example, in Matthew 16, Jesus is explicit.

> ¹³ When Jesus came to the region of Caesarea Philippi, he asked his disciples, "Who do people say the Son of Man is?" ¹⁴ They replied, "Some say John the Baptist; others say Elijah; and still others, Jeremiah or one of the prophets." ¹⁵ "But what about you?" he asked. "Who do you say I am?" ¹⁶ Simon Peter answered, "You are the Messiah, the Son of the living God." ¹⁷ Jesus replied, "Blessed are you, Simon son of Jonah, for this was not revealed to you by flesh and blood, but by my Father in heaven. ¹⁸ And I tell you that you are Peter, and on this rock I will build my church, and the gates of Hades will not overcome it. ¹⁹ I will give you the keys of the kingdom of heaven..." Matthew 16:13-19

If Peter is given the keys to heaven, he is certainly on the inside with eternal life. He is the gatekeeper. This same doctrine about who Jesus is also emphasized in John 11, shortly after Lazarus has died and just before Jesus is about to bring him back to life. Jesus is talking to Lazarus' sister Martha.

> ²³ Jesus said to her, "Your brother will rise again." ²⁴ Martha answered, "I know he will rise again in the resurrection at the last day." ²⁵ Jesus said to her, "I am the resurrection and the life. The one who believes in me will live, even though they die; ²⁶ and whoever lives by believing in me will never die. Do you believe this?" ²⁷ "Yes, Lord," she replied, "I believe that you are <u>the Messiah, the Son of God</u>, who is to come into the world." – John 11:23-27

Just like Peter's confirmation, Jesus was making it clear that not only was He the Son of God but that Martha needed to believe and proclaim it. If she only thought that Jesus was simply a kind, smart prophet, this was not going to cut it. If she wanted to see her brother in heaven someday, she needed to believe that He was indeed the promised Messiah.

As another example that salvation is dependent on the belief that Jesus is the Son of God, we can look at the event immediately following the conversion of Saul (who later would be called Paul). Saul had been persecuting people who believed in Jesus. When he was on the road traveling to Damascus, he was struck blind. He heard Jesus' voice asking why he has been persecuting him. He was blind for three days, and the incident was so impactful on Saul that he did not eat. The disciple Ananias is sent to Saul to restore his vision. After Ananias lays his hands on Saul, we read:

> 18 Immediately, something like scales fell from Saul's eyes, and he could see again. He got up and was baptized, 19 and after taking some food, he regained his strength. Saul spent several days with the disciples in Damascus. 20 At once he began to preach in the synagogues that *Jesus is the Son of God. –* Acts 9:18-20

So what is the point? The point is that in the case of Peter, Martha, and Paul, Scripture places great emphasis on the acknowledgment that Jesus is the Son of God. This emphasis is so significant that we could be led to believe that this is the only fact we must hold near to our hearts to obtain eternal salvation.

I find it fitting that similarly Peter, Martha, and Paul proclaimed that Jesus was the Messiah and the Son of God, the Apostle John also makes the same claim. But in his case, his profession of faith was not because Jesus asks him. Instead, he makes a claim based on the fact that this was the very reason Jesus performed so many miracles. Sure, miracles changed the lives of many people. Some had had infirmities since they were born, and the healings provided for a much better life. And certainly, these miracles showed the love Jesus had for people. He healed many people without judgment or promise of anything in return. But John claims that Jesus performed miracles to prove without a doubt that Jesus was both the Messiah (the Savior) and truly the Son of God.

If all the above verses are not enough to make a point that Jesus
wanted everyone in Israel to know that He was the Son of God,
consider the Bible verse where Jesus pointedly makes this belief a
defining doctrine. He tells the religious leader Nicodemus that he
must either believe He is the Son of God and have eternal life or
doubt/deny His claim and be forever condemned.

I am guessing that the profession of faith that Jesus is the Christ,
the Son of God, is why so many churches today require that those
who are to be baptized should make this claim. They reason that if
people make this claim and believe it, they will be saved forever.
This statement is often made in front of a congregation, and it
serves to be a witness to others. It should inspire others to proudly
proclaim their faith and stand up in the face of persecution.

Believing that Jesus is the Son of God is important, but we should
not think that accepting this doctrine, by itself, will earn us eternal
life. After all, even Satan believed Jesus was the Son of God
(Matthew 4:3).

My dad believed that Jesus was born of the virgin Mary and is the
Son of God. He believed in the many miracles He performed. He
believed that He was the Messiah. He came to save the world. He
had heard from ministers about God's Grace and believed that God
is a loving God who forgives the many sins of those who repent
despite their imperfections. He had heard how that Jesus showed

grace to sinners, some of which He healed. He also heard how Jesus showed mercy to the woman at the well by not condemning her even though she had been married five times.

My dad was never an evil man, although, like many people, he had become angry at times, but certainly not often. He had never killed anyone, and to my knowledge, he never hit anyone (except for spankings that my brother and I occasionally received). No, my dad appeared to be a good man and someone who went to church fairly often. By many accounts, my dad is like a lot of people in America. They hear of God's extraordinary Grace, and they believe that all past sins are forgiven.

Based on the Bible verses already shown, it is not difficult to see why my dad believed as he did. He would call himself a "believer." And yet he had a scotoma.

As I pointed out from the beginning, we all have blind spots…, but not all blind spots are equal. Some are relatively unimportant; others are significant. The problem is that because they are blind spots, we never see them…, unless we get lucky or someone else points them out to us. What we need to do is to hope…, no, hope is not strong enough; we should *PRAY*! Pray to God that He doesn't allow you or a loved one to have a scotoma, a blind spot, a misunderstanding that is so important that it affects where you or he/she will spend eternity.

CHAPTER

4 What Did the Apostle Paul Teach About Salvation?

The man referred to in the Bible as "Saul of Tarsus" was born a Roman citizen and grew up in a devout Jewish family. He was sent to Jerusalem and received his education by noted Rabbi Gamaliel (Acts 22:3). He had described himself as very zealous for God. He developed a belief that he should do all that was possible to oppose the name Jesus of Nazareth.

After Saul's conversion (a few years after Jesus' resurrection), he initially confessed that Jesus was the Son of God (Acts 9:20). His understanding was consistent with the knowledge of other Jews at that time. However, a few years later, he received through revelation that his profession by faith that Jesus is the Son of God is NOT what saves us. Let that sink in for a moment. The Apostle Paul believed this at one time, but then later, Jesus revealed that believing He is the Messiah and the Son of God is not enough to save a person. Likewise, people are not spared because of any religious practice they perform. This includes going to church, trying to obey the 10 Commandments, being baptized, taking communion, or doing their best to lead a good life. True, no one can dispute the love of God. He has shown us grace and mercy. But according to Paul, we are not saved just by knowing who Jesus is or by doing good works (Ephesians 2:8,9)!

He emphasizes that God is a very loving God, but He is also a just God. This theology means that all of our sins are not forgotten or overlooked, but they must be atoned (paid for by complete restitution). All sin, great and small must be reconciled. God accomplished this by having his Son severely whipped, causing extreme bloodshed, being spit upon, and dying on the cross.

This concept sounds unimaginable to most people. After all, who would ever say they would torture their own Son so that others could have eternal life? However, this was the principle Paul taught and not just once, but he mentioned this theme repeatedly throughout his many letters.

Paul emphasizes in his epistles that we must realize the Spiritual impact when Jesus was crucified. We must understand his great suffering. He shed His blood for our benefit. We must realize that the shedding of blood makes the atoning sacrifice for us (pays for *our* sins). Without this understanding and belief, then our sins are not forgiven, *and* we are unacceptable to God. Here are just some of the verses that emphasize this theology;

> For God presented Jesus as the sacrifice for sin. People are made right with God when they believe that *Jesus sacrificed his life, shedding his blood.* - Romans 3:25

> And since we have been *made right in God's sight by the blood of Christ,* he will certainly save us from God's condemnation. - Romans 5:9

> But now you have been united with Christ Jesus. Once you were far away from God, but now you have been *brought near to him through the blood of Christ.* - Ephesians 2:13

> He is so rich in kindness and grace that *he purchased our freedom with the blood of his Son and forgave our sins.* - Ephesians 1:7

> For he has rescued us from the kingdom of darkness and transferred us into the Kingdom of his dear Son, *who purchased our freedom and forgave our sins.* - Colossians 1:13,14 (NLT)

> … and through him God reconciled everything to himself. *He made peace with everything in heaven and on earth by means of Christ's blood on the cross.* - Colossians 1:20 (NLT)

> In fact, according to the law of Moses, *nearly everything was purified with blood. For without the shedding of blood, there is no forgiveness.* - Hebrews 9:22 (NLT)

When we read a few verses of Scripture in just one place, we can take them out of context. But when several verses in different books of the Bible provide the same concept (although stated a little differently), it is a firm doctrine on which we can rely. God planned it this way to emphasize what He wants us to believe. In this case, I have used only the most prominent examples (but there are many more) which specify how we are forgiven; how we have been freed from the bondage of Spiritual death when we accept God's free gift. Only through our acceptance of Jesus' shed blood does God determine that we are saved. According to Paul, this must be a central and essential doctrine of Christianity. From his perspective, believing that Jesus is both the Messiah and the Son of God is not enough. It *was* enough for the Jews to believe *before* Jesus' crucifixion, but Paul was given a revelation that salvation now requires a fuller, more complete explanation. Jesus suffering should mean something special to us. God poured out His wrath on His own Son so that our sins would be paid in full, and we could enjoy eternal life. This is the true meaning of the grace of God!

As I relate this truth, I should reiterate that my dad *did* believe that Jesus was the Messiah and the Son of God; however, he would never admit that Jesus died for his sins. My dad had heard about the Grace of God, but to him, it meant that God would overlook his sins. Furthermore, because he had never killed anyone nor committed any law that put him in prison, then God was merciful and gave him the free pass he deserved.

Unfortunately, there are a whole lot more people that have this same philosophy. They believe that unless they have committed a horrible sin, then God realizes that he/she is not perfect, and He forgives them because He is a good, loving God. However, according to the teachings of Paul, this is a false belief! The Bible never says God doesn't hold us accountable out of the goodness of his Deity. If He did this, He would not be a just God. No, somebody has to pay for these sins; they can't just be swept under the rug. Paul has mentioned this many times in his letters. It was Jesus who paid for our sins.

I tried to explain this concept to my dad and got very frustrated when he would not believe me. Oh, I will admit that this philosophy goes against our human understanding; nevertheless, this is the concept Paul taught. When I would tell him this and show him in the Bible the verses that emphasized the importance of believing that Jesus' blood atoned for our sins, he would simply say he didn't believe it. To him, Paul was just like many other (but not all) preachers of today. Paul was a man who stands up in front of a podium and reads a few lines of Scripture. He then elaborates on a point and then stretches it to confirm his ideas. In the eyes of my dad, if Jesus didn't say pointedly that He would die and as a result of his suffering would pay for our sins, then it wasn't true. So I thought that if he didn't believe the Apostle Paul, perhaps he would believe some Old Testament prophecy. I had my dad read Isaiah 53: I asked him who the prophet was talking about when he said:

> 4 Surely he took up our pain
>   and bore our suffering,
> yet we considered him punished by God,
>   stricken by him, and afflicted.
> 5 But he was pierced for *our transgressions*,
>   he was crushed for *our iniquities*;
> the punishment that brought us peace was on him,
>   and by his wounds we are healed. - Isaiah 53:4,5

For me, these verses indicated that someone suffered and was afflicted for our sins, transgressions, and iniquities. Nevertheless, my dad was not convinced it was referring to Jesus. I asked him if he knew of anyone else in the Bible who was convicted for someone else's sins, and he said, "No." But that still didn't convince him that Isaiah's prophecy was referring to Jesus. For him, he needed to see the name "Jesus" (even though Isaiah wrote these words about 700 years before Jesus was born). I did not know how to react to my dad's rejection. Paul's teachings, along with consistent verses from the Old Testament, convinced me, but then I read my Bible on a regular basis. I continued to emphasize to my dad the importance of reading the Bible so he would, in time, understand the truths contained within, but he did not take the challenge. To him, reading the Bible was a boring waste of time.

Consistent Verses Worth Contemplating

My dad was never convinced Jesus was sent to die for our sins. Would he believe it if he had read in the Bible that Jesus told his disciples he was going to die for everyone's sins? Perhaps, but for him, everything had to be spelled out precisely in a specific way. So if Jesus never told his disciples he was going to die on the cross and his blood was to pay for the sins of everyone, then why should he believe Paul when he tells us so plainly that this is what Jesus did?

Jesus did make several comments that implied he would be a sacrifice for others; however, as with so many things in life, we can be blind to what is in front of us but see very clearly with 20/20 vision hindsight. With that in mind, consider these confirming themes and Bible verses.

1. Jesus did not explicitly tell his disciples that He was about to die so that everyone could enjoy a relationship with God. However, He did tell them how His blood was to confirm a new covenant between them and God. It is this promised covenant that we affirm each time we take communion. Granted, the disciples probably did not recognize its significance when they drank the wine. Still, we should realize the significance in light of all the verses that Paul wrote emphasizing how Jesus shed His blood for us all. The event is recorded in the Gospels of Mathew, Mark, and Luke, but Luke 22 provides the clearest example:

> After supper he took another cup of wine and said, "This cup is the new covenant between God and his people—an agreement confirmed with my blood, which is poured out as a sacrifice for you."
> -Luke 22:20

Just like many things that Jesus said, the disciples probably didn't have a clue what this meant. But even at that, the disciples may have assumed that his blood was only important to "God's people," that is, the Jews.

2. Jesus could have asked his disciples, "Do you believe that the Son of man must die on the cross and will be raised up on the third day?" But he didn't, and probably the main reason he didn't was because he knew they couldn't comprehend it. The disciples were focused on Jesus being the Messiah, and being the Messiah indicated that a revolt was about to take place. The Messiah was going to free all the Jews from the Roman dictatorship. Jesus was getting ready to set up his Kingdom. The Son of man could not die. If he did, then how was he going to set up his Kingdom? This is not something a dead person can do.

However, Jesus told the disciples three times what was to befall him. They just never understood. And probably they never should have. God planned that the disciples should not understand too much. However, when they wrote the Gospels, then it was time to reveal what Jesus had told them. The scriptures make this point very clear. First, there is the incident with Peter in Matthew 16:

> 21 From that time on Jesus began to explain to his disciples that he must go to Jerusalem and suffer many things at the hands of the elders, the chief priests and the teachers of the law, and that he must be killed and on the third day be raised to life.

Jesus told the disciples three times how He was going to suffer greatly, die, and be resurrected, but each time He told them, they didn't understand. Luke 18 proclaims their lack of understanding after his third announcement.

You talk about a scotoma; this is a huge one! My wife tells me some things three times, but I am old and forgetful, so it is understandable. But here Jesus is telling his young disciples three times, and they just don't get it.

But suppose they had understood. What would it have looked like? Imagine your friend who you believe is going to rule the world comes to you and says, "Oh, by the way. Before I become the Savior of the world, I am going to be mocked, spit on, flogged and killed! After I die, I will be resurrected and come back to you." If this would happen I am certain that most people, (including me), would be running away as fast as we could. This guy is nuts!

No, the message of Jesus had to be hidden from them.

3. The third reason we should believe Paul is because of all the references in the Old Testament about the need to atone

(which means to make amends or compensate) for sins using blood. Now the Old Testament does not state clearly that Jesus' blood paid for our sins, but after Paul made this claim, it is easy to see. First, there are many verses in Leviticus stating that an unblemished (theoretically perfect) animal had to be sacrificed when the Jews sinned. This was usually a male sheep. There are two important references to Jesus with this concept.

1) Jesus was referenced as the Lamb of God (John 1:29).
2) Jesus was without blemish; he was perfect (1 Peter 2:22, 1 John 3:5).

While these verses lead us to the conclusion about the purpose of Jesus' death, the most straightforward one line of Old Testament scripture that indicates Jesus' blood paid for our sins is Leviticus 17:11.

> For the life of a creature is in the blood, and I have given it to you to make atonement for yourselves on the altar; *it is the blood that makes atonement for one's life.*

So even though Jesus never directly said that he shed his blood and died on the cross to pay for our sins, many biblical references point to this truth. He is our redeemer. Jesus paid back what was owed to God for the sins of the world so that we could be made whole again in His sight.

> "… all are justified freely by his grace through the redemption that came by Christ Jesus." - Romans 3:24

What Did Peter Say About Salvation?

So we see how Jesus fulfilled his mission, and Paul explained it through his letters. But what about Peter? Did he explain it like Paul did…, that Jesus' suffering and blood atoned for our sins? Well, no, he didn't…, at least he never explained it as such in the book of Acts, which covers at least 30 years from the time Jesus was crucified until Paul took his message to the Gentiles.

For example, we see Peter addressing Jews in Acts 2. Peter reads from the Old Testament about what the prophet Joel had said. He explains how the Jews had put Jesus on the cross and killed him. He gives an account of how Jesus performed many mighty miracles, signs, and wonders. He tells how God raised him from the dead and how the promised Holy Spirit had been given to Jesus and had come upon Peter as he was speaking. So Peter did acknowledge that Jesus had died and that God resurrected him. But, as great as this speech was, Peter never said that Jesus' suffering and death paid for their sins. This message was not the same as Paul's. There was no discussion about atonement; instead, it was about the acknowledgment that Jesus was the Messiah, which was the same thing that Peter had acknowledged when asked by Jesus as recorded in Matthew 16. As you read Acts 2, pay particular attention to the words of Peter. You might interpret that he was saying repentance and baptism resulted in the forgiveness of sins.

> [36]"Therefore let all Israel be assured of this: God has made this Jesus, whom you crucified, both Lord and Messiah." [37]When the people heard this, they were cut to the heart and said to Peter and the other apostles, "Brothers, what shall we do?" [38]Peter replied, "Repent and be baptized, every one of you, in the name of Jesus Christ for the forgiveness of your sins. And you will receive the gift of the Holy Spirit. [39]The promise is for you and your children and for all who are far off—for all whom the Lord our God will call." [40]With many other words he warned them; and he pleaded with them, "Save

yourselves from this corrupt generation." [41]Those who accepted his message were baptized, and about three thousand were added to their number that day. – Acts 2:36-41

In this example, Peter told the Jews they would be saved by their acknowledgment that Jesus was the Messiah; but *not* because of his sacrifice on the cross, nor that His death paid for their sins. Peter does not state this critical fact that Paul repeatedly proclaimed.

Another example of Peter's belief about salvation is provided in Acts 10, where Peter is sent to the first Gentile (non-Jew) convert, Cornelius, a devout but lost man. We must remember that Peter went to Cornelius's house, not by his own volition, but instead, he was directed by the Holy Spirit to go. When Peter arrives, he tells his audience:

[34] "I now realize how true it is that God does not show favoritism [35] but accepts from every nation the one who fears him and does what is right. [36] You know the message God sent to the people of Israel, announcing the good news of peace through Jesus Christ, who is Lord of all. [37] You know what has happened throughout the province of Judea, beginning in Galilee after the baptism that John preached— [38] how God anointed Jesus of Nazareth with the Holy Spirit and power, and how he went around doing good and healing all who were under the power of the devil, because God was with him. [39] "We are witnesses of everything he did in the country of the Jews and in Jerusalem. They killed him by hanging him on a cross, [40] but God raised him from the dead on the third day and caused him to be seen. [41] He was not seen by all the people, but by witnesses whom God had already chosen—by us who ate and drank with him after he rose from the dead. [42] He commanded us to preach to the people and to testify that he is the one whom God appointed as judge of the living and the dead.

> ⁴³ All the prophets testify about him that everyone who believes in him receives forgiveness of sins through his name." – Acts 10:34-43

We might even assume from verse 35 that Cornelius was accepted by God because "he feared Him and did what was right." But then we read in verse 43 that everyone who believes in Jesus receives forgiveness of sins *"through his name"* Regardless, Peter never mentions that they are forgiven of their sins by Jesus' atoning blood, shed on the cross. In other references, we read where Jesus, Peter, and John all teach that salvation comes through the Holy Name of Jesus (John 3:18, Acts 4:11-12, John 20:31).

It is only Paul who teaches the essential but detailed doctrine of the shedding of blood.

To Peter's credit, he did realize this when he wrote 1 Peter (which most theologians believe was 30+ years after the death of Jesus.) Likewise, John realized it when he wrote 1 John (which was about 30+ years after Peter's crucifixion). However, all during the book of Acts, there is no indication that *any* disciple realized that Jesus died for everyone's sins. Don't take my word for this! Read all of Acts and see if you can find any mention of it.

Did Peter know the message of Paul but not say it? Possibly, but probably not. The reason I say this is because of what Peter had written in his epistle 2Peter 3.

> ¹⁵ Bear in mind that our Lord's patience means salvation, just as our dear brother Paul also wrote you with the wisdom that God gave him. ¹⁶ He writes the same way in all his letters, speaking in them of these matters. His letters contain some things that are hard to understand, which ignorant and unstable people distort, as they do the other Scriptures, to their own destruction. – 2 Peter 3:15-16

Why does Peter say that Paul's letters are hard to understand? Peter walked daily with Jesus for three years! What was Paul saying that Peter thought was difficult to understand? There could have been many things, but I think one of the items was possibly because Paul was talking about how Jesus had shed his blood for us. This was not something Jesus had explicitly taught his disciples; therefore, they did not understand.

Why Paul's Message of Salvation Was Different Than Jesus' and Peter's

When we consider historical prophecy, it makes sense why Jesus did not make the claim about believing that His blood sacrifice was necessary to obtain salvation. The well-known prophecy was that the Messiah was coming to set up a new Kingdom and be the ruler. Therefore, because the disciples believed Jesus was the Messiah, then how could they reconcile He was going to be put on a cross and bleed to death? They simply could not understand. In their minds, if He died, then He couldn't be the reigning King. It wouldn't make sense. Therefore, if they couldn't grasp His sacrifice, then they certainly weren't going to comprehend that His blood was about to be shed for everyone's sins, nor were they going to understand that He would be resurrected.

I have contemplated that if the disciples did in fact, realize Jesus was going to die; then maybe they would have tried to change the course of history. Perhaps they would have attempted to hide Him, or perhaps all the disciples would have fought the Roman soldiers when they came to take Jesus away. Had it turned out this way, it would have been ugly. Several or all of the disciples could have ended up in jail…, or dead. Therefore, for prophecy to be fulfilled, I believe that the truth had to be hidden from the disciples, yet they had to be told during their time with Him so that when it was time to write their Gospels, they could recall it and testify to it.

Even though the concept of animal sacrifice is difficult for most people to believe, God required it of the Jewish people to pay for their sins. It needed to be from a perfect (unblemished) animal. The blood sacrifice was necessary for atonement (as described in Leviticus 17:11).

Likewise, the concept of Jesus needing to die for our sins doesn't make sense from the human view (in a world where everyone is punished for their own mistakes). However, verses from both the Old and the New Testament tells us it does make sense from God's viewpoint. All the Biblical references are there. The necessity for a substitute shedding of blood; the warnings by Jesus that He would be severely tortured and die; the analogy of pouring the red wine and his blood being poured out as a human sacrifice.

Why would Jesus sacrifice himself? We may see where a policeman, a fireman, or a soldier deliberately puts themselves in harm's way to protect others. This takes a level of self-sacrifice we rarely see, but even then, there is a question in the hero's mind whether they will suffer; the outcome is unknown. So maybe they will go through an ordeal without too much suffering. Who knows? But in Jesus' case, He knew precisely what would happen. He was completely innocent of any wrongdoing; He also knew that He would be stripped naked, humiliated, and suffer greatly. He allowed others to put a crown of thorns on His head. He allowed individuals to drive spikes thorough His hands and feet. He hung on a cross pushing bone on steel and pulling cartilage on steel just to try to take another breath. Above all, there was no need for it! He didn't do anything wrong!

I said that the concept of Jesus dying for our sins is difficult for many people to accept, but I don't say this as if I grasp the idea better than anyone else. I struggle with this concept myself, especially when I consider I wasn't around when Jesus was crucified. How could His shedding of blood pay for the sins of so many people years after His death? How could Jesus' crucifixion pay for my sins 2000 years in advance? How could *His* suffering equate to me and millions more escaping judgment?

The only possible explanation is that He knew from His Father that it needed to be done and He did it is because of his great love for us. He did it so we could have eternal life; certainly *not* because we deserved to be saved.

For the disciples who were experiencing the event first hand, they missed it. They couldn't see it. And we would have missed it too had it not been for Paul's many proclamations in his letters to help clarify it. We should all be thankful for the insight and wisdom given to him by God.

CHAPTER

5 Are We Saved Only by Jesus' Atoning Blood?

Paul's letters indicate that simply believing Jesus died for our sins is not enough to have eternal salvation. We must also realize that it was His resurrection that proves God's power over the grave. If we don't believe in His resurrection, then we are still lost. The power of the Holy Spirit raised Him, and we will be too if we believe it. But many people don't. Instead, they believe in what's known as "swoon theory." According to the swoon theory, Jesus did not die, but instead, He became unconscious and appeared dead. Later in the tomb, He recovered and "beat death."

Jesus made his claim about his resurrection, not pointedly about himself, but in a veiled way.

> "For as Jonah was three days and three nights in the belly of a huge fish, so the Son of Man will be three days and three nights in the heart of the earth." - Matthew 12:40

Matthew's verse does not explicitly say Jesus was to die, but the verse in Luke does. And just like Matthew 12, these words came from the lips of Jesus.

> And he said, "The Son of Man must suffer many things and be rejected by the elders, the chief priests and the teachers of the law, and he must be killed and on the third day be raised to life." - Luke 9:22

Either His claim was true or it wasn't. If it wasn't true, how can we be sure of all the other things He said? No, it must be true, or the entire Christian doctrine is on thin ice. Paul affirms the death of Jesus and the power it took to raise Him from the dead in Ephesians.

¹⁸I pray that the eyes of your heart may be enlightened in order that you may know the hope to which he has called you, the riches of his glorious inheritance in his holy people, ¹⁹ and his incomparably great power for us who believe. That power is the same as the mighty strength ²⁰ *he exerted when he raised Christ from the dead* and seated him at his right hand in the heavenly realms, ²¹ far above all rule and authority, power and dominion, and every name that is invoked, not only in the present age but also in the one to come. – Ephesians 1:18-21

Resurrection was not a central doctrine in the Bible until Jesus raised Lazarus back to life. Just before He did this, He told Martha,

²⁵ "I am the resurrection and the life. The one who believes in me will live, even though they die; ²⁶ and whoever lives by believing in me will never die. Do you believe this?" – John 11:25-26

Similar to wanting others to believe He was the Messiah and the Son of God, Jesus wanted others to confirm the power of the resurrection. He was claiming that God can bring people back to life. All Jesus had to do was to give the command, "Lazarus, come out!" and when He did, this became a defining moment in Biblical history. It separated those who wanted to follow Jesus from those who didn't. We read about the impact after this incident:

⁴⁵ Therefore many of the Jews who had come to visit Mary, and had seen what Jesus did, believed in him. ⁴⁶ But some of them went to the Pharisees and told them what Jesus had done. ⁴⁷ Then the chief priests and the Pharisees called a meeting of the Sanhedrin.

"What are we accomplishing?" they asked. "Here is this man performing many signs. ⁴⁸ If we let him go on like this, everyone will believe in him, and then the Romans will come and take away both our temple and our nation." ... ⁵³ So from that day on they plotted to take his life. – John 11:45-48, 53

It is hard to imagine that the matter at the top of the religious leaders' minds was their concern that their religion might be dissolved. Instead, we would think the most important topic would be, "Who is this Jesus who brought Lazarus back to life?!" At least that is what I would be wondering. I would be astounded to see someone who was probably starting to stink from decay walk out from their grave! But similar to 2000 years ago, many people today are skeptical that God raises people from the dead. It is similar today in that the belief in resurrection separates those who believe from those who don't. Through resurrection, we have certainty that God has sovereignty over life and death. If we can't be certain of Jesus' own resurrection, then we are spiritually blinded. The Bible will have lost its credibility. Therefore, while Paul makes the claim that we are saved by Jesus' atoning blood, he also emphasizes the importance of Jesus' resurrection. This is all part of Paul's Gospel, which he called his good news. His gospel is stated plainly in 1 Corinthians.

> ¹ Now, brothers and sisters, I want to remind you of the gospel I preached to you, which you received and on which you have taken your stand. ² _By this gospel you are saved_, if you hold firmly to the word I preached to you. Otherwise, you have believed in vain.
> For what I received I passed on to you as of first importance: that Christ died for our sins according to the Scriptures, that he was buried, that he was raised on the third day according to the Scriptures, ⁵ and that he appeared to Cephas[Peter], and then to the Twelve. –
> I Corinthians 15:1-5

These five verses sum up the gospel of Paul. Sure, Jesus' death on the cross paid for our sins, but his good news was that after Jesus was put in the grave, He was raised by the Father through the Holy Spirit. This was a whole lot more than merely believing that Jesus was the Messiah and the Son of God.

Can we exclude the resurrection from the Gospel and still be saved? According to Paul, the answer is no. He stated in verse 2 above that we are _saved_ by the gospel he just stated. But it is not only here that he makes the point. He continues in 1 Corinthians 15 about the importance of believing in Jesus' resurrection:

> 14 And if Christ has not been raised, our preaching is useless and so is your faith. 15 More than that, we are then found to be false witnesses about God, for we have testified about God that he raised Christ from the dead. But he did not raise him if in fact the dead are not raised. 16 For if the dead are not raised, then Christ has not been raised either. 17 And if Christ has not been raised, your faith is futile; you are still in your sins. 18 Then those also who have fallen asleep in Christ are lost. 1 Corinthians 15:14-18

There is no doubt in Paul's mind that Jesus was raised from the dead. It is an essential part of his Gospel and we should not try to ignore it or lightly pass over it. He claims that if Jesus was not raised, then we are still in our sins. We are saved from our sins by *both* Jesus' blood *and* by his resurrection. Without believing both, we are lost individuals.

Professing a Belief in the Resurrection

Believing in actual resurrection has been a debate for thousands of years. This is just as true today as it was back in the day of the Apostle Paul. In today's world, arguments may become a little heated, but it usually doesn't spark such a debate that one person would likely kill another. However, as we read about the events of Paul's life in Acts 23 – 26, we see that Paul was nearly killed for professing the concept of resurrection. It is interesting to note that these verses were not written in the beginning or the middle of his ministry. Instead, these verses were written near the end of his ministry. This shows the continued opposition to his teachings.

> 6 Then Paul, knowing that some of them were Sadducees and the others Pharisees, called out in the Sanhedrin, "My brothers, I am a Pharisee, descended

from Pharisees. I stand on trial because of the hope of the resurrection of the dead." 7 When he said this, a dispute broke out between the Pharisees and the Sadducees, and the assembly was divided. 8 (The Sadducees say that there is no resurrection, and that there are neither angels nor spirits, but the Pharisees believe all these things.)

9 There was a great uproar, and some of the teachers of the law who were Pharisees stood up and argued vigorously. "We find nothing wrong with this man," they said. "What if a spirit or an angel has spoken to him?" 10 The dispute became so violent that the commander was afraid Paul would be torn to pieces by them. He ordered the troops to go down and take him away from them by force and bring him into the barracks. – Acts 23:6-10

This first account happened in Jerusalem. Problems started because of some of Paul's teachings in the temple. People were so angry that they started a riot. A Roman regiment was sent out and the account in Acts 23 was a result between the commander of the regiment and Paul. As a result of this incident, the commander placed Paul under heavy guard and sent him to appear before the governor Felix in Caesarea. When Paul appeared before the governor, he said:

'It is concerning the resurrection of the dead that I am on trial before you today.' – Acts 24:21

According to Paul, it wasn't his testimony about Jesus dying for our sins that was an issue; instead, it was his testimony about Jesus' resurrection. Felix didn't know what to do about Paul, so he left him in prison for two years.

Porcius Festus replaced Felix. Because Paul was a Roman, he asked to be tried before Caesar. While he was waiting for his trial,

Festus brought Paul before King Agrippa. Paul presented his case to Festus and the king and said:

> 22 … God has helped me to this very day; so I stand here and testify to small and great alike. I am saying nothing beyond what the prophets and Moses said would happen — 23 that the Messiah would suffer and, as the first to rise from the dead, would bring the message of light to his own people and to the Gentiles."
>
> 24 At this point Festus interrupted Paul's defense. "You are out of your mind, Paul!" he shouted. "Your great learning is driving you insane."
>
> 25 "I am not insane, most excellent Festus," Paul replied. "What I am saying is true and reasonable. 26 The king is familiar with these things, and I can speak freely to him. I am convinced that none of this has escaped his notice, because it was not done in a corner. 27 King Agrippa, do you believe the prophets? I know you do." – Acts 26:22-27

Overall, three things strike me as interesting in this scripture in Acts 26:23-26. The text implies that Paul had offended the Jewish leaders about several things; however, it was the subject of resurrection that evoked the most emotion. At first, the general idea of anybody being resurrected was presented. Paul was talking about his hope of the resurrection. We could interpret this as his hope for strictly his own resurrection, but instead, I think we should think of it in a broader sense. It was the resurrection of Jesus that was the most important. He knew it took the power of the Holy Spirit to raise Jesus, a clear sign from God that Jesus was indeed the Son of God and that even if He lost all his blood, God could return Him to life. It was this confrontation that was the most serious and continues to challenge people to this day.

That is why Paul made this part of his Gospel. That is why he said in his letter to the Corinthians:

… For what I received I passed on to you as of first importance: that Christ died for our sins according to the Scriptures, that he was buried, that he was raised on the third day according to the Scriptures – I Corinthians 15:2-4

In addition, there is Biblical confirmation that there is a blessing for believing in Jesus' resurrection.

And with great power the apostles gave witness to the resurrection of the Lord Jesus. And great grace was upon them all. - Acts 4:33 (NKJV)

6 Do We Need to Obey All God's Laws?

Once we see that the blood sacrifice of Jesus was necessary for us to have eternal life, then most Christians get hung up on the need to obey all of God's laws in order to be saved. Why is this such a problem? It is because this is another area where the things Jesus said were much different from what the Apostle Paul said. When Jesus walked the earth, he taught that all the laws God had given to Moses and the Jews should be obeyed, including all civil, moral, and ceremonial laws. There were no exceptions.

My dad was resolute and unwavering when it came to this point. "We must obey all of God's laws."

So I asked him pointedly, "Dad, have you sinned?"

His response was predictable. "Yes, I have sinned. But I try not to sin."

To which I replied, "So you are just like many other Christians. I don't try to sin either, but I do. So how do you know if your sins are forgiven?"

His answer was like those from many others, "I believe in God's Grace. He knows none of us are perfect. Therefore, if we try not to sin, then He forgives us."

First, I explained again how Jesus' shedding of blood paid for our sins. Then I explained that according to the writings of Paul, we are not saved by obeying God's laws but that He gave laws to show us just how sinful we really are.

Again, knowing my dad's feelings about Paul, his response was predictable. "Aw, hogwash!"

I should have handled the situation better, but I didn't. I knew what Paul had taught, and I was adamant that we are not saved by trying to obey God's Commandments. Likewise, my dad was familiar with the Gospels of Matthew, Mark, Luke, and John. He knew what Jesus had said, and he was just as adamant that God does judge us by the sins we commit. In this chapter, we will look at his side of the argument.

First, we should clarify these various types of laws. There were three different types; Civil laws, Ceremonial laws, and Moral laws.

Civil laws were given by God to protect the rights of citizens. They offered legal remedies that may be sought in a dispute and covered such areas as contracts, torts, property, and family law. Civil law is similar to the laws of ancient Rome which used doctrines to determine the outcome of legal issues.

Ceremonial laws identify the customs of a nation. These would have included sacrifices of perfectly good animals, and rejection of food sources such as pork. It was also a necessity that a man be circumcised. These were customs that God required so that the Jews would be set apart and recognized as His people.

God gave moral laws as they related to justice and judgment. They reflect His Holy nature. As such, these ordinates are Holy, just, and unchanging. They encompass regulations on justice, respect for others, and sexual conduct.

As we read the Gospels of Matthew, Mark, Luke, and John, we see that Jesus' view of these laws was obvious. All of God's laws should be followed to the letter and there were no exceptions. Well, He did make an exception for working on the Sabbath, compared to what the Pharisees believed. Because Jesus was the Son of God, He could have determined that some of the laws were not useful and He could have said they were no longer necessary, but He didn't. Instead, He emphasized how important they were. Here are the words of Jesus about the law :

17 "Do not think that I have come to abolish the Law or the Prophets; I have not come to abolish them but to fulfill them. 18 For truly I tell you, until heaven and earth disappear, not the smallest letter, not the least stroke of a pen, will by any means disappear from the Law until everything is accomplished. 19 Therefore anyone who sets aside one of the least of these commands and teaches others accordingly will be called least in the kingdom of heaven, but whoever practices and teaches these commands will be called great in the kingdom of heaven.20 For I tell you that unless your righteousness surpasses that of the Pharisees and the teachers of the law, you will certainly not enter the kingdom of heaven." – Matthew 5:17-20

This is strong language. We could not misinterpret these words to think that it is unnecessary to obey all of God's Laws. To reinforce what Jesus means, He elaborated on the intent of the law by saying such things as:

21 "You have heard that it was said to the people long ago, 'You shall not murder, and anyone who murders will be subject to judgment.' 22 But I tell you that anyone who is angry with a brother or sister will be subject to judgment. Again, anyone who says to a brother or sister, 'Raca,' [a term of contempt] is answerable to the court. And anyone who says, 'You fool!' will be in danger of the fire of hell." 23 "Therefore, if you are offering your gift at the altar and there remember that your brother or sister has something against you,24 leave your gift there in front of the altar. First go and be reconciled to them; then come and offer your gift." – Matthew 5:21-24

(Notice He does not say that bringing gifts to the alter is not necessary! The law of making animal sacrifice was still in effect at that time.)

Nor does Jesus imply that the laws God gave Moses thousands of years earlier should be discarded, but instead, we should put great emphasis on obeying them. He made statements about sinning that many people would consider extreme by today's standards that emphasizes this point. Here are references from Matthew:

> 27 "You have heard that it was said, 'You shall not commit adultery.' 28 But I tell you that anyone who looks at a woman lustfully has already committed adultery with her in his heart. 29 If your right eye causes you to stumble, gouge it out and throw it away. It is better for you to lose one part of your body than for your whole body to be thrown into hell.30 And if your right hand causes you to stumble, cut it off and throw it away. It is better for you to lose one part of your body than for your whole body to go into hell." – Matthew 5:27-30

Not only should the Jews obey the original laws God handed to Moses, but they were also to observe the expanded laws given by Jesus. The penalty for disobeying was the risk of going to hell! Yikes!! These were severe threats!!!

In another example, Jesus tells people not only that they shouldn't be revengeful but that enemies should be given respect in an extreme way.

> 38 "You have heard that it was said, 'Eye for eye, and tooth for tooth.' 39 But I tell you, do not resist an evil person. If anyone slaps you on the right cheek, turn to them the other cheek also. 40 And if anyone wants to sue you and take your shirt, hand over your coat as well. 41 If anyone forces you to go one mile, go with them two miles. 42 Give to the one who asks you, and do not turn away from the one who wants to borrow from you." - Matthew 5:38-41

Jesus taught that we should love not only our neighbors but also our enemies. This teaching not only sounds difficult, but it also seems impossible! If this isn't extreme enough, Jesus expands that concept and professes the need to be perfect!

> 43 "You have heard that it was said, 'Love your neighbor and hate your enemy.' 44 But I tell you, love your enemies and pray for those who persecute you, 45 that

you may be children of your Father in heaven. He causes his sun to rise on the evil and the good, and sends rain on the righteous and the unrighteous. 46 If you love those who love you, what reward will you get? Are not even the tax collectors doing that? 47 And if you greet only your own people, what are you doing more than others? Do not even pagans do that? 48 Be perfect, therefore, as your heavenly Father is perfect." – Matthew 5:43-48

Are we to be perfect? Really? How can we be perfect? That's understandable for Jesus, who was perfect, but anyone else? No way!

Let's assume we know we fail, and we try to make up for it by performing various good works to atone for our failures. Let's even assume we had the power to perform some miraculous acts, and we miraculously healed afflicted or injured people. Certainly, we would expect we would be forgiven, but what else should we expect to receive from God? The answer is in Matthew 7:

21 "Not everyone who says to me, 'Lord, Lord,' will enter the kingdom of heaven, but only the one who does the will of my Father who is in heaven. 22 Many will say to me on that day, 'Lord, Lord, did we not prophesy in your name and in your name drive out demons and in your name perform many miracles?' 23 Then I will tell them plainly, 'I never knew you. Away from me, you evildoers!'" – Matthew 7:21-23

Ok, so we can't make atonement for our own sins regardless of what we do, even if we perform wonderful, kind, miracles. I think this makes it clear that based on the statements made by Jesus, heaven will be a pretty desolate place! Who can keep all his commandments? The impression we get is that we need to obey all the laws and commandments…, and if we don't, then we won't have any chance of being in heaven someday.

By reading the Gospels, we could infer that obeying God's laws is extremely important and that we should also have the internal fortitude to do it. In other words, we should all have the power to

obey the commandments. We shouldn't try to make excuses that it
is too difficult; anybody ought to be able to be loving, kind-
hearted, and obey all laws.

CHAPTER

7 The Law

The Law According to Paul

I don't know anyone who would say that obeying God's laws is a bad idea. Even the Apostle Paul said that God's laws are good. However, he also has a much different take than Jesus on the need to obey all of God's laws. Jesus indicated that everyone should be able to obey God's laws, but Paul said that it is impossible. First, he wrote in Romans 3:23 that we are all sinners and fall short. In Romans 5, he describes why we are all sinners. It is because we are all born as sinners.

> When Adam sinned, sin entered the world. Adam's sin brought death, so death spread to everyone, for everyone sinned. – Romans 5:12

This is our default mode. It is in our very makeup. When Adam committed the first sin, it affected everyone as if we all inherited a "sin" gene. If sin is our default mode, then can we overcome it? What are the chances we will change, at least change to the point that we can satisfy Jesus' commandments?

In Romans 5, Paul makes it sound like sin is fatalistic. It happens to everyone, and there is nothing we can do about it. He makes this same argument in Romans 7. It is not like he is pointing his finger at us, but he, like any good teacher, describes himself and how he is a prisoner of sin. He doesn't want to sin; he wants to break free, but he is always a slave to sin.

> 21 So I find this law at work: Although I want to do good, evil is right there with me. 22 For in my inner being I delight in God's law; 23 but I see another law at work in me, waging war against the law of my mind and making

67

me a prisoner of the law of sin at work within me. 24 What a wretched man I am! Who will rescue me from this body that is subject to death? – Romans 7:21-24

Without a doubt, the views of Jesus and Paul appear very contradictory. Jesus gave commands, not just suggestions that all of God's laws should be obeyed. If any part of the body wants to sin, then remove it before it causes sin, an eye, a limb, regardless of how painful it is. Do not be angry or hostile towards enemies, but love others to a fault. Turn the other check, do what your enemy asks of you, and then do more. There is no way to compensate for sin by serving God in some other way. Whatever we attempt is futile; Jesus said that even if we perform great works, we would still be rejected. The only acceptable behavior is perfection!

On the other hand, Paul admits the sinfulness of mankind. We are born as sinners. Paul confesses his continual temptation to sin. There is no way to escape it.

Most of us have probably heard church members who are quick to point out the sins of others. It's not that they are perfect, but it always makes a person feel better to talk about someone else's faults rather than their own. They can quote all of Jesus' words of advice on the subject. Likewise, many of us have heard ministers preach at great length about how some people commit many evil sins. They also feel a certain amount of satisfaction by quoting Jesus' rebuke of lawbreakers. "We should all try to be non-sinners, and if giving 99 or 100 percent effort doesn't give us success, then we should put forth 110 percent or more." The theory is that while we can't be perfect, we can get close, and doing the best we can is what satisfies God. And if we do the best we can do, then that determination and effort earns our way into heaven.

While this makes sense to most people, this is bad theology. Paul contradicts many aspects of this argument. First, he says we *cannot* be saved by obeying God's law. Here are some scriptural examples:

³¹But the people of Israel, who tried so hard to get right with God by keeping the law, never succeeded. ³²Why not? Because they were trying to get right with God by keeping the law instead of by trusting in him. They stumbled over the great rock in their path. - Romans 9:31, 32

These few verses require some explanation. After Moses had parted the Red Sea and the Jews crossed on dry ground to the other side, God told them that all they had to do was go into the land He had shown them (present-day Israel), and He would drive out the people living there and give them the wonderful land of milk and honey. Because the Jewish people were skeptical, they sent men to scout the countryside. They saw many large men and decided that God couldn't make good on His promise. Therefore, rather than give them the land He graciously offered, God punished them because they were essentially calling Him a liar. He left them in the desert for 40 years. The people were still under the law and they obeyed it the best they could, but the real rub was that they didn't totally trust God. If they did, they would have simply walked in and taken the land. So they did only part of what God commanded but not everything He commanded. They only followed Moses through the Red Sea but no further. They erroneously believed that if they only obeyed some of His commandments, then God would approve them. They were wrong! This is why Paul said they didn't believe God (totally), and that is why He punished them.

Like the Israelites of the Old Testament, this was true for the people of Israel during Paul's ministry, and it is also true for us today. God declares us as sinners not only when we break a specific Commandment but also when we don't trust Him completely.

We must trust God completely! How? By trusting that He is a loving God and He lets us get away with minor sins? No! No! No! By trusting that He sent his Holy Son to pay for/redeem us of our sins!

> ²⁰ For no one can ever be made right with God by doing what the law commands. The law simply shows us how sinful we are. ²¹ But now God has shown us a way to be made right with him without keeping the requirements of the law, as was promised in the writings of Moses and the prophets long ago. ²² We are made right with God by placing our faith in Jesus Christ. And this is true for everyone who believes, no matter who we are. – Romans 3:20-22

Let that sink in. We need to read this over and over again. _No one_ can ever be made right with God by doing what the law commands. _The law simply shows us how sinful we are. We are made right with God by placing our faith in Jesus Christ. And this is true for everyone who believes, no matter who we are._

Notice also what this does _not_ say. It does not say we are made right by being baptized, going to church, taking communion, helping the poor, etc. While these things are good, according to Scripture, they are _not_ necessary to be made right with God. We are only made righteous by following one command, and that command is not physical; it is mental. We must believe that Jesus died for our sins!

While the words of Paul sound good, how could anyone take him at his word? Did the Jews at that time, listen to Paul and take his words to heart. No way! According to Paul, Jesus sacrificed Himself for everyone's sins, and there was no longer a need to continue with animal sacrifice. But the temple was still in full operation even after the death of Jesus, and people continued to make sacrifices until the temple was destroyed in 70 A.D. According to Flavius Josephus, a historian during biblical times, he wrote in his work "The Jewish War", that 256,000 lambs were sacrificed during Passover. This is a large number! Even as Paul was preaching that obeying the law was unnecessary, many Jews were still practicing the ceremonial laws.

The Law According to Peter

We know what Jesus and Paul thought about obeying the law; but what about the other disciples? What did they think? They strictly followed Jewish law. We see an example of their attitude in Acts 10 and 11. God's law was that Jews should not intermingle with Gentiles (non-Jews), and the disciple Peter knew it. However, he eventually yielded after having a supernatural vision that indicated he should visit the Gentile Cornelius. He was very puzzled by this vision. Should he go? No! But the revelation was telling him it was okay. What should he do? He was given this vision not only once, but then twice, and finally a third time. Associating with a Gentile was a sin, and Peter was a strict adherer to the law, so he was not going to see a Gentile unless he was positive it was acceptable with God. He initially had reservations, but finally he was convinced he should go. And what did the other disciples say after Peter made his visit? They were up in arms. They were on him like a wet blanket. We read about their objection in Acts 11.

> 2 So when Peter went up to Jerusalem, *the circumcised believers criticized him* 3 and said, "*You went into the house of uncircumcised men and ate with them.*" - Acts 11:2-3

There were no punctuation marks in the original text of the Bible; however, my Bible has a period at the end of verse 4. But I think it should have been at least a double exclamation mark!! I picture the other disciples, almost yelling at him. "Peter, how could you!!"

Jesus had drilled into Peter and the other disciples that they should obey the law very strictly. Never were they told that they were allowed to make any exceptions. The only time that may have seemed like an exception was when Jesus gave the disciples the Great Commission. The task given to them was to go out among *all* nations and make disciples (Matthew 28:18-20). We would have thought they would have all believed that they not only *could* go to the Gentiles but that they *should* go and spread the message of Jesus. However, it never occurred to them; instead, they avoided Gentiles.

According to a timeline provided by Biblehub[11], Peter did not have his interaction with Cornelius until 37A.D., which was about seven years after the ascension of Jesus. Furthermore, the disciples were still avoiding interaction with Gentiles in 42 A.D. (Acts 11:19). Therefore, perhaps the disciples never understood that they were supposed to spread the message of Jesus to the Gentiles (except for Peter's visit to Cornelius).

You may be thinking, like my dad, that Paul was not serious when he wrote that our approval by God does not depend on obeying His laws. The concept of being approved by God without obeying His commandments is a direct contradiction to what God told Moses, what Jesus said, and it seems contrary to everything we have learned while growing up! We have had it drilled into us that we are only acceptable to our parents, teachers, police, and other people in our community by being law abiders, not lawbreakers. How can God approve of us if we break His commandments?

Some people might think that perhaps Paul only wrote about the concept that we don't need to obey God's laws only in his letter to the Romans. Others might think he really meant that our approval by God depends on following God's laws, but translators distorted his letter over many years through faulty interpretations. Let me be clear; this is *not* the case!

Paul has peppered the theme of being given God's grace and not held accountable to the law throughout his letters. Furthermore, we cannot earn eternal life through any of our own efforts; we are saved/made acceptable to God based strictly on our faith in Jesus' atoning sacrifice. We can not be law abiders under our own power

---

[11] *Acts Bible Timeline*. (2010). Rich Valkanet. https://biblehub.com/timeline/acts/1.htm

so let's not assume that even the most disciplined person can abide by all of God's laws. Here are Bible verses proclaiming this critical doctrine.

> I do not treat the grace of God as meaningless. *For if keeping the law could make us right with God, then there was no need for Christ to die.* - Galatians 2:21

> 21Is there a conflict, then, between God's law and God's promises? Absolutely not! If the law could give us new life, we could be made right with God by obeying it. 22But the Scriptures declare that we are all prisoners of sin, so *we receive God's promise of freedom only by believing in Jesus Christ.* - Galatians 3:21, 22

> 2 If you are counting on circumcision to make you right with God, then Christ will be of no benefit to you. 3I'll say it again. If you are trying to find favor with God by being circumcised, you must obey every regulation in the whole law of Moses. *4For if you are trying to make yourselves right with God by keeping the law, you have been cut off from Christ!* You have fallen away from God's grace. - Galatians 5:2-4

> 8*God saved you by his grace when you believed.* And you can't take credit for this; it is a gift from God. 9Salvation is not a reward for the good things we have done, so none of us can boast about it. - Ephesians 2:8, 9(NLT)

According to Paul, there is one and only one way to be made right with God. We are *only* acceptable to Him by believing that Jesus died for our sins.

The Jerusalem Showdown

During Paul's ministry, he emphasized how no one was made acceptable to God by obeying His laws. Conversely, the disciples were teaching that everyone needed to obey all God's laws, including all the rituals and customs initially given to the Jews.

Their disagreement went on for quite a while. Even 14 years after Paul's conversion and ministry, they still had their differences. Paul felt like he was fighting an uphill battle. Finally, he decided that enough was enough. He and his co-worker, Barnabas, went to Jerusalem to settle their differences with the other Jewish disciples. Their argument was fierce. In Acts 15:2, the NIV says that they had a "Sharp dispute," while the NLT says they vehemently disagreed. In either case, it was nasty.

Through this meeting, they worked out their differences and the Jerusalem council led by James, Peter, and John conceded that the Gentiles were no longer required to obey Jewish law (Galatians 2:9).

Why Did God Give Jews the Law?

Therefore, people want to have the following questions answered. "Why did God give us the commandments in the first place? Why is the obeying of His laws now no longer necessary?"

Paul said that part of the reason we were given the law is to show how sinful we are, but the other part is to show us that we need to rely on Jesus' shed blood to pay for our sins. Paul explains this in a little different way in Galatians 3.

> [19] Why, then, was the law given? It was given alongside the promise to show people their sins. But the law was designed to last only until the coming of the child who was promised. God gave his law through angels to Moses, who was the mediator between God and the people… If the law could give us new life, we could be made right with God by obeying it. [22] But the Scriptures declare that we are all prisoners of sin, so we receive God's promise of freedom only by believing in Jesus Christ. – Galatians 3:19-22

The promised child Paul referred to in verse 19 was obviously Jesus Christ. Paul's explanation of sin made it clear that we never could obey God's laws completely. And after Jesus came, the only way we could be made right with God was to believe in His work; to understand and accept that Jesus died on the cross for our sins. Paul continues in Galatians with more details about why we were given the law.

> 23 Before the coming of this faith, we were held in custody under the law, locked up until the faith that was to come would be revealed. 24 So the law was our guardian until Christ came that we might be justified by faith. 25 Now that this faith has come, we are no longer under a guardian. - Galatians 3:23-25

Some versions of the Bible use the word "tutor" (verse 24) instead of "guardian," but I think the term tutor is misleading in this case. Tutor refers typically to a teacher. A guardian does more than just teach. A guardian helps keep a person in check and protect them. As Paul used the term, the law was not just to teach, but it helped safeguard their minds; it served as a reminder of their limits. They should not shamelessly go out to do whatever they wanted to do at the expense of someone else. They shouldn't even wish/desire (covet) what other people had, for eventually coveting often leads to physical sin.

While society's laws should serve as a method to teach (and be a guardian) to what is acceptable and unacceptable in the community, God's laws, as given in the Old Testament, should have taught the Jewish people what was acceptable and unacceptable in His mind.

The breaking of God's laws should have been a reminder to the Jewish people of just how sinful they were. After all, the laws given by God to Moses were in effect for about 1500 years. They had plenty of time and opportunity to sin (and they took advantage of it). As an acknowledgment of their sins, they were required to make animal sacrifices repeatedly as a reminder that they were not perfect. This was the process that helped maintain the law as their guardian. But once they accepted that Jesus' blood had paid for their sins, their consciences were cleaned. Notice I did not say that Jesus paying for sins cleansed their mind; I said it was *their acceptance* that Jesus atoned for their sins that renewed their minds. This is true today. Jesus' suffering and death mean nothing by themselves to set us free. It is only our acceptance (our acknowledgment and belief) through faith that cleanses our conscience. This concept is explained more fully in Hebrews 9.

> 13 With the Old Way of Worship, the blood and ashes of animals could make men clean after they had sinned. 14 How much more the blood of Christ will do! He gave Himself as a perfect gift to God through the Spirit that lives forever. Now your heart can be free from the guilty feeling of doing work that is worth nothing. Now you can work for the living God.- Hebrews 9:13-14 (NLT)

Notice what is said here. The people were performing sacrificial activities not because they wanted to but only out of guilt. Now that Jesus had come to pay for their sins, they didn't have to make any more sacrifices. There was no need to feel guilty. Once and for all, the requirements of obeying the laws was finished.

> 8 First he said, "Sacrifices and offerings, burnt offerings and sin offerings you did not desire, nor were you pleased with them"—though they were offered in accordance with the law. 9 Then he said, "Here I am, I have come to do your will." He sets aside the first to establish the second. 10 And by that will, we have been made holy through the sacrifice of the body of Jesus Christ once for all.

> 11 Day after day every priest stands and performs his religious duties; again and again he offers the same sacrifices, which can never take away sins. 12 But when this priest had offered for all time one sacrifice for sins, he sat down at the right hand of God, 13 and since that time he waits for his enemies to be made his footstool.

¹⁴ For by one sacrifice he has made perfect forever those who are being made holy. - Hebrews 10:8-14

What was true for the Jews of Paul's time was also true for the Gentiles; the law was intended to lead them to Christ. And what was true for the Gentiles in Paul's day is valid for Gentiles today. We are no more under the law today than we were at the time of Paul. So not only have our sins been wiped away by the sacrifice of Christ, our consciences have been cleansed as well; at least they should be. The problem is that many Christians don't want to admit that they are not under the requirements of God's laws. Instead, they want to keep us under the law and make us feel guilty. They want to wag their finger and tell us how we should obey the law and that we will not go to heaven unless we obey every law. Furthermore, they also emphasize that we are unworthy unless we are baptized, go to church every Sunday, take communion every time it is offered, tithe, etc. That is what the minister did to my grandparents, and I guess it was the same for my dad.

For those who have faith that Jesus died for their sins and arose to prove God's power, they are made right in God's eyes by their faith. Their faith eliminated the need for the law and the guardian. So now we can have a clear conscience and are free to serve God. We have something better than the law. Now that we have faith, we have the Holy Spirit indwell us (Ephesians 1:13). The Holy Spirit should be guiding us (as long as we allow Him to).

CHAPTER
8 Jews and Gentiles

When people read their Bible, many of them are uncertain who the writers were talking about when they use the term "Gentile." Here is a brief explanation.

During the time of Jesus, there were seven nations of people who were classified as Gentiles. They were the Canaanites, Amorites, Girgashites, Hittites, Hivites, Jebusites, and Perizzites. These were the main groups of people living in and around what is present-day Israel. They lived in the area before God led his people (the Jews) there. Therefore, the people living at that time were classified as either Jews or Gentiles. Because we are ancestors, we too are either a Jew or a Gentile. According to Wikipedia, in 2018 the world's core Jewish population, those identifying as Jews above all else, was 14.6 million.[12] The world's Gentile population (everyone else) in 2020 is 7.8 billion.

Did Jesus Come to Save the Gentiles?

Did Jesus come to save the Gentiles? To many people, this is a seemingly strange question. Ministers will quickly admit, "Of course Jesus came to save everyone." Then they will start skipping through their Bible, spouting verses that state explicitly, "Jesus died on the cross for our sins. We are saved according to his suffering and shedding of blood. He came to save the whole world of their sins, not just a particular class of individuals, etc."

---

[12] *Jews.* (2020, October 25). Wikipedia. https://en.wikipedia.org/wiki/Jews

Admittedly, most Christians believe that Jesus came to save both the Jews and the Gentiles. Why would I even ask such a question? I ask because I have read some Bible verses that initially caused me to doubt whether it is true.

When I have asked ministers about these verses, they gave me explanations that did not sound correct, but because I believed church leaders, I said, "Oh, okay, thanks." And then I walked away, still not understanding. I concluded that the verses were either too deep or that the ministers didn't know the answer themselves, but they didn't want to admit it.

Let me give an example from Matthew 15 that I found troubling.

> 22 A Canaanite [Gentile] woman from that vicinity came to him, crying out, "Lord, Son of David, have mercy on me! My daughter is demon-possessed and suffering terribly."
>
> 23 Jesus did not answer a word. So his disciples came to him and urged him, "Send her away, for she keeps crying out after us."
>
> 24 He answered, "<u>I was sent only to the lost sheep of Israel.</u>"
>
> 25 The woman came and knelt before him. "Lord, help me!" she said.
>
> 26 He replied, "It is not right to take the children's bread and toss it to the dogs."
>
> 27 "Yes it is, Lord," she said. "Even the dogs eat the crumbs that fall from their master's table."
>
> 28 Then Jesus said to her, "Woman, you have great faith! Your request is granted." And her daughter was healed at that moment. - Matthew 15:22-28

So why wouldn't Jesus heal the woman's daughter when she first asked? Why didn't He just say no and let it go? Why was there an additional dialogue? Indeed, it would have been easy for Jesus to heal the woman's daughter. I don't believe it was because he was feeling weak and experienced a temporary power shortage. When I asked a more mature Christian, he told me that Jesus was testing her faith. Another mature Christian said that this was a difficult passage, and he dropped it like a hot potato. Because ministers and my parents had told me that Jesus loved everyone, I found it difficult to understand why Jesus initially denied helping the woman who made a passionate plea. So what did Jesus mean in the key verse 24 when He said, "I was sent *only* to the lost sheep of Israel."

Didn't that mean that he was sent only to the Jews and *not* sent to minister to the Canaanite/Gentile people? It sounded like it to me.

Likewise, I found it difficult to understand a passage in Matthew 10 when Jesus was sending out his disciples unto Israel:

> 5 These twelve Jesus sent out with the following instructions: "Do not go among the Gentiles or enter any town of the Samaritans. 6 <u>Go rather to the lost sheep of Israel.</u> 7 As you go, proclaim this message: 'The kingdom of heaven has come near.' 8 Heal the sick, raise the dead, cleanse those who have leprosy, drive out demons. Freely you have received; freely give." - Matthew 10:5-8

Again, I was told that this is another "difficult" passage. How can we rationalize Jesus, who has the same love as God, yet He tells his disciples explicitly in verse 5 to *not* go to the Gentiles. There is a common thread to these two passages, but I don't want to accept it in my mind. "Lord, say it ain't so!" I want to believe that you came for the salvation of all of us. Despite my rejection that Jesus only came to minister to Jews, I couldn't get out of my mind the verses Matthew 15:24, "I was sent only to the lost sheep of Israel." and Matthew 10:6 – "Go rather to the lost sheep of Israel."

How can this be? This concept goes against everything I was taught! I thought God loved everyone. I thought He didn't discriminate. I thought He wanted everyone to be saved. Did my mom, dad, Sunday school teachers, and ministers lie to me about this my whole life? These verses quote words from the lips of Jesus himself.

Peter Tries to Avoid the Gentiles

So let's put this concept on the back burner for a few moments and review Jesus's Great Commission. After Jesus died and was resurrected, he appeared to the disciples and told them:

> [18] "All authority in heaven and on earth has been given to me. [19] Therefore go and make disciples of all nations, baptizing them in the name of the Father and of the Son and of the Holy Spirit, [20] and teaching them to obey everything I have commanded you. And surely I am with you always, to the very end of the age." - Matthew 28:18-20

Jesus had given this command to all his disciples, but as I said earlier, Peter rebelled at going to Cornelius's house (a Gentile). Wasn't it time for him and the other disciples to change their modus operandi? Curiously, their opinion to avoid Gentiles didn't change.

Jesus was a law-abiding Jew, and He did not explicitly tell his disciples that they should violate Jewish law.

Were Jews Really Supposed to Avoid Gentiles?

There are at least 15 Bible verses that emphasize the great love of God (John 3:16, 1 John 4:7-8, 1 John 4:9-11, 1 John 4:16, Romans 8:37-39, Isaiah 54:10, Romans 5:8, Psalm 136:26, Ephesians 2:4-5, Psalm 86:15, Exodus 34:6, Zephaniah 3:17, 1 John 3:1, 1 Peter 3:9, Deuteronomy 7:9). Therefore, it may seem difficult to believe that the loving Almighty told the Jews to avoid Gentiles. But the reason was simple; the native people living in these seven nations were worshipping false gods. As part of everyday life, they were violating the first three commandments of God's great Ten Commandments.

"3 I am the Lord your God, who brought you out of Egypt, out of the land of slavery. 4 You shall have no other gods before me. You shall not make for yourself an image in the form of anything in heaven above or on the earth beneath or in the waters below. 5 You shall not bow down to them or worship them; for I, the Lord your God, am a jealous God, punishing the children for the sin of the parents to the third and fourth generation of those who hate me - Exodus 20:3-5

God reiterated His command to the Jewish people when they were about to embark on their journey to the promised land. As they were getting ready to leave the Sinai region, God told them:

23 My angel will go ahead of you and bring you into the land of the Amorites, Hittites, Perizzites, Canaanites, Hivites and Jebusites, and I will wipe them out. 24 Do not bow down before their gods or worship them or follow their practices. You must demolish them and break their sacred stones to pieces. – Exodus 23:23-24

God had given them the reason for his action; the Gentiles were idolatrous people. They worshipped many other gods. God had called out the Jewish people to be His people and not be influenced by the Gentiles.

The avoidance of the Gentiles did not end here. God also commanded them to *not* marry them either.

3 Do not intermarry with them. Do not give your daughters to their sons or take their daughters for your sons, 4 for they will turn your children away from following me to serve other gods… - Deuteronomy 7:3,4

God, the Creator of all people, is a tolerant God, but he also knows human nature. He knew that if the Jews married Gentiles, then His people would be tempted. Even good people who associate with unlawful and immoral people frequently take on their lifestyles (the evil tends to pull down the good rather than the moral pulling up the corrupt). Therefore, if the Jews were associating with and marrying Gentiles, they would become like them, and no longer would they be a separate people.

Sometimes we pay attention to God's commandments, and other times we blow them out of proportion. That is what happened this time. He only told His people to avoid Gentiles, but additionally, their attitude turned into discrimination, retort, and despise. Sure, the Israelites were God's favored people. Sure, the Gentiles were idol worshippers. But the hatred had grown to an intemperate level.

"How could anyone associate with a lowly Gentile?" One of the best accounts in the Bible of this attitude is described in Acts 22. In this chapter, Paul gives his testimony before other Jews and tells them how that as a Pharisee, he gave the command to have the disciple Stephen stoned to death. He continues with his testimony describing how he fell into a trance, and the resurrected Jesus spoke to him after this event.

> 21 "Then the Lord said to me, 'Go; I will send you far away to the Gentiles.' " - Acts 22:21

This was a crushing blow to the listening Jews. How dare this guy named Paul claim that God told him to go to the Gentiles. God had told the Jews explicitly that they were not to associate with them. Avoid them lest you become like them! Now God told Paul to go minister to them? His statement was blatant blasphemy. Their reaction is recorded in verse 22:

> 22 The crowd listened to Paul until he said this. Then they raised their voices and shouted, "Rid the earth of him! He's not fit to live!" - Acts 22:22

Wow! Those are harsh words. Before Jesus crucifixion, Paul did not advocate ministering to any Gentiles. But after his Damascus road conversion, he claimed this as his primary objective; and we should be glad he did.

God Separates His Mission

It is apparent that the disciples didn't want to go to the Gentiles, but the question is whether they were supposed to. True, Jesus did command them to go throughout the world and make disciples (Matthew 20:18-20). But also remember that the Jews had been dispersed and scattered throughout Judea and Samaria (Acts 8:1). Therefore, perhaps they thought that the Great Commission meant that they were supposed to go only to the Jews dispersed through other areas.

But this is not the only reason why they directed their energy towards ministering to the Jews and not the Gentiles. They also remembered the other commands of Jesus. Don't forget, He explicitly told them:

> 5 ..."*Don't* go to the Gentiles or the Samaritans, **6** but *only* to the people of Israel—God's lost sheep. - (Matthew 10:6)

Peter also had been told three times by Jesus in three consecutive verses to go feed and take care of His sheep (referring to Israel) (John 21:15-17). Consequently, when Paul confronted the disciples regarding whether the Gentiles needed to obey Jewish law (described in Galatians 2), they agreed that they would continue ministering to the Jews. Paul would minister to the Gentiles.

> 7 ...they [the disciples] saw that God had given me [Paul] the responsibility of preaching the gospel to the Gentiles, just as he had given Peter the responsibility of preaching to the Jews. 8 For the same God who worked through Peter as the apostle to the Jews also worked through me as the apostle to the Gentiles. - Galatians 2:7,8

Does God Change His Mind?

We might ask, "Did Paul decide to minister to the Gentiles by his own volition, or was this God's plan?" How was it that God didn't want the Jews to associate with Gentiles, but suddenly these become favored people to whom He would show grace?

This line of thought might cause us to contemplate whether God ever changes his mind. From some of the Bible verses in the Old Testament, I believe that God has possibly changed his mind. The one incident that sticks out most prominently is described in Exodus 32:11-14 where Moses convinces God not to destroy the Israelites for creating a golden calf idol.

Or, we may ask, "Did God know that man would become so evil that He would destroy them all with a great flood? Or did He originally think He wouldn't but then changed His mind?" Such instances are subject to debate; some people believe God has changed His mind while others believe God wanted to test the people He was interacting with, but He did not change His mind.

Regardless of which way you believe, we can be confident from scripture that God did not change His mind about initially favoring the Jews, then rejecting them, and then favoring the Gentiles. True, God had decided to give the Gentiles grace, and this was a change from the way it was in the Old Testament, but the Old Testament documents that the change would be taking place sometime in the future. After all, He told Abraham that He would bless the whole world through him; this obviously included Gentiles. We will look at specific verses about the apparent change in blessing the Gentiles in the next chapter, but first, let's look at the cause of the change.

Why Jesus Was Rejected by Jews During His Ministry

Sometimes my mind wanders, and I think of the strangest things. I question in my mind that if I had been a Jew living during the time of Jesus' ministry, would I have believed He was the Messiah? After all, most Jews at that time were taught Old Testament scripture. If I were living then, I too would have been very familiar with verses from the book of Isaiah and Jeremiah. When the rumors about Him had circulated to my home town, and I saw Him on the street with His disciples, would I have thought, "Aha! That's the guy described in the scriptures!" Put more pointedly, would I have associated the following Bible verses with the Jesus walking around town?

6 For to us a child is born, to us a son is given, and the government will be on his shoulders. And he will be called Wonderful Counselor, Mighty God, Everlasting Father, Prince of Peace.
7 Of the greatness of his government and peace there will be no end. He will reign on David's throne and over his kingdom, establishing and upholding it with justice and righteousness from that time on and forever. The zeal of the Lord Almighty will accomplish this. - Isaiah 9:6,7

1 A shoot will come up from the stump of Jesse; from his roots a Branch will bear fruit.
2 The Spirit of the Lord will rest on him— the Spirit of wisdom and of understanding, the Spirit of counsel and of might, the Spirit of the knowledge and fear of the Lord—
3 and he will delight in the fear of the Lord. He will not judge by what he sees with his eyes, or decide by what he hears with his ears;
4 but with righteousness he will judge the needy, with justice he will give decisions for the poor of the earth. He will strike the earth with the rod of his mouth; with the breath of his lips he will slay the wicked.
5 Righteousness will be his belt and faithfulness the sash around his waist. - Isaiah 11:1-5

5 "The days are coming," declares the Lord, "when I will raise up for David a righteous Branch, a King who will reign wisely and do what is just and right in the land.

⁶ In his days Judah will be saved and Israel will live in safety. This is the name by which he will be called: The Lord Our Righteous Savior. - Jeremiah 23:5,6

Looking at events in hindsight always appear much more apparent when we have a lot of other information. If I was a mature man when Jesus was born, I might have missed it also; the coming of Jesus might not have been that clear. Perhaps I would have been more like my dad in that I needed to see the actual name of Jesus in the scripture before I would have connected scripture with reality.

We might think that the Jewish people should have been expecting the coming of their Messiah based on the Old Testament scripture just mentioned. But actually, there were many more verses that pointed to a coming Messiah. For example, in 2 Samuel 7:12,13, God promised that King David's offspring was to have an eternal kingdom. God promised a particular sign; a baby would be born of a virgin and his name would be "Immanuel" (Isaiah 7:14). A great ruler of Israel would be born in the little town of Bethlehem (Micah 5:2). An offspring of Eve would destroy the devil's work (Genesis 3:15). The Messiah would become the perfect sacrifice (Psalm 40:6-8), and He would teach in parables (Psalm 78:1,2). The Messiah would be a stone that causes people to stumble (Isaiah 8:14). A Redeemer would open blind eyes, unstop the ears of the deaf, cause the lame to leap like a deer, cause the mute to talk (Isaiah 35:5,6). The Messiah would come to Jerusalem riding on a donkey (Zachariah 9:9).

For those who didn't know Old Testament scripture well, there had been conversations about this rugged guy named John the Baptist (John 1:31), who was baptizing people in the river. The Jews should have been questioning what he meant when he said that the kingdom of heaven was near:

> [1] In those days John the Baptist came, preaching in the wilderness of Judea [2] and saying, "Repent, for the kingdom of heaven has come near." - Matthew 3:1,2

And they should have taken Jesus at His word when He was proclaiming He was getting ready to set up His Kingdom:

> From that time on Jesus began to preach, "Repent, for the kingdom of heaven has come near." - Matthew 4:17

> Jesus went through all the towns and villages, teaching in their synagogues, proclaiming the good news of the kingdom and healing every disease and sickness. - Matthew 9:35

The local people should have listened to Jesus' disciples, who were sent to the mission fields proclaiming that the kingdom of heaven was near.

> [6] Go … to the lost sheep of Israel. [7] As you go, proclaim this message: 'The kingdom of heaven has come near.' - Matthew 10:6-7

The concept of a coming kingdom was so prevalent that the disciples were asking Jesus which of them would be greatest in the Kingdom.

> At that time the disciples came to Jesus and asked, "Who, then, is the greatest in the kingdom of heaven?" - Matthew 18:1

James and John petitioned Jesus to sit at His right and left when He set up His Kingdom. (Mark 10:37) Even their mother asked the same of Jesus (Matthew 20:21).

So it was not like the setting up of the Kingdom was a secret. Jesus was not trying to hide it from anyone. In fact, the opposite was true. He wanted everyone to know it and believe it.

Looking back through history, we wonder why Jesus could not convince the Jewish nation that He was a special emissary sent from God. It was not like He was trying to convince them of something utterly foreign to them like radio waves or cell phone technology where people could hear voices from the other side of the world using a small handheld device. This would have seemed like voodoo magic. Nor was He trying to convince them of the possibility to drive people from one city to another at blinding speed on a motorized machine. At the time, this would have seemed far-fetched. Nor was He trying to convince them of the possibility to send people to a distant planet. Had He taught this concept, the people would have had him committed. No, He was not trying to persuade the Israelites of anything foreign to their knowledge. Instead, He was just trying to convince them that He was the promised Messiah and the Son of God.

If the Old Testament prophecies and the words of Jesus and His disciples didn't convince the Jews who He was, then we must ask about all the miracles He performed. Shouldn't they have been convincing evidence that He was the Son of God? After all, He walked on water, controlled the winds, fed thousands with only a few fish, and healed those afflicted with illness for a very long time. Yes, the miracles should have convinced everyone who saw them, but they didn't.

The Apostle Paul wrote in 1 Corinthians 1 a very insightful verse about what it took for people to believe in God in his time:

> "Jews demand signs and Greeks look for wisdom" -
> 1 Corinthians 1:22

Of course, there are always exceptions, but if you want to convince a Jew that you are a messenger from God, you perform some sign or miracle. This might be different today, but this was true in Paul's day. The Jewish people were always looking for signs and miracles. Perhaps this is still true for many Jews and non-Jews today. We all would like to see an astounding miracle, and yet if we do, are we convinced it is real? The first thing that enters my mind is whether it is a miracle or a magic trick.

We have to wonder what it was like for the Jews of Jesus day who saw him perform perform miracle after miracle. What did they think when they saw a man who they passed every day and who could not walk, all of a sudden get up and walk at the command of Jesus? Or what did they believe when they saw Jesus spit on some mud, rub it on some man's eyes who had been blind since birth and all of a sudden he could see? Or what did they think when they saw a few fish and loaves of bread multiplied to feed 5000 people? Even more impressive was when Jesus raised Lazarus from the dead. Certainly, not every Jewish person saw all the miracles performed by Him. but the Apostle John writes at the very end of his book:

> Jesus did many other things as well. If every one of them were written down, I suppose that even the whole world would not have room for the books that would be written.- John 21:25

This is a remarkable statement; it makes me wonder, "How many astounding miracles did Jesus actually perform? How many would a person have to see Him perform before they would believe He was truly the Son of God? How many parables would a person have to hear from Jesus before they would be convinced that He had wisdom far beyond that of a normal man?"

Without a doubt, Jesus was an extraordinary person, but as a result of all the things he said and done, how many lost sheep would come to believe that he was the Son of God? Unfortunately, not many. The question is, "Why?" Why didn't people believe he was the Son of God? Here are three reasons worth contemplating:

1) He didn't act like a king. Many were asking themselves, "Was this the man who was supposedly the Messiah?" The Messiah was supposed to be the King, a benevolent king, but one with a flowing, royal robe. He would live in a palace and have guards.

He would not mingle among commoners and hang out with sinners.

Theoretically, He would give commands, root out corruption, and use His power to turn the oppressive, dictatorial Roman government on its head. Jesus wasn't anything like they imagined. He didn't talk about holding arrogant, self-serving officials accountable; instead, He lectured about love, forgiveness, and mercy. They wanted to believe Jesus was going to be their new King, but He wasn't acting like the forceful person they imagined.

2) Jesus was claiming that salvation came from believing in Him.

> 16 For God so loved the world that he gave his one and only Son, that whoever believes in him shall not perish but have eternal life. 17 For God did not send his Son into the world to condemn the world, but to save the world through him. 18 Whoever believes in him is not condemned, but whoever does not believe stands condemned already because they have not believed in the name of God's one and only Son.- John 3:16-18

The Jews were to take this message based on faith and nothing else. For the most part, there was no other explanation. How could the Jews confirm what Jesus said? Everything they had heard in the past said that their forgiveness was based on animal sacrifice. Jesus never told them to stop animal sacrifice for their sins. But this new method of forgiveness, based on faith, was a radical idea and a change to what was written in the Torah (the first five books of the Bible).

The Jewish priests had ingrained in them that they earned their righteousness by obeying Jewish law and making sacrifices when they sinned. They just couldn't wrap their heads around a new way of thinking. All they had to do was to believe Jesus was the Son of God. There was nothing written in the Old

Testament that explained this new concept of acceptance by God. For these people, who had been making animal sacrifices for 1500 years, this seemed like utter nonsense! His statement put into question H what are you breathing like that Comfort medsis credibility. No one could go to a book and study more in-depth about this theology. The people just had to take Jesus' word for it. No skeptic would have readily accepted this statement based only on a person's testament about himself.

Realistically, I don't think God expected people to believe it based on no other evidence. However, the Jews were told by their ancestors all of the miraculous events that God performed for their relatives. They knew the promises of a future Messiah made by the Old Testament prophets. They knew that Jesus was superior by His knowledge of scripture and the wisdom contained in His parables. They also heard about and witnessed several examples of superhuman abilities provided by the Holy Spirit and performed by Jesus. Everything considered, this was overwhelming evidence that He was credible.

3) The religious leaders of the day had created rules and regulations that were not Biblical. These Jewish leaders were offended by many of the things that Jesus said. They, too, were amazed by His ability to perform miracles, yet their jealousy of Him having the ear of so many people made them frustrated. And when Jesus made statements stating that the religious leaders were hypocrites, pompous, and that they really didn't care about the ordinary Jew, then their jealousy, shame, and frustration turned to anger and hatred towards Him (Matthew 23).

Just how great was their hatred towards Jesus? Again, we should refer to John 11 after Jesus raised Lazarus from the dead. The priests were talking among themselves:

> "...Here is this man performing many signs. [48] If we let him go on like this, everyone will believe in him, and then the Romans will come and take away both our temple

and our nation." … 53 So from that day on they plotted to take his life. - John 11:47,48,53

The Jewish leaders were not going to say or do anything to convince the typical Jew to believe in Jesus. Their goal was to destroy His credibility

Jesus is Rejected as the Messiah Even After Crucifixion

If Jesus couldn't convince Jews before they crucified Him that He was their Messiah, then we would have thought that those who knew scripture would have realized it afterward. There are several verses in the Psalms and Isaiah that describe how Jesus would be a man of little means, how He would suffer both physically and emotionally for others, and how others would reject him. Here are some of the more well-known verses from Isaiah and Psalms that point to the great suffering of Jesus.

3 He was despised and rejected by mankind, a man of suffering, and familiar with pain. Like one from whom people hide their faces he was despised, and we held him in low esteem. 4 Surely he took up our pain and bore our suffering, yet we considered him punished by God, stricken by him, and afflicted. 5 But he was pierced for our transgressions, he was crushed for our iniquities; the punishment that brought us peace was on him, and by his wounds we are healed. 6 We all, like sheep, have gone astray, each of us has turned to our own way; and the Lord has laid on him the iniquity of us all. 7 He was oppressed and afflicted, yet he did not open his mouth; he was led like a lamb to the slaughter, and as a sheep before its shearers is silent, so he did not open his mouth. - Isaiah 53:3-7

6 … I am a worm and not a man, scorned by everyone, despised by the people. 7 All who see me mock me; they hurl insults, shaking their heads. 8 "He trusts in the Lord," they say, "let the Lord rescue him. Let him deliver

him, since he delights in him." 9 Yet you brought me out of the womb; you made me trust in you, even at my mother's breast. 10 From birth I was cast on you; from my mother's womb you have been my God. 11 Do not be far from me, for trouble is near and there is no one to help. 12 Many bulls surround me; strong bulls of Bashan encircle me. 13 Roaring lions that tear their prey open their mouths wide against me. 14 I am poured out like water, and all my bones are out of joint. My heart has turned to wax; it has melted within me. 15 My mouth is dried up like a potsherd, and my tongue sticks to the roof of my mouth; you lay me in the dust of death. 16 Dogs surround me, a pack of villains encircles me; they pierce my hands and my feet. 17 All my bones are on display; people stare and gloat over me. 18 They divide my clothes among them and cast lots for my garment. - Psalm 22:6-18

CHAPTER

9 **God's New Plan**

There were several reasons why the Jewish people should have recognized and believed that Jesus was the Messiah and the Son of God. They had witnessed the fulfillment of much Old Testament prophecy, John the Baptist's preparatory work, Jesus' superior wisdom, and a multitude of His miracles. But even with all this evidence, they didn't recognize Him when he arrived.

In the last chapter, I gave three reasons why the Jews had rejected Jesus as their Messiah, but there is a fourth reason, and it is one which we should all be acutely aware of. The prophecies in the Old Testament were written somewhere between 500 to 1000 years before Jesus was born. After 500 years or so, the people had become complacent. They had given up believing that the Messiah would show up in their lifetime. Here is a vital point. Beware! This is similar to the same situation where we are now. It's been 2000 years since Jesus walked the earth. How many people are anticipating his return in their lifetime? Not many. We have become complacent during our waiting. Jesus predicted His second coming in Matthew 24, Luke 21, and Mark 13. His disciple, John, predicted it in Revelation. His disciple, Peter, predicted it in Acts 3:20, 21 and 2 Peter 3:10. The Apostle Paul predicted it in 1 Thessalonians 4:16. We should all have our eyes open, recognize the signs, and eagerly await His arrival.

God is faithful; Jesus fulfilled the prophecy about His first coming. Likewise, He will also fulfill the prophecy of His second coming. We just don't know when God's patience dealing with hardened, unbelieving people will run out. But one day, it will, and when it does, the accompanying world events will be dramatic and

95

devastating! The book of Revelation describes the events in gory detail.

It was not nearly as evident to the world when God ushered in His relationship of Grace through the Apostle Paul. It was dramatic to Paul on that famous incident on his trip to Damascus, but only a few people witnessed it. Most Jews didn't have a clue that their rejection of Jesus had affected their relationship with God, but Paul knew. It must have been a shock to his system. He had been persecuting those who believed in Jesus, but now he was the Apostle telling the world how God had brought Gentiles into the fold through Jesus. He explained that the reason he was being sent to the Gentiles with the message of Grace was that the Jewish people rejected Jesus as their Messiah.

> 11 …because of their transgression, salvation has come to the Gentiles to make Israel envious. - Romans 11:11

God gave us salvation to make Israel envious for their rejection of their Messiah, Jesus.

Knowing all this history begs the question, "Did God know along time ago that Israel would reject Jesus, and consequently, He would offer Grace to the Gentiles?" Paul acknowledges that, of course, God knew. In Romans 10, he repeats Scripture written by Isaiah explaining this very fact, and why: because the Israelites were a disobedient and obstinate people.

> 19 …"I will make you envious by those who are not a nation; I will make you angry by a nation that has no understanding."
> 20 And Isaiah boldly says,
> "I was found by those who did not seek me; I revealed myself to those who did not ask for me."
> 21 But concerning Israel he says, "All day long I have held out my hands to a disobedient and obstinate people." - Romans 10:19-21

Several other seemingly obscure scriptures in the Old Testament foretold a change in God's future plan. He knew all along He was going to offer Grace to the Gentiles.

> "Behold! My Servant whom I uphold, My Elect One *in whom* My soul delights! I have put My Spirit upon Him; He will bring forth justice to the <u>Gentiles</u>." - Isaiah 42:1(NKJV)

> "And in that day there shall be a Root of Jesse, who shall stand as a banner to the people; for the Gentiles shall seek Him, and His resting place shall be glorious." - Isaiah 11:10 (NKJV)

> The Gentiles shall come to your light, and kings to the brightness of your rising. - Isaiah 60:3 (NKJV)

> The Gentiles shall see your righteousness, and all kings your glory. You shall be called by a new name, which the mouth of the Lord will name. - Isaiah 62:2(NKJV)

The above verses refer to Jesus and His effect on Gentiles. Unlike the Jews, the prophecy was that the Gentiles would embrace him.

God told Abraham that He would bless him and his many Jewish descendants (Genesis 12:1-3). They enjoyed this special privilege for 2000 years. When Isaiah wrote these verses some 700 years later, I doubt that any Jew realized their special privilege would end; they were still proclaiming it during the time of Jesus (Matthew 3:9). Yet it did end…, at least for the next 2000 years. They probably had focused on the part of God's promise to Abraham that he was a special blessing. Consequently, they did not think much about how God would bless the entire world through him. That was their scotoma.

Like so many life events, we often don't see what is immediately in front of us. But afterward, it is a lot more apparent. John 12 records an event where some Greeks (Gentiles) had come to meet with

Jesus. Remember how that Jesus had come for the Jews, not Gentiles.

> 20 Now there were some Greeks [Gentiles] among those who went up to worship at the festival. 21 They came to Philip, who was from Bethsaida in Galilee, with a request. "Sir," they said, "we would like to see Jesus." 22 Philip went to tell Andrew; Andrew and Philip in turn told Jesus.- John 12:20-22

The disciples were well aware that Jesus had come only for the Jews (Matthew 10:5,6). So when the Gentiles approached Philip, he wasn't sure how to turn them down. Consequently, he went to Andrew, and they both went to Jesus. At first glance, Jesus' response seems puzzling.

> 23 Jesus replied, "The hour has come for the Son of Man to be glorified. 24 Very truly I tell you, unless a kernel of wheat falls to the ground and dies, it remains only a single seed. But if it dies, it produces many seeds. 25 Anyone who loves their life will lose it, while anyone who hates their life in this world will keep it for eternal life. 26 Whoever serves me must follow me; and where I am, my servant also will be. My Father will honor the one who serves me." - John 12:23-26

Notice that the verses do not read that Jesus actually met with the Gentiles. However, He subtly announces that He is about to be crucified, buried, and resurrected. Furthermore, He also reveals that His sacrifice is for whoever follows Him (including Gentiles). However, at the time, the disciples never realized it.

Likewise, James makes this confession about how God opened the door for the salvation of Gentiles in Acts 15:

> James spoke up. "Brothers," he said, "listen to me. 14 Peter has described to us how God first intervened to choose a people for his name from the Gentiles. 15 The

words of the prophets are in agreement with this, as it is written:
16 "'After this I will return and rebuild David's fallen tent. Its ruins I will rebuild, and I will restore it, 17 that the rest of mankind may seek the Lord, *even all the Gentiles* who bear my name, says the Lord, who does these things'— 18 things known from long ago. - Acts 15:14-18 (quoting Amos 9:11,12)

James said that God had initially chosen His people, the Jews, from the Gentiles, but after they fell (David's fallen tent), the rest of mankind (even the Gentiles) might seek the Lord.

If there is any doubt whether God intended for Jesus to pay for the sins of everyone (including both Jews and Gentiles), here are some additional verses:

> This is good, and pleases God our Savior, 4 who wants <u>all</u> people to be saved… - 1 Timothy 2:3,4

> "<u>Everyone</u> who calls on the name of the Lord will be saved." - Romans 10:13

> But we do see Jesus, who was made lower than the angels for a little while, now crowned with glory and honor because he suffered death, so that by the grace of God he might taste death for *everyone*. - Hebrews 2:9

> The Lord is not slow in keeping his promise, as some understand slowness. Instead he is patient with you, not wanting anyone to perish, but *everyone* to come to repentance. - 2 Peter 3:9

A Couple of Amazing Bible Verses

In Matthew 8 is recorded an interesting event. A Roman centurion, a Gentile, asked Jesus to heal his paralyzed, suffering servant.

> 7 Jesus said to him, "Shall I come and heal him?"

⁸ The centurion replied, "Lord, I do not deserve to have you come under my roof. But just say the word, and my servant will be healed. ⁹ For I myself am a man under authority, with soldiers under me. I tell this one, 'Go,' and he goes; and that one, 'Come,' and he comes. I say to my servant, 'Do this,' and he does it."
¹⁰ When Jesus heard this, he was amazed and said to those following him, "Truly I tell you, I have not found anyone in Israel with such great faith. ¹¹ I say to you that many will come from the east and the west, and will take their places at the feast with Abraham, Isaac and Jacob in the kingdom of heaven. ¹² But the subjects of the kingdom will be thrown outside, into the darkness, where there will be weeping and gnashing of teeth."- Matthew 8:7-11

I have been dumbfounded by verse 10. The verse says that Jesus was "amazed." The dictionary defines "amazed" as a great surprise. How could this be? I believe Jesus is the Son of God, and therefore I wonder how He could ever be a little surprised, let alone greatly surprised (amazed). After all, Jesus knew that the woman at the well (John 4:18) had previously been married five times without anyone telling Him. How could Jesus be amazed by the statement of the centurion?

There have been times I have been somewhat surprised, but I can't remember a time I was amazed. Synonyms include: astonished, dumbfounded, stunned awestruck. For me, the miracles Jesus performed were amazing. With this being the case, how could Jesus be astonished?

I have heard these verses in Matthew taught by ministers, and their emphasis is always on the Roman soldier's faith. Even Jesus said He was amazed by his faith. And while I agree that faith is an integral part of the story, it doesn't tell the whole story. The reason why Jesus was amazed was because Gentiles, (which included Roman soldiers), were not given all of the historical background and prophecy provided by Old Testament scripture. They may have extraneously heard Jesus speak or had come upon one of his miracles, but for the most part, they were not exposed to Jesus. Why would any Gentile have great faith? God had given all the previous blessings only to the Jews. It would not be a surprise for a Jew to have great faith…, but a Gentile? No way!

There are only two incidents in the Bible (but repeated in the Gospels) where Jesus said He was amazed. There is the verse above from Matthew 8/Luke 7. The second place is in Matthew 8/ Mark 6:

> Jesus left there and went to his hometown, accompanied by his disciples. 2 When the Sabbath came, he began to teach in the synagogue, and many who heard him were amazed.
> "Where did this man get these things?" they asked. "What's this wisdom that has been given him? What are these remarkable miracles he is performing? 3 Isn't this the carpenter? Isn't this Mary's son and the brother of James, Joseph, Judas and Simon? Aren't his sisters here with us?" And they took offense at him.
> 4 Jesus said to them, "A prophet is not without honor except in his own town, among his relatives and in his own home." 5 He could not do any miracles there, except lay his hands on a few sick people and heal them. 6 *He was amazed at their lack of faith.* - Mark 5:1-6

If Jesus is amazed at anything, it should be about these two events regarding faith. At this time, Jesus was not trying to convince them that He would shed His blood to pay for the sins of the world. Nor was He trying to convince the Jews that He was going to die and be resurrected. No, He was simply trying to convince the Jews that He was the Messiah and the Son of God. He was doing everything correctly. He was citing ancient scripture and relating it to Himself. He was sharing God's wisdom through parables. He was performing miraculous healings. He dedicated his ministry primarily to Jews only so that they would be convinced that He was the Son of God and the Messiah. But as it turned out, the Gentile who had little reason to believe in Jesus actually had great faith in Him. Secondly, the Jews who had many reasons to believe in Jesus and were astounded by the things He said and did, yet they had no faith in Him. This was an inexplicable, confounding mystery!

Paul's Attitude Change That Gentiles *Are* Accepted by God

As a law-abiding Pharisee, Paul (originally called Saul) had an attitude toward the Gentiles initially like Peter's and all the other disciples; he didn't have any use for them. He knew it was unlawful to associate with them. Indeed, he wasn't going to meet or be friends with them. However, after he was struck blind on the road to Damascus and was confronted by Jesus asking him why he is persecuting other believers, his mind should have been preparing him that a significant change was coming his way. The Jesus who he thought was an imposter and was dead, approached him in a dramatic way. A light flashed from heaven, and he heard his voice, "Saul, Saul, why do you persecute me?"

In the meantime, the believer Ananias, is told to lay his hands on Paul to give him his sight back. Ananias was the first person told that Paul was to be the Apostle to the Gentiles:

> 15 ... the Lord said to Ananias, "Go! *This man is my chosen instrument to proclaim my name to the Gentiles* and their kings and to the people of Israel." – Acts 9:15

It is unclear exactly when Paul realized he was to be the Apostle to the Gentiles. Was it while he was walking blindly down the Road to Damascus? Was he given a revelation at the same time when Ananias was told? Or was it during his three-year "boot camp" in the desert? Considering all he had learned earlier about the Jews being given preferential treatment by God, this new direction had to be a big surprise to him.

Regardless, he was convinced he was the new Gentile Apostle, and consequently, he makes this claim in Galatians 1:1, 1 Corinthians 1:1, 1 Timothy 2:7, Romans 11:13, and Romans 15:16. Because Old Testament scripture forbids the Jews to associate with Gentiles, convincing others that he was now the Apostle of the Gentiles would be one of the biggest challenges of his life.

Did it Surprise God That Jews Rejected Jesus?

Scripture states that God sent Jesus only to Israel's lost sheep and that He gave grace to Gentiles to make Israel jealous. Therefore, today's Christians are possibly wondering, "If Israel had accepted Jesus as their Messiah, would Gentiles have been excluded from God's Grace forever?"

If you assume that the answer is "Yes," then you might take this logic to the next step and think that God didn't, and perhaps still doesn't really love Gentiles. He was merely getting back at the Jews because they never believed in Jesus. So let's review the reasons why God chose the Israelites.

First, it was because God had made a promise to Abraham. He had promised that He would bless the whole world through him. Remember, this wasn't just because of His random choice to pick Abraham. Instead, it was because Abraham had shown extraordinary faith. God told him to sacrifice his son (as a type of prophecy of God sacrificing His Son, Jesus, on the same mount Moriah). Abraham was obedient, believing that God could bring his son, Isaac, back to life (Hebrews 11:19).

Second, because God gave the Jews all of the Old Testament Scripture, spelling out much prophecy about the coming Messiah, it only made sense that Jesus would go to them first. Had he gone to the Gentiles first, they would have no way of authenticating a coming Messiah.

Third, the Israelites had a history of experiencing God's power. They were aware of how He supernaturally freed the Jews from Egypt. God had sent plagues to convince the Pharaoh of His power. He also parted the Red Sea, which allowed His people to escape Pharaoh's army. Then while His people were in the desert, He supernaturally fed them and prevented their clothes from wearing out. The Gentiles had possibly heard about these miracles, but none had personally experienced God's protection.

Fourth, remember that the Gentiles were idolatrous people. They were worshipping many false gods. They didn't know the one, true God.

After reviewing these events, it becomes easier to understand that Jesus was *not* trying to avoid Gentiles because they didn't deserve His righteousness and His blessings. Instead, it was because of the history the Jewish people had with God. It seems only reasonable that Jesus would give the Israelites the first opportunity to accept or reject him.

Paul wrote in Romans 11:7 that God purposely blinded the Jews so that they couldn't recognize Jesus for who He was.

To many people, this makes no sense. Why did God send Jesus to the Jews knowing full well that they would not accept Him? One point worth consideration is that their rejection of Jesus was not the first and only sign of their obstinance. There are many examples in Isaiah, Psalms, Jeremiah, and Ezekiel that documents how Israel rebelled against God. Furthermore, some Jews killed the prophets (1 Thessalonians 2:15). God knew that because they killed the prophets, they also would reject and crucify Jesus.

It is interesting to note that God blinded Paul, a Pharisee for many years, on his road to Damascus trip. As a result of this experience, he became humbled, and he became a usable vessel to minister to Gentiles. Conversely, the other Pharisee religious leaders had seen Jesus many times. They could have humbled themselves and accepted Him, but they did not. They were spiritually blinded, and their pride and jealousy caused them to become more antagonistic towards Jesus; so much that they had Him crucified.

Would we conclude then that it was to Israel's advantage to be offered salvation first, compared to being a lowly Gentile? Absolutely not. God knew all along what would happen. As it turns out, it was a more generous benefit to Gentiles.

What does all this mean regarding my dad? If he was familiar with Old Testament Scripture regarding faithless, idol-worshipping Gentiles; he may have developed the opinion that he could earn God's respect by not worshipping idols. Likewise, if he focused on the things Jesus said in the four Gospels and disregarded what Paul said, then he could have possibly believed that Jesus came only to benefit the Jews. He may have considered that Gentiles (including himself), were afterthoughts; a group of people who were unimportant in the eyes of God. It is assumptions like this that keeps people from developing a closeness to the Loving Father.

But for us who have the writings of Paul, we get the full picture. We know that Jesus came for our benefit. Because of what Paul said, we can be confident that Jesus came to save us all.

CHAPTER

10 God's Secrets

My dad understood the Old Testament containing God's Commandments. He didn't know that they were directed to the Jews. Nor did he realize that Jesus' comments were primarily directed to Jews. Therefore, what he believed was that all mankind was held accountable to God's Commandments. To him, this was how we are all judged as being acceptable to God. "God gave these Commandments to Moses thousands of years ago, and because the nature of God does not change, everyone is still found acceptable to God based on the same set of laws." He believed we see His blessings when we abide by His commandments.

The last chapter focused on God's New Plan. Although we have seen scripture from Paul that revealed a change in how God interacted with humans, many people are still skeptical. Therefore, I provided scripture from the Old Testament of how God was not surprised. While it seemed like a massive change to us, He knew all along that He would extend His Grace to the Gentiles. We can look at a verse from Deuteronomy where God chooses to keep some things secret until He decides to reveal them:

> The secret things belong to the Lord our God, but the things revealed belong to us and to our children forever… - Deuteronomy 29:29

Some people still argue, "God detested the Gentiles (Leviticus 20:23) for thousands of years because they worshiped false idols. On the opposite end, He greatly favored Abraham and all his relatives because of Abraham's faithfulness (Romans 4:3). Now He turned this all around and offered grace to the Gentiles

106

and blinded the Jews (Romans 11:7-10). Many people think this happened just too quickly to be believable. Furthermore, God required the Jews to obey all His laws and make animal sacrifices when they sinned, but now, Gentiles who believe that Jesus paid died for them are not held accountable for their sins? Again, for many people, "This is just too bizarre to be true!"

I must admit that this change in plan happened quickly. Likewise, it is hard to fathom how God placed the sins of the world on his sinless Son so that we all could be forgiven. Nowhere else have we seen such a dramatic change in His approach to mankind…, or have we?

There is a theological concept and a term used in some versions of the Bible called "dispensation." The word is not used in all versions, but it is used in the King James Version. The Apostle Paul uses it in two different places in his letter to the Ephesians. Here are the references:

> … in the <u>dispensation</u> of the fullness of the times He might gather together in one all things in Christ - Ephesians 1:10 KJV

> … if indeed you have heard of the <u>dispensation</u> of the grace of God which was given to me for you - Ephesians 3:2 KJV

These examples might not mean much by themselves, but once the concept of "dispensation" is understood in the broader context, it is more meaningful. It is a big word, but it is not complicated.

To better understand the term "dispensation," think about having a prescription filled at the drugstore. The druggist writes down the instructions for taking the medication; therefore we say the druggist dispenses it. What God has chosen to do is to "dispense" His nature, will, and character to us; therefore, it should be considered as part of the big picture while reading the Bible. This means that He has leaked it out to us over time, and it has changed.

In the example of Ephesians 1:10 from above, Paul is referring to a mystery that God reveals. In Ephesians 3:2 example, Paul is writing about God's dispensation of Grace. In a broad perspective, anytime God specifies His will, it can be referred to as a dispensation. He has done this in a limited way ever since the creation of Adam. But the will He has projected has changed over the millenniums. In the early years of humanity, He did this by either direct communication or revelation. Eventually, Moses and other prophets would write down what God revealed and told them so we could read the history and progression of how God has chosen to dispense His will. Some people would prefer to call this disclosure as progressive revelation.

Why Is Dispensation Important?

Dispensationalists, those who study dispensation, break down the history of the Bible into basically seven different dispensations.

During each dispensation period, God chose what He intends for man to learn from Him and He also communicates what is acceptable and sometimes unacceptable. For some people, this concept is confusing. They had been told that God is unchanging; therefore, they begin to have questions. "God chooses to interact with humans differently? He changes His mind about what is acceptable and what is unacceptable? He has handed down different guidelines to different people? This doesn't make sense."

However, when we look at biblical history, this is precisely what has happened. Consider God's relationship with Adam. In Genesis 1:28,29, He initially gave three simple commands:

1) Be fruitful and fill the earth with children.
2) Subdue the earth.
3) Have dominion over the animals. He gave him every fruit with seed to eat.-Genesis 1:28-29

After putting Adam in the garden of Eden, He added to the original commands and told him to:
4) Care for the garden.
5) Abstain from eating the fruit from the tree of knowledge of good and evil. God warned of the punishment of death if he ate its fruit. Genesis 2:15,17

It is important to note that there were no ten commandments or any other laws at this time. Adam (and Eve) had the freedom to do pretty much whatever they wished! There were only five commandments. The first dispensation could have lasted a long time, but it didn't. When Adam and Eve sinned, everything changed. Their relationship with God was fractured.

Therefore, Dispensation two began after Adam and Eve sinned. It lasted from their sin until the Great Flood (about 1650 years later) (Genesis 3:8–8:22). The significant aspects of this dispensation were:
1) Adam and Eve were kicked out of the garden. - Genesis 3:23
2) The serpent was cursed. - Genesis 3:14
3) God promised that Christ is the seed who would bruise the serpent's head (Satan). - Genesis 3:15
4) Women would incur pain during childbearing. - Genesis 3:16
5) The ground was cursed and would produce thistles and thorns. - Genesis 3:17-19
6) The "free lunch" went away. From then on, mankind had to work to produce food. - Genesis 3:17-19

As a result of Adam and Eve's sin, all men had inherited a sinful nature and it affected everyone from then on (Romans 5:12). After God saw how evil most men had become, He chose Noah, a man he declared righteous, and commanded him to build a large boat. This boat was to be big enough to hold all varieties of animals and hold enough food to last through the duration of the flood. God then flooded the earth to destroy all the other remaining people and animals. I believe it is significant that God did not destroy man because we broke any particular laws, i.e., " committed adultery, murdered, worshipped idols, stole, coveted, etc." After all, at this time in history, God had still not given the Ten Commandments. It was plain and simple:

> "Then the LORD saw that the wickedness of man was great on the earth, and that every intent of the thoughts of his heart was only evil continually"- Genesis 6:5.

Therefore, God had morals for us, and even though he hadn't expressed them specifically, our motives and actions were way off track of what He had intended.

Dispensation three began after the Great Flood. God promised never again to send a flood to destroy all the creatures of the earth. He permitted eating animals. He then told Noah and his sons that they should:

1) Be fruitful and repopulate the earth - Genesis 9:1.
2) Man should not eat animals with blood still in them - Genesis 9:4.
3) Man was not to kill other men. Anyone who sheds the blood of another will have their blood shed. - Genesis 9:5-6.

During this third dispensation, mankind fails to fulfill God's commandment to disperse and populate the earth. Instead, they get the idea to stay together and build a great city with a tower (Babel) to "reach the skies – a monument to their greatness" (Genesis 11:4). God could have handled the rebellion in several different ways. In this case, God changed people's language so that instead of assembling with foreign speaking people, everyone would be motivated to split and go with those who spoke the same language as their own. This dispensation lasted about 325 years.

Dispensation four began with God's promise and commitment to a man named Abram. This dispensation is one of the most well known because it contains the Abrahamic covenant. Because of Abram's faith, God promised him that he would become the father of a great nation. Abram's descendants would be given the land of "milk and honey," i.e., what we now know as present-day Israel. This was the beginning of the Jewish nation. While we can argue all we want that it wasn't fair that God made the promise to just one people group, this was God's choice. (If you feel it wasn't fair, then after your death, you can take it up with Him face to face.) Later, Abram's name was changed to Abraham (meaning in Hebrew, "Father of many"). Christians believe that the most crucial part of God's promise was that the whole world would be blessed through Abraham, so the blessing wasn't limited to just the Jews. – Genesis 12:1-3. Instead, it was about Jesus, the Savior, who was a descendant of Abraham.

During this dispensation, God spoke to Abraham in a vision that he would "protect him and his reward would be great" (Genesis 15:1 NLT). Many ministers and pastors have used this Bible verse, and others like it to declare it as a Biblical doctrine relevant to current times. They make the analogy that if God protected and rewarded Abraham for his faithfulness, then God will protect and reward us for our faith.

This "protect and reward" doctrine was prominently taught by the PTL "Praise the Lord" Ministry (1974-1989). People were encouraged to give the church large sums of money, with the expectation that God would protect and reward them. The result was that people drained their savings accounts, based on the belief that the more they gave, the more God would recompense them.

Unfortunately, it was then, and still is today, easy for the clergy to take Bible verses out of context.

It is true that God promised the Jewish people that they would inherit a land of "Milk and Honey" in the Old Testament. Likewise, He promised a "financial reward" to Abraham (later confirmed to his son Isaac - Genesis 26:3 and also confirmed to his grandson Jacob - Genesis 28:13). But the New Testament makes no mention of earthly financial reward for having faith.

The sign of the covenant with Abraham was circumcision, and the dispensation lasted for about 430 years, until the people exited Egypt. All Jews were to be circumcised as their commitment to the promises of God.

Dispensation five is the one that most people are familiar with, primarily because of the movie "The Ten Commandments." I can still recall Charlton Heston climbing down Mount Sinai carrying the stone tablets. This is the dispensation that generated the "law." And while most people are familiar with the Ten Commandments, there were over 600 laws given to Moses pertaining to diet, temple sacrifice, cleanliness, how to treat strangers, who not to marry, tattoos, and many other things (Exodus 20-23).

This dispensation was also given strictly to the Jews. God required them to obey His laws, and the failure to do so could result in death. Obviously, God has the right to determine appropriate justice for violating His laws, but the penalty for breaking them certainly was severe compared to current laws in the United States. For example, the Bible states:

> "If a man commits adultery with another man's wife, both the man and the woman must be put to death." -Leviticus 20:10

> "The penalty for homosexual acts is death to both parties."- Leviticus 20:13

"Men and women among you who act as mediums or psychics must be put to death by stoning." - Leviticus 20:27

"All who curse their father or mother must be put to death." - Leviticus 20:9

Work six days only, but the seventh day must be a day of total rest. I repeat: Because the LORD considers it a holy day, anyone who works on the Sabbath must be put to death. - Exodus 31:15

If a priest's daughter becomes a prostitute, defiling her father's holiness as well as herself, she must be burned to death. - Leviticus 21:9

"You must carefully obey all my laws and regulations; otherwise the land to which I am bringing you will vomit you out. -Leviticus 20:22

Do not live by the customs of the people whom I will expel before you. It is because they do these terrible things that I detest them so much. - Leviticus 20:23

While we understand that these laws define God's character and justice, we also need to realize that they were given only to the Jews 3300 to 3600 years ago. We like to dwell on God's great love without realizing that He is a righteous God who stipulates that sin is unacceptable. Today, we must rely on the suffering of Jesus to atone for our sins, but there was no alternative to the prescribed penalty during this dispensation.

Fortunately, our country has decided not to adopt the same penalties as the Israelites had. If we had, and enforced them, our population would be significantly less!

Dispensation 6 is that of Grace, the one in which we currently live. It began with the death of Christ. It is the New Covenant provided by Christ's blood (Luke 22:20) through his crucifixion. This dispensation is worldwide and includes both Jews and Gentiles. In this dispensation, the Holy Spirit indwells believers as the Comforter (John 14:16-26) and the moral guidance system. It has lasted for over 2,000 years, and no one knows when it will end. Many Christians believe it will end with the Rapture of all born-again believers from the earth to go to heaven with Christ (1 Thessalonians 4:16-18). Following the Rapture will be the judgments of God.

This current dispensation was only made known to the Apostle Paul. It had been revealed to him by Jesus after His resurrection (Galatians 1:12). It included his complete Gospel message, i.e., that Christ died for our sins, He was buried, and on the third day, God raised from the dead (1 Corinthian 15:1-4). At that time, Paul was the only one who understood the complete plan of salvation. This was not the message being dispensed by the other disciples; it was hidden from them. He writes this in his letter to the Romans:

> Now all glory to God, who is able to make you strong, just as my Good News says. This message about Jesus Christ has revealed his plan for you Gentiles, *a plan kept secret from the beginning of time.* But now as the prophets foretold and as the eternal God has commanded, this message is made known to all Gentiles everywhere, so that they too might believe and obey him. - Romans 16:25-26 [NLT]

Paul states that God kept the plan secret since the beginning of time. Nobody knew it but him; until he released it to Gentiles.

Jesus had made statements about His pending crucifixion to His disciples during their first communion (Matthew 26:28), but they never picked up on it. Just like when He foretold them that He would be killed, and on the 3rd day, He would rise again (Matthew 12:40, Luke 18:33). But they did not understand.

So how long will this dispensation last? We don't know…, but then we do also have an idea. Paul tells us in Romans 11 of a mystery. Israel (generally as a nation but not individually), was blinded to

God's grace. But God will eventually restore them. They will come to know the truth about salvation so that some of them will be saved:

> 25 I do not want you to be ignorant of this mystery, brothers and sisters, so that you may not be conceited: Israel has experienced a hardening in part *until the full number of the Gentiles has come in,* 26 and in this way all Israel will be saved. - Romans 11:25, 26

Many people are not aware of this verse. They believe that because it has been 2000 years since the death of Christ, then it may go another 2000 or so years. Anything is possible, but this verse makes it clear that there is a limit. Whenever God determines that the Gentiles have filled all their reservations, He will raise the blinders from the nation of Israel. They will again have another opportunity to recognize Jesus' sacrifice.

Now here is the critical part about the dispensation of grace. According to Paul, believing that Jesus died for our sins, He was buried, and He rose from the dead by the power of the Holy Spirit is what now makes us acceptable to God. He also writes that the obeying of God's laws does not make us more acceptable to Him.

Moses has been credited with writing the books of Exodus, Leviticus, and most of Deuteronomy. In these books, he clearly states that we are held accountable for obeying God's laws. Therefore, the concept that we are no longer held accountable to obey the law is very difficult to accept. Every discipline experience we had while growing up is contrary to this concept. If we did something wrong and got caught, then we had to pay the penalty. No one else paid it for us. To quote an old cliché, "Don't do the crime if you can't do the time!"

However, the present time is the dispensation of Grace. It replaces the dispensation of law. The Apostle Paul makes this very clear.

Unfortunately, millions of people do not believe what Paul has taught about Grace. They say they believe it, but actually, they don't. What they really believe is that, because God is a loving God, He gives us all a limited amount of Grace regardless of the actions of Christ.

The seventh dispensation is the one to come and is predicted in the Bible. It is the one spoken of by the Apostle John in the book of Revelation. After the full number of Gentiles has been saved, then this book predicts a horrible punishment by God that will last for seven years. However, after the seven years, the Millennial Kingdom of Christ will be ushered in by Jesus and will last for 1,000 years as Christ Himself rules on earth. This Kingdom will fulfill the prophecy to the Jewish nation that Christ will return and be their King. The only people allowed to enter the Kingdom will be born-again believers from the Age of Grace and the few righteous survivors of the seven years of tribulation (Ephesians 2:8-9, Romans 10:9-10, Matthew 25:31-46, Revelation 20:12-14). No unsaved person is allowed access into this Kingdom. Satan will be bound during the 1,000 years. This period ends with the final judgment (Revelation 20:11-14). The old world will be destroyed by fire, and the New Heaven and New Earth of Revelation 21 and 22 will begin.

You may look at these dispensations and say, "So what? What do they have to do with me?" I believe that when viewed at a deeper level, we inductively develop some conclusions. For example, because God knew that Abraham was a faithful man, He promised him that he would be incredibly blessed…, and he was! He had a beautiful wife, was wealthy, and although he had only one child (Isaac) with his wife, he ended up with many descendants; as numerous as the stars in the sky (Hebrews 11:12). Therefore, we incorrectly assume that faithful people will be blessed with Abrahamic like earthly blessings.

Does God's Love Equate to Protection and Prosperity on Earth?

From the Pew study I referenced in Chapter 1, eighty percent of adults think God has protected them and two-thirds say that the Almighty has rewarded them. Considering that only a little over half of them believe in the God of the Bible, I wonder how they arrive at this concept.

My explanation comes from two widely held beliefs. One, most people believe that the God who created the world is a God of love. Two, people want to believe that God's love manifests itself in both healings and prosperity. After all, isn't that what most people think of when they mention love. I want the best for you. I don't want to see you suffer from illness, depression, or loneliness. I don't want to see you and your family go hungry or struggle to pay mounting bills. No, I want to see you healthy and prosperous.

If we use these human concepts of love to describe God, He has undoubtedly disappointed His most faithful. That's not to say that God hasn't blessed people because He has. He protected and gave great wealth to Abraham and King David. He made Solomon very prosperous and blessed him with great wisdom. But these were individuals from a different dispensation. They were all Jews from the lineage of Abraham. However, if we consider the faithful believers of the current dispensation, we see something entirely different.

Jesus did not live a life of earthly comfort. There were no luxuries for Him. He did not depend on people or animals to carry Him around. Near the end of His three years of ministry, His life got even worse. He was despised and mocked by the religious leaders, spit upon, given severe lashings with whips that ripped open His skin, causing profuse bleeding, and finally He was crucified. King David prophetically wrote Psalms 22, describing what Jesus was feeling just before and during the time He was put on the cross…; and yet He knew what was going to happen to Him. Psalms 22 describes a horrible human life, including being hated, ridiculed, helpless, lonely, and physically miserable:

My God, my God! Why have you forsaken me? Why do you remain so distant? Why do you ignore my cries for help? Every day I call to you, my God, but you do not answer. Every night you hear my voice, but I find no relief. Yet you are holy. The praises of Israel surround your throne. Our ancestors trusted in you, and you rescued them. You heard their cries for help and saved them. They put their trust in you and were never disappointed. I am a worm and not a man. I am scorned and despised by all! Everyone who sees me mocks me. They sneer and shake their heads, saying, "Is this the one who relies on the LORD? Then let the LORD save him! If the LORD loves him so much, let the LORD rescue him!" Yet you brought me safely from my mother's womb and led me to trust you when I was a nursing infant. I was thrust upon you at my birth. You have been my God from the moment I was born. Do not stay so far from me, for trouble is near, and no one else can help me. My enemies surround me like a herd of bulls; fierce bulls of Bashan have hemmed me in! Like roaring lions attacking their prey, they come at me with open mouths. My life is poured out like water, and all my bones are out of joint. My heart is like wax, melting within me. My strength has dried up like sunbaked clay. My tongue sticks to the roof of my mouth. You have laid me in the dust and left me for dead. My enemies surround me like a pack of dogs; an evil gang closes in on me. They have pierced my hands and feet. I can count every bone in my body. My enemies stare at me and gloat. They divide my clothes among themselves and throw dice for my garments. O LORD, do not stay away! You are my strength; come quickly to my aid! Rescue me from a violent death; spare my precious life from these dogs. Snatch me from the lions' jaws, and from the horns of these wild oxen. – Psalms 22:1-21

If there was anyone who had a reason to question the love of God because of His physical life, it should have been Jesus. He never had an easy life from the time He was born in a manger until His crucifixion, yet He was faithful; He knew God loved Him.

Of course, we can look at Jesus and exclude Him. He came with a special purpose. He came as a servant and died for us. We wouldn't expect Him to have lived a privileged life.

Therefore, let's look at Jesus' disciples. Did they have it easy? Were they protected or given special privileges? Did they lead a life of posh and luxury? No, it was just the opposite. The Romans and other Jews despised them also. They were considered insurrectionists who were trying to overthrow the government. Consequently, of Jesus' eleven faithful disciples, ten were scourged and executed by some torturous method.[13]

Consider how their contemporary, the Apostle Paul lived. Granted, while he was a Pharisee, he lived a luxurious life. But everything turned south when he became a believer in Jesus. He writes in 2 Corinthians11:

> 24 "Five times I received from the Jews the forty lashes minus one. 25 Three times I was beaten with rods, once I was pelted with stones, three times I was shipwrecked, I spent a night and a day in the open sea, 26 I have been constantly on the move. I have been in danger from rivers, in danger from bandits, in danger from my fellow

---

[13] Nelson, R. (2020, July 2). *How Did the Apostles Die? What We Actually Know*. OverviewBible. https://overviewbible.com/how-did-the-apostles-die/

> Jews, in danger from Gentiles; in danger in the city, in danger in the country, in danger at sea; and in danger from false believers. [27] I have labored and toiled and have often gone without sleep; I have known hunger and thirst and have often gone without food; I have been cold and naked." -
> 2 Corinthians11:24-27

Paul was tortured repeatedly, and his suffering and abuse weren't because he didn't believe God; it was because he did!

Wealth is one thing, but sometimes there are more important things than money…, like friends. How did God bless Paul in this area? Paul had made several converts and had developed many friendships, but near the end of his ministry, he writes in 2 Timothy:

> As you know, all the Christians who came here from the province of Asia have deserted me; even Phygelus and Hermogenes are gone. - 2 Timothy 1:15

After the many sacrifices Paul had made, all his friends have left him. How would you feel if all your friends had deserted you? Pretty lonely, I bet.

Sometimes we need to think about what was *not* written in the Bible, as well as what was. Think for a moment; where did Jesus, any of the twelve disciples, or the Apostle Paul, write that anyone will receive earthly blessings. They didn't!

These examples should in no way make you think that God is uncaring. No, He loves us very much. But it is a misconception to believe that He will reward us on earth for our work, faithfulness, and suffering. True, He protected Abraham and rewarded him; but it was for a different reason. This was the dispensation of God's promise and commitment. It was to benefit the Jewish people and to provide an avenue for the Messiah. The documentation in the Old Testament also serves as proof that God is a Deity of His word. He made promises and He fulfilled them. God does not need to do this for people in the dispensation of Grace. Unfortunately, many people believe that the "love of God" translates to wealth and prosperity.

Our problem is that we are too attuned to earthly life. We see, we feel, and we believe what we experience. But when it comes to the spiritual, we have doubts. Again, the scripture talks about this, but the question is whether we believe it. Will there be benefits in our next life? According to words spoken by Jesus, God has made several promises concerning our faithfulness in this life to rewards in eternal life. For example, consider the following verses:

> "God blesses you when you are mocked and persecuted and lied about because you are my followers. Be happy about it! Be very glad! For a great reward awaits you in heaven. And remember, the ancient prophets were persecuted, too." – Matthew 5:11,12

> "I assure you that when the world is made new and the Son of Man sits upon his glorious throne, you who have been my followers will also sit on twelve thrones, judging the twelve tribes of Israel. And everyone who has given up houses or brothers or sisters or father or mother or children or property, for my sake, will receive a hundred times as much in return and will inherit eternal life. But many who are the greatest now will be least important then, and those who seem least important now will be the greatest then." – Matthew 19:28-30

"Look, I am coming soon, bringing my reward with me to repay all people according to their deeds. I am the Alpha and the Omega, the First and the Last, the Beginning and the End." – Revelation 22:12,13

I press on to reach the end of the race and receive the heavenly prize for which God, through Christ Jesus, is calling us. – Philippians 3:14

24 It was by faith that Moses, when he grew up, refused to be called the son of Pharaoh's daughter. 25 He chose to share the oppression of God's people instead of enjoying the fleeting pleasures of sin. 26 He thought it was better to suffer for the sake of Christ than to own the treasures of Egypt, for he was looking ahead to his great reward. – Hebrews 11:24-28

The one who plants and the one who waters work together with the same purpose. And both will be rewarded for their own hard work. – 1 Corinthians 3:8

Now this I say, he who sows sparingly will also reap sparingly, and he who sows bountifully will also reap bountifully. – 2 Corinthians 9:6

And when the Great Shepherd appears, you will receive a crown of never-ending glory and honor – 1 Peter 5:4.

And now the prize awaits me—the crown of righteousness, which the Lord, the righteous Judge, will give me on the day of his return. And the prize is not just for me but for all who eagerly look forward to his appearing. – 2 Timothy 4:8

Yes, there will be a reward, but it is in heaven, not on earth.

CHAPTER
11 Revisiting the Law - Overcoming brainwashing

Why did Paul eventually conclude that we could not be made right with God by obeying all His laws? Where did he get such an idea? This concept seemed so contradictory to what Jesus taught.

First, we should acknowledge that Paul had not always held this belief. In fact, he had just the opposite opinion. God was very explicit in the Old Testament that the Jews should obey His laws. If they didn't, then there were severe consequences, up to and including death! This was the lesson that Paul was taught over and over. I believe that almost anyone who had been educated as he had would develop the same opinion. We wouldn't expect that God suddenly create a new way of relating to Him.

Paul thought that everyone needed to obey every little detail of Jewish law. Furthermore, he believed that the better a person showed he was following God's laws, the better his approval rating was by God. This was one of the reasons why Paul became a Pharisee. He was a zealous religious leader who worked diligently to obey every law.

Most Pharisees tried to obey all laws all of the time to the nth degree. They were in a tough spot dealing with Jesus, a devoted law abider. They hated Him because He was performing miracles and proving that He had more authority and knowledge than them. In the meantime, Jesus was ridiculing them for their hypocrisy. In many cases, they were obeying the letter of the law, pretending to be righteous, yet secretly they had selfish motives. They were living a lavish lifestyle. They were cheating others when they brought their animals to be sacrificed, telling them that their animals were not "pure" enough, and then would sell them a "more perfect" animal at a considerable markup.

It irritated the religious leaders when Jesus cleared their exchange tables (Matthew 21:12-17). It also grated on them that this pauper who didn't know where He was going to lay his head at night was claiming to have a special relationship with God. Who was this guy who thought He was so righteous? He made the Pharisees look bad, and the greater the miracles He performed, the worse it looked for them. They had a big problem on their hands. How could they portray this man called Jesus to look like a villain who should be crucified? He threatened their way of life, their religion, and their income.

The religious leaders convinced the Roman officials that Jesus was claiming to be King of the Jews, which was an act of sedition. The Roman government would not tolerate anyone who claimed that they were a king. Jesus should be executed! … And He was!!

Meanwhile, the Pharisee called Saul believed the other religious leaders. They brainwashed him. Consequently, he too ridiculed this man named "Jesus of Nazareth." He knew that Jesus was no ordinary man; he had heard that Jesus performed miracles. But now that Jesus had been crucified and was dead, He certainly could not have been the Messiah He claimed to be. He mistakenly assumed that if He were truly the Son of God, God would never have allowed Him to be hung on a cross.

Ironically, Saul believed that all of the followers of Jesus had been brainwashed. He considered them a threat to Judaism; therefore, He decided to track them down and get rid of them. Saul admits by his own words of his former life as a Pharisee in Galatians 1:

> [13] For you have heard of my previous way of life in Judaism, how intensely I persecuted the church of God and tried to destroy it. [14] I was advancing in Judaism beyond many of my own age among my people and was extremely zealous for the traditions of my fathers. - Galatians 1:13,14

Saul was teaching that eternal life was earned by obeying all laws, and the disciples were teaching that God would give salvation to anyone who believed that Jesus was His Son. Their disagreement was fierce. Saul was convinced that the more righteous a person acts, then the greater likelihood that they would earn eternal life.

Saul was searching for and destroying everyone who believed in Jesus. But then! How quickly things changed. Saul saw a bolt of lightning, and he had to rethink all he had been doing:

> 3 As he neared Damascus on his journey, suddenly a light from heaven flashed around him. 4 He fell to the ground and heard a voice say to him, "Saul, Saul, why do you persecute me?"
> 5 "Who are you, Lord?" Saul asked.
> "I am Jesus, whom you are persecuting," he replied. 6 "Now get up and go into the city, and you will be told what you must do."
> 7 The men traveling with Saul stood there speechless; they heard the sound but did not see anyone. 8 Saul got up from the ground, but when he opened his eyes he could see nothing. So they led him by the hand into Damascus. 9 For three days he was blind, and did not eat or drink anything. - Acts 9:3-9

During those 3 days, Saul must have been doing a lot of thinking. Was he wrong about Jesus? He believed that the crucified man was dead and gone for good. He must have been greatly perplexed.

God knows our hearts and motivation. In the case of Paul, God identified him as a man true to his beliefs. So when we read in Galatians that Paul had a zeal for persecuting the followers of Jesus, we should not be surprised. Paul was initially doing what he thought was right. God can use a man or woman of conviction and integrity if He gets their mind pointed in the right direction. God can turn them into useful servants.

I believe that Paul was not like other Pharisees, but I have no way of proving it. All we know for sure is that Paul admitted how he was a strict adherer of the law and then after he met Jesus, he became a changed man. He learned the fallacy of his previous life. He still had zeal, but his understanding of Christ's sacrifice had changed his teaching.

What A Revelation!

Many people today still believe that the idea of eliminating the requirement to obey all of God's laws is absurd. Their logic is, "If God created laws for us to obey and Jesus affirmed it, how can we believe a mere mortal like Paul?" They would agree with my dad, "Paul is out in left field." Indeed, the Son of God must have the correct doctrine.

Furthermore, it just makes sense that we must obey the Creator's laws. While most of us chose to rebel at a young age, as we grew older, we have concluded that to have a functioning, somewhat cohesive society; then there must be rules and laws to obey. That does not mean we all agree with what those rules and regulations should be, but only that we should all abide by some standards for everyone's safety and well-being. Therefore, for Paul to say we don't need to obey God's laws sounds blasphemous and just like downright nonsense.

From a conceptual view, Paul's theology just doesn't seem rational. We may reason, "If we don't obey our Creator's laws, then we have been given a license to commit as many vile sins as we wish without a second thought. Is this what God intended?"

While we may develop this attitude, it is certainly not true. Thinking that we can commit gross sins repeatedly is a total misrepresentation of what Paul was emphasizing.

However, Paul tells us in his letter to the Galatians why his theology changed after his Damascus Road experience.

He was given this concept by direct revelation from Jesus Christ. He didn't make it up, nor was he given this doctrine by anyone else:

> 11 I want you to know, brothers and sisters, that the gospel I preached is not of human origin. 12 I did not receive it from any man, nor was I taught it; rather, I received it by revelation from Jesus Christ. - Galatians 1:11,12

So it wasn't like he fabricated this concept. Had he met with the other disciples who had walked with Jesus throughout his ministry, they would have told him that everyone *must* obey all God's laws. After all, that is what their Master had taught. However, what they would not have mentioned was that Jesus' death on the cross paid for everyone's sins. They never expressed any knowledge of this essential concept.

Jesus' payment for our sins was a new revelation given by God. Just like when He gave Moses the Ten Commandments, it was a new dispensation, a completely new model of how God interacted with people. He spoke, and He expected people to obey.

Most of the Jewish people had rejected Jesus. Only a relatively few accepted Him as their Messiah. Therefore, it was time to announce the new game plan. He had suffered and died on the cross. He had paid for the sins of *everyone*, but only a small percentage of the Jewish people accepted it. For those *who accepted* this simple concept, they would *not* be subject to God's Commandments again. For those who *did not accept* it, they *were* subject to God's judgment of every sin, both great and small. Furthermore, because the Jews rejected Him, Saul was sent with this message of God's Grace to the Gentiles.

A Change in Pharisee Mentality

I believe that Saul's change of opinion was not quick but took him a relatively long time. After all, the necessity to obey God's laws had been in existence for a couple of thousand years. Until Saul had met Jesus on the road to Damascus, all he knew was to practice God's laws. In all, God had given 613 religious laws, and the Pharisees added to these laws all with the intent to make them "more religious" and more favorable to God.

Our brains are wired so that when a concept is reinforced over and over, it is next to impossible to change our opinion. Saul had been taught from the time he was a little shaver that acceptance by God was based on obeying laws. Suddenly he is confronted with a new doctrine. "No one is made acceptable to God by obeying His laws!" This concept had to be a shock to his system.

Some people have speculated that Saul needed to spend three years in the desert with Jesus because it took him that long to get his mind re-oriented to a new way of thinking.

I can imagine Saul questioning Jesus, "Now I know you told me this every day for the last couple of years, but please tell me again that we are *not* accepted by obeying God's commandments."

However, after Jesus revealed (probably just as many times) that we are saved only by His atoning blood on the cross, Saul eventually realized how wrong he was. And like most people, when they realize how blatantly wrong they are, it sticks in their crawl. I think Saul might have been thinking, "Oh, what a fool I was!! Jesus *is* who He claimed to be. He really is the Messiah and the Son of God. Although He died, the rumors that He was resurrected are true! He truly has the Holy Spirit in Him! How could I have been so wrong going after the disciples of Jesus!"

The Bible gives only a brief explanation of Saul's experience during those three years in the desert, but I believe this was intense training. He had learned many mysteries about Jesus, His relationship to God, what He gave up to come to earth, and how much He sacrificed for us. Finally, he had an "*aha*!" moment.

The Typical Pharisee

While Paul initially had the wrong opinion of how God views us as acceptable or not, I believe he wasn't as insincere as other Pharisees. Many of the other Pharisees were hypocrites; much of what they did was for show. In Matthew 6, Jesus points this out to the everyday Jew. He warns them not to be like the Pharisees regarding giving to the needy or saying prayers. In fact, He says to do the opposite of what they do:

> 2 "So when you give to the needy, do not announce it with trumpets, as the hypocrites do in the synagogues and on the streets, to be honored by others. Truly I tell you, they have received their reward in full. 3 But when you give to the needy, do not let your left hand know what your right hand is doing, 4 so that your giving may be in secret. Then your Father, who sees what is done in secret, will reward you.
>
> 5 "And when you pray, do not be like the hypocrites, for they love to pray standing in the synagogues and on the street corners to be seen by others. Truly I tell you, they have received their reward in full. 6 But when you pray, go into your room, close the door and pray to your Father, who is unseen. Then your Father, who sees what is done in secret, will reward you. 7 And when you pray, do not keep on babbling like pagans, for they think they will be heard because of their many words. - Matthew 6:2-7

Jesus and Paul Agree about Obeying God's Laws

While it appeared that Paul disagreed with Jesus when he said that we could not be saved by obeying God's laws, at a deep level, they were both emphasizing a complementary concept. Jesus was saying, "Don't be like the Pharisees who act like they are obeying God's laws. They aren't. They are mocking God's laws, and it is all for show. They want you to believe that they are generous towards the needy. They are saying prayers that make them look like they are godly men, but it is all a performance; an appearance of looking good; when in reality, their minds are not focused on God at all."

Many people are familiar with the fit of rage Jesus displayed when he overturned the tables of the money changers in the temple (Matthew 21:12-13). He was distraught because the religious leaders took advantage of the ordinary Jews who had come to make animal sacrifices. But Jesus displayed as much verbal angst when He spewed out his criticism of the Pharisee in Matthew 23. He begins with several verses explaining in detail how they do things only for attention. He followed up with other things they did, which showed that they didn't really love God or others. Six times he said:

"Woe to you, teachers of the law and Pharisees, you hypocrites!"

Another time he said:

"Woe to you, blind guides!"

Near the end of his rant, He said:

"You snakes! You brood of vipers! How will you escape being condemned to hell?"

The people that Jesus was condemning were not typical Jews; no, they were the religious leaders. The problem was their heart. They taught about the letter of the law without emphasizing or practicing the intent of the law. They taught about God, but they did not love Him. They thought their knowledge about God's laws and their Pharisee title should earn them respect, …but they were as fake as a three dollar bill.

Even though Saul was not around to hear Jesus' sermon, I am certain that he understood these attitudes and behaviors as a Pharisee. He had probably been guilty of some of these same traits. After his eyes had been opened to his own deceitfulness, he rebelled against the idea of being saved by works. He knew that no person could do enough to save themself. Instead, it takes the love and sacrifice of Christ, combined with the Grace of God, to save us.

> 8 For it is by grace you have been saved, through faith—
> and this is not from yourselves, it is the gift of God— 9 not
> by works, so that no one can boast. - Ephesians 2:8-9

If we consider the wisdom that Jesus spoke to the Pharisees, we would realize that He was talking to more than just the Jewish hypocritical religious leaders. He was also talking to us. We are all born with the desire and inclination to sin(Romans 5:12). We all try to think of ourselves as loving God and loving others at some high level, but we all fail (to some degree). We cannot live the perfect life that God demanded; only Jesus could do that.

Saul, who was later renamed Paul, used words that were not the same as Jesus, but he was making a similar point. "Do not think that all the things you do are earning you points with God. You are not nearly as good as you try to make yourself appear. And even if you are honest and truly have a repentant heart, you can't earn your own righteousness. No, you must believe in and accept the sacrifice that Jesus made for you."

Paul gave us this wisdom through his writings. Even though it appears Jesus and Paul seem to be in disagreement, we can be at peace knowing that their words were, in fact, in perfect harmony.

Paul's Embarrassment

After Paul realized his theology mistake, I think his previous actions were embarrassing and foolish to him personally. He probably had thoughts running through his mind, such as, "What made me think I could be made right with God by trying to obey all 613 laws. How absurd! And who did I think I was kidding when I was saying long prayers and tried to act pious in front of others?

If the resurrected Jesus knew how to track me down, then He probably saw all my actions, knowing that I was trying to "work" my way to heaven. How could I think that my pretenses fooled the Almighty God?"

All of his attempts to earn God's favor by obeying his laws were meaningless. They had earned him nothing. He made this confession in Philippians:

> 4 If someone else thinks they have reasons to put confidence in the flesh, I have more: 5circumcised on the eighth day, of the people of Israel, of the tribe of Benjamin, a Hebrew of Hebrews; in regard to the law, a Pharisee; 6 as for zeal, persecuting the church; as for righteousness based on the law, faultless.

> 7 But whatever were gains to me I now consider loss for the sake of Christ. 8 What is more, I consider everything a loss because of the surpassing worth of knowing Christ Jesus my Lord, for whose sake I have lost all things. I consider them garbage, that I may gain Christ 9 and be found in him, not having a righteousness of my own that comes from the law, but that which is through faith in Christ—the righteousness that comes from God on the basis of faith. - Philippians 3:4-9

Before Paul's conversion, he thought it made a difference that he had been circumcised (which was required by God). He believed it was important he was from God's chosen nation of Israel and that both his father and mother were Hebrews. He had been faultless in his observation of God's written law. He would persecute those who did not try to obey every detail of the law. But later, he realized how wrong he had been. Everything he had done was worthless garbage compared to knowing Christ as his Lord and Savior.

It drove him to the other end of the spectrum, denying any relationship between obeying the law and attaining eternal life. Therefore, he made statements in his letters, such as:

¹⁵ "We who are Jews by birth and not sinful Gentiles ¹⁶ know that a person is not justified by the works of the law, but by faith in Jesus Christ. So we, too, have put our faith in Christ Jesus that we may be justified by faith in Christ and not by the works of the law, because by the works of the law no one will be justified. - Galatians 2;15, 16

You foolish Galatians! Who has bewitched you? Before your very eyes Jesus Christ was clearly portrayed as crucified. ² I would like to learn just one thing from you: Did you receive the Spirit by the works of the law, or by believing what you heard? ³ Are you so foolish? After beginning by means of the Spirit, are you now trying to finish by means of the flesh? - Galatians 3:1-3

I have looked at a few of the Pharisees' extended rules and laughed at their ridiculousness. For example, they reasoned that if a person spits on the Sabbath, then when their spit hits the dirt, it could roll and create a mud-ball; therefore, it was deemed "work" and was a sin. Baloney!

How could they have dreamed up a law like this? And while we don't have such rules today, many of us have developed a similar attitude in that we believe we can earn God's favor through performing some activity. For example, we think, "If I go to church every Sunday, then God will look at me with favoritism. Every week, I should take communion to show God (and others) how much I believe in Him. I know the church keeps track of how much money I give them, and because I got a raise last year, I should put a little more in the offering plate. I should help others because it is the Christian thing to do. I shouldn't work on Sunday because we are supposed to rest and go to church on that day." These are often the unspoken thoughts that run through our minds, or sometimes we even speak them. If we could ask Saul, the man who became Paul, he would say, "Nonsense! God knows your heart and motivations better than you know yourself!"

CHAPTER
12 The Alternative to Law

Before we try to build a relationship with God, our intent is mostly self-seeking. We are born with the desire to sin and be rebellious. This nature was bred into us by the first man and sinner, Adam(Romans 5:12). Our desire to love others (for their benefit) is limited. Although few people admit it, the instinct of trying to love others comes from a desire of wanting to be loved.

However, once we believe that Jesus died for our sins, then the Holy Spirit enters our body:

> And you also were included in Christ when you heard the message of truth, the gospel of your salvation. When you believed, you were marked in him with a seal, the promised Holy Spirit... - Ephesians 1:13

This is the single most important event in our life! Several things happen when a person takes this step of faith, but I will state only two of them. First, let me be clear. The two promises I declare are only guaranteed if we are sincere. (It doesn't make a difference to who on earth you make a promise of your sincerity. It only counts if you are honest in your heart to God.)

1. We are sealed for eternal Salvation!

2. Our desires and our nature changes! This means that we become convicted not to want to sin (break God's laws). We will still sin because we are human, but we will not want to sin. In addition, the Holy Spirit should be guiding us (by reminding us) how we should try to be understanding and forgiving of others. He will give us the heart to be helpful to others.

Some people get confused about what this should look like. It is not like a little angel sits on your shoulder, whispering in your ear. Instead, it is something you sense internally, sensing the difference of right from wrong; trying to love others (compared to indifference); wanting to help but not necessarily knowing how to help.

I thought it was interesting to hear my dad question other believers (including me) about whether it was a sin to lie. I asked myself, "Why did he want to know? Did he want to lie but was afraid God would hold him accountable, or had he already lied, and he felt guilty about it?" I never did discover his motivation, but my answer to him was, "It depends on why you lie. If you are lying for personal gain, keeping from being held responsible, or getting someone else in trouble, it is absolutely a sin. However, if you are trying to keep from hurting someone, it falls into a grey area. For example, if a friend asked me my opinion and I thought my answer would be hurtful, then I would try not to lie; but I might." I thought that was the best answer I could give to my dad, who was sometimes very exacting.

The point is that once we believe in what Jesus did for us, we have a new nature. We want to do what is right; what is loving. We shouldn't have to question whether it is okay to lie; the Spirit should be motivating us to do the greater good for a person.

This new nature affects our thoughts, feelings, and promptings. Over time, it will affect any misconceptions we have about trying to earn our way into heaven. Let me state this again as a summation of these last two sentences. The Holy Spirit should guide us to be loving, forgiving, compassionate, and helpful, but we should *not* think that we are earning our way into heaven through human effort. This is one of Paul's main principles; we are saved by Grace, *not* by works (Ephesians 2:8,9). Through the work of the Spirit, we become aware of how much God loves us. Our mind becomes renewed, guiding us to do what is loving and considerate towards others. This concept is expressed in Romans 12.

¹ Therefore, I urge you, brothers and sisters, in view of God's mercy, to offer your bodies as a living sacrifice, holy and pleasing to God—this is your true and proper worship. ² Do not conform to the pattern of this world, but be transformed by the renewing of your mind. Then you will be able to test and approve what God's will is—his good, pleasing and perfect will.
³ For by the grace given me I say to every one of you: Do not think of yourself more highly than you ought, but rather think of yourself with sober judgment, in accordance with the faith God has distributed to each of you. ⁴ For just as each of us has one body with many members, and these members do not all have the same function, ⁵ so in Christ we, though many, form one body, and each member belongs to all the others. ⁶ We have different gifts, according to the grace given to each of us. If your gift is prophesying, then prophesy in accordance with your faith; ⁷ if it is serving, then serve; if it is teaching, then teach; ⁸ if it is to encourage, then give encouragement; if it is giving, then give generously; if it is to lead, do it diligently; if it is to show mercy, do it cheerfully. - Romans 12:1-8

I believe Paul's words were not given just because they are foreign to us (as non-believers). But when the Holy Spirit prompts us to be loving and helpful, how should we respond? We are all given different talents. What options are available to us? You might think these things should be obvious, but they weren't for me. If they were all that obvious and given to us by the Holy Spirit, then Paul would not have had to write about them. But he did…, because they are not obvious! I am thankful he gave slow learners like me specific ideas.

He continues with more words of advice for believers. It is one thing to be prompted by the Spirit, but having our conscious triggered does not mean that we will follow through with action. We live in a busy world where we see many different types of behavior. It is not uncommon for me to see such actions and say to myself, "That person is too political; he is too far right… or left. That person is too aggressive. I can't help people like that." In essence, I can find a reason to avoid almost everyone if I so desire. But who am I kidding? God doesn't want me to do this. Therefore, the next several verses are very practical for me.

> 9 Love must be sincere. Hate what is evil; cling to what is good. 10 Be devoted to one another in love. Honor one another above yourselves. 11 Never be lacking in zeal, but keep your spiritual fervor, serving the Lord. 12 Be joyful in hope, patient in affliction, faithful in prayer.
> 13 Share with the Lord's people who are in need. Practice hospitality.
> 14 Bless those who persecute you; bless and do not curse. 15 Rejoice with those who rejoice; mourn with those who mourn. 16 Live in harmony with one another. Do not be proud, but be willing to associate with people of low position. Do not be conceited.
> 17 Do not repay anyone evil for evil. Be careful to do what is right in the eyes of everyone. 18 If it is possible, as far as it depends on you, live at peace with everyone. - Romans 12:9-18

With this advice, I can now say, "Ah! Now I see what I am supposed to do. I may disagree with it. I may not feel like doing it, but at least I understand what it is supposed to look like." With my new attitude, I should try to do these things.

Some people develop the expectation that this transformation, i.e., the renewing of our mind, will suddenly happen when we trust Jesus. While this sounds great, it has been my experience that this just isn't true. Because we had a sinful and rebellious mind for many years, we will not change overnight. You may think that you will break a destructive drug or alcohol problem upon professing your faith in Christ, and there have been a few people who have, but this is not the norm. The Spirit will try to change our desires and attitudes, but it is up to us to recognize and give in to those changes. Galatians 5:16-18 reads:

> 16 So I say, walk by the Spirit, and you will not gratify the desires of the flesh. 17 For the flesh desires what is contrary to the Spirit, and the Spirit what is contrary to the flesh. They are in conflict with each other, so that you are not to do whatever you want. 18 But if you are led by the Spirit, you are not under the law. - Galatians 5:16-18

I find these words helpful. It explains that there is a war going on; the flesh (our human desires) wants to do fleshly, worldly activities to indulge ourself and the Spirit wants us to do loving, caring activities for others. We may understand what is going on within us, but which way will we go? The reality is that undesirable, fleshly habits are easy to follow and difficult to break. Paul tells us that we were created from the lineage of Adam and we have adopted his sin nature (Romans 5:12), therefore, it is going to take submissiveness to the Holy Spirit on our part in order to change.

The Holy Spirit points out sin in our life. He tries to help us to break free of our sin nature and to commit no sins. He tries to break us from a destructive lifestyle. However, it is still up to us to give in to Him. Paul states this more clearly in Romans:

> 4 So, my brothers and sisters, you also died to the law through the body of Christ, that you might belong to another, to him who was raised from the dead, in order that we might bear fruit for God. 5 For when we were in the realm of the flesh, the sinful passions aroused by the law were at work in us, so that we bore fruit for death. 6 But now, by dying to what once bound us, we have been released from the law so that we serve in the new way of the Spirit, and not in the old way of the written code. - Romans 7:4-6

So when we believe what Jesus has done for us, then the Holy Spirit indwells us. Once the Holy Spirit indwells us, then we get new desires. Will we follow the passions? The Holy Spirit will try to change us, but He still gives us free will. God has not and will not take that away from us. I believe that is why Paul tells us how we should behave in Romans 12. Do not be surprised if you have new desires after you believe what Jesus did for you. This should be your new normal. Your inclinations should change. But once you receive these promptings, will you recognize them, or will you dismiss them. He is saying, "Listen! I am telling you how you may be conflicted between your old fleshly habits and your new desires. Drop your old habits and follow your new desires."

In many of Paul's letters, he tells us how we should give up worldly desires. Instead, focus on what Jesus Christ did for you. Follow your new promptings provided by the Holy Spirit. Listen to Him. Love, support, encourage and serve others.

Does Grace Give a License to Sin?

If Paul writes that our sin does not determine our salvation, then it seems like we can sin as much as we want, and we are forgiven. Right? That may be the way it appears, but that is not the case.

We just covered what the effect of the Spirit should be on us. The Spirit should affect our heart and attitude. The Spirit should give us a desire to think less about ourselves and to think more about others. The Holy Spirit should have produced in us a desire to be considerate towards others, thinking about their needs. Within us, we should be thinking about how to help others for their good.

We saw specifics from (Romans 12:9-18) how a changed attitude should affect us. Likewise, with a transformed mind, we shouldn't have a desire to sin. So you might ask, "So what are those specific sins?" You might be wondering, like my dad asked, "Is lying a sin?" Or you attend a church where they teach that dancing and card-playing are sins. Maybe your church emphasizes that alcohol should not touch your lips.

Fortunately, Paul has identified sinful behaviors. As he gives those details, he also offers severe warnings. He makes it clear that people should not indulge in such behaviors. Paul does not tell this to only one of the churches he is mentoring, but he gives warnings and specific "don'ts" in his letters to the Corinthians, Galatians, and Ephesians.

9 Or do you not know that wrongdoers will not inherit the kingdom of God? Do not be deceived: Neither the sexually immoral nor idolaters nor adulterers nor men who have sex with men 10 nor thieves nor the greedy nor drunkards nor slanderers nor swindlers will inherit the kingdom of God. 11 And that is what some of you were. But you were washed, you were sanctified, you were justified in the name of the Lord Jesus Christ and by the Spirit of our God. - 1 Corinthians 6:9-11

19 The acts of the flesh are obvious: sexual immorality, impurity and debauchery; 20 idolatry and witchcraft; hatred, discord, jealousy, fits of rage, selfish ambition, dissensions, factions 21 and envy; drunkenness, orgies, and the like. I warn you, as I did before, that those who live like this will not inherit the kingdom of God. - Galatians 5:19-21

3 But among you there must not be even a hint of sexual immorality, or of any kind of impurity, or of greed, because these are improper for God's holy people. 4 Nor should there be obscenity, foolish talk or coarse joking, which are out of place, but rather thanksgiving. 5 For of this you can be sure: No immoral, impure or greedy person—such a person is an idolater—has any inheritance in the kingdom of Christ and of God. 6 Let no one deceive you with empty words, for because of such

things God's wrath comes on those who are disobedient. [7] Therefore do not be partners with them.

[8] For you were once darkness, but now you are light in the Lord. Live as children of light [9] (for the fruit of the light consists in all goodness, righteousness and truth) [10] and find out what pleases the Lord. [11] Have nothing to do with the fruitless deeds of darkness, but rather expose them. [12] It is shameful even to mention what the disobedient do in secret. [13] But everything exposed by the light becomes visible—and everything that is illuminated becomes a light. [14] This is why it is said:
"Wake up, sleeper, rise from the dead, and Christ will shine on you."
[15] Be very careful, then, how you live—not as unwise but as wise, [16] making the most of every opportunity, because the days are evil. [17] Therefore do not be foolish, but understand what the Lord's will is. [18] Do not get drunk on wine, which leads to debauchery. Instead, be filled with the Spirit, [19] speaking to one another with psalms, hymns, and songs from the Spirit. Sing and make music from your heart to the Lord, [20] always giving thanks to God the Father for everything, in the name of our Lord Jesus Christ. - Ephesians 5:5-20

[15] Outside are the dogs, those who practice magic arts, the sexually immoral, the murderers, the idolaters and everyone who loves and practices falsehood. Revelation 22:15

As you read these verses, you probably couldn't help but think you were sitting in a Baptist church with the minister shouting hellfire and brimstone. And while I don't want to soft-soap these verses, I believe we should view them in a little different light; something other than a threat of either straightening up our act or going to hell. Instead, we should compare these verses with our lifestyle. Are we living our lives in a way that is contrary to the guiding Spirit? If so, then we should question whether the Spirit is really in us. If we are genuinely not saved, we should be concerned that we will not spend eternity with God. However, if we truly accept and believe Christ to be our Lord and Savior, then we can't continue to sin without compunction for very long. I say this because the Holy Spirit will have given us a new nature, and He will convict us when we do things that are opposed to that nature.

Our nature is that which provides desires, intent, and motivation. So if we maintain our old nature, then we have no feelings of guilt when we sin. However, if our new nature is not to sin, we will feel guilty when we do. Does that mean that once we are given a new heart, we will not sin again? No, we are emotional beings, and as such, we can perform foolish and rebellious behaviors on the spur of the moment. But even if we do such things, our nature will not change. Once we become a believer in all Christ has done, the Holy Spirit will not only indwell us (Ephesians1:13, 1Corinthians3:16, 1Corinthians6:19), but He will also seal our nature (Ephesians 4:30). We will not want to sin.

These verses make it clear that there is a distinction between wanting to sin and sinning without intent. Let's remember that Paul said the purpose of sin was for us to recognize it and to realize that we all sin. But that still doesn't give us a legitimate excuse to sin whenever we feel like it. Instead, Paul tells us that we should be convicted when we desire to sin. If we are not, then something is wrong. The Holy Spirit should convict us and remind us like a parent would when we think that sinning is okay.

There was thought back in Paul's day that the more a person sinned, this exemplified God's greater grace. Therefore, if we want to show the world how great and loving that God is, then we should sin frequently and watch how the love of God becomes greater and greater. What?? What a sick and demented mind! This is nothing more than the flawed thinking of someone who has too much time on his hands and likes to develop vain philosophies. There is nothing in the Bible that indicates this is God's thinking. Jesus made this very clear, and Paul agreed. We should try to obey God's moral laws. We should not interpret that Jesus' atoning death on the cross gives us a license to commit sins without giving it a second thought.

In contrast, we have seen many verses where Paul explicitly states that we shouldn't sin. There is a distinction between wanting to sin and sinning without consciousness.

Can We Outsmart the Holy Spirit?

How does this understanding of the Holy Spirit and what Jesus said tie together? Jesus said we are guilty of sin not only by what we do but also by what we desire (Matthew 5:28). Now, if we are true believers, then the Holy Spirit lives in us. And because the Spirit lives in us, then He knows our mind and what we are thinking. So, for instance, if you are a man and you see a beautiful woman on the street or on television, or you see a picture of a scantily dressed woman in a store window, then you might develop lust in your mind. Do not be deceived, thinking that it doesn't make a difference that you feel lust or that the Holy Spirit doesn't know. The Spirit lives in you; He knows your mind; otherwise, He couldn't give you a new attitude. What kind of Spirit would He be if He could only see your "action" sins but didn't know your motivations? If He didn't know your mind, He would guess your intentions and give you wrong signals. No, most sins are committed first in your heart/mind. He knows this, and He tries to warn and change you, i.e., in your heart/mind.

So what do you do? Are you so concerned with what others think that you say to yourself, "It's okay if I sin only in my mind and no one else knows? It's not that big a deal. We are human. Everyone sins in their mind." Therefore, you may think, "Just as long as I don't act on my thought, then I'm okay. And even if I do act out physical sin every now and then, God realizes I'm not perfect and will forgive me."

I do not recommend these mental gymnastics. I honestly and genuinely believe in the grace of God, but the words of Jesus and the Apostle Paul put enough fear in me that if I don't try to control myself, then I will start down a slippery slope. Therefore, I try to control it.

Some people may take this one step further. They may trust in the power of prayer and say something like, "I am a sinful person. I don't want to sin, but I do. I pray that you forgive me. Amen."

This is an appropriate response, however, perhaps a little premature. Yes, we certainly want to admit we're sinful people. We never want to hide or deny our sinfulness. But we need to ask ourselves more in-depth questions. "Why am I sinning? Why do I want to sin?" Part of the answer is obvious; it is because we still have the sin nature of Adam living in us; and he will be in us until the day we die! However, there are probably other underlying reasons that are related to past experiences. If there is a method to make those events known, it may help us become aware of triggers we can avoid.

The alcoholic may keep a bottle of gin or whiskey around just to serve others. Those who are prone to lust may keep magazines of women in bikinis or ads of women in lingerie lying around. Those prone to covet may watch commercials advertising the latest car, the new high tech gadget, or fancy jewelry. We are bombarded with many forms of advertising which affect our desires in subtle ways. In any event, we never want to take an attitude that we are so saturated with enticing pictures and advertising that we must just accept it. Likewise, we never want to develop a fatalistic attitude that our personality (and therefore our behavior) is preordained and uncontrollable. The power of the Holy Spirit is always greater than our weak human power.

The Holy Spirit wants to saturate us with a new nature but it takes our willingness to cooperate with Him for the transformation to take affect. Therefore we need to take some active steps for ourself.

The most active movement we can take is to turn away. In the NIV version of the Bible, there are 122 incidences of the term "turn away." More than half of those verses refer to humans sinning. These verses say we turn away from God, truth, faith, and belief. These references are all sinful. But we can also look at the converse to this. Our trust(truth), faith, and confidence in the power of God are manifested by turning away from sin.

Therefore, it is in our best interest to actively turn away from sin whenever we can. The most straightforward examples to see this principle in action are covetousness, lust, or any unhealthy desire (even if you do not personally consider it a sin). Stop your looking at them! Turn your head away. You are not doing yourself any favor by continuing to look. To do so only enhances the desire. God made us humans so that we move in the direction of those things we continually think about. To continue to focus on those things that are against God's will cause a person to want to sin more.

Here are some practical examples. Do not keep your eyes on beautiful, worldly possessions such as fancy cars, expensive homes, or flashy jewelry. Do not repeatedly think about what others have and you don't.

Do not dwell on beautiful bodies at the beach. Instead, throw a frisbee, play volleyball, build a sandcastle, look for shells, or take a swim. If you know you repeatedly lose control when you drink alcohol, then avoid it. Drink other types of refreshing drinks. Do other age-appropriate physically exerting activities like walking, running, playing tennis, riding a bike, etc. Purposely try to turn your mind to something else, like reading an engaging story, listening to music, playing games that require strategy, or more in-depth thinking.

Last and certainly not least, if we are turning away from sin, we should also turn towards God. Study your Bible. Don't just read it and put it down but use a study Bible that provides a more in-depth explanation of scripture. Look up references. Try to become engaged with it. Memorize Bible verses. Remember that this is God's love letter to you. Contained with-in are words of His love and advice. Dwell on verses assuring His spiritual promises.

In association with your studying, think about Christ and his sacrifice for you. Think about where He now is. As I write, the Bible verses of Colossians3:1-3 come to mind:

> [1]Since, then, you have been raised with Christ, set your hearts on things above, where Christ is, seated at the right hand of God. [2] Set your minds on things above, not on earthly things. [3] For you died, and your life is now hidden with Christ in God. - Colossians 3:1-3

CHAPTER
13 Is Water Baptism Necessary?

Over the last few years of my father's life, my dad and I had quite a few discussions about various religions. He asked, "Why are there so many different views about God?" He was correct in asking the question. According to the Pew Research Center, the top four major religions range from 2.3 to 1.1 billion people each. The greatest of these is Christianity, with 31.7 percent of the world following it.[14] However, if any one of those views were really the correct one, why wouldn't the numbers be more lopsided? Why wouldn't the predominant world view of God be something more like 85%?

Although no religion approaches anywhere near 85%, I believe that Christianity has more followers than others because of the Bible. I would argue that it is an incredible book that contains lots of fulfilled and future prophecies. Furthermore, it was written by many writers over a period of 1500 years with great coherency.

Given what I considered a legitimate question by my dad, he expanded his question. "If the Bible is so easily understood, then why are there so many different denominations who have their niche views? Why does one group have one philosophy, and another group believes something different? Aren't they all supposed to be in accordance?"

---

[14] Hackett, C. (2017, April 5). *Christians remain worlds largest religious group, but they are declining in Europe.* Pew Research Center. https://www.pewresearch.org/fact-tank/2017/04/05/christians-remain-worlds-largest-religious-group-but-they-are-declining-in-europe/

I must admit this is a difficult question to answer. For example, there are Episcopalians, Methodists, Baptists, Catholics, Lutherans, Presbyterians, Church of Christ, Seventh Day Adventists, Jehovah's Witness, and on and on. These groups claim to use the same Bible as the basis of their doctrine, yet they all interpret it differently. How can this be?

Do not be too quick to dismiss this question. Of course, there is only one Bible, even though the translations are somewhat different. So most of us agree. There is only one correct interpretation; … it's just we don't know which one it is.

One of the doctrines I discussed with my dad was regarding baptism. When he was a boy, the church he attended thought it was necessary for salvation, and therefore, he was baptized. He remembered sermons regarding John the Baptist and recalled that he had baptized Jesus. To his recollection, he thought Jesus taught that baptism was essential.

Sure enough, my dad was correct; Jesus had taught about the significance of baptism. In Matthew 3, we read where Jesus had a discussion with a Pharisee named Nicodemus. Jesus told him that no one can enter the Kingdom of God unless they are "born again." Nicodemus is confused. "How can someone be born again when they are old? Surely they cannot enter into their mother's womb a second time to be born!"

Jesus answered in verse 5 and 6:

> … "Very truly I tell you, no one can enter the kingdom of God unless they are born of water and the Spirit. 6 Flesh gives birth to flesh, but the Spirit gives birth to spirit." – Matthew 3:5,6

Does this mean that everyone must be baptized with water to enter the Kingdom of God? Certainly, my dad thought so. And though he didn't know if he was good enough to merit heaven on his own, he believed that his baptism was at least one qualification he met.

These two Bible verses have caused a lot of controversy among Christians. Some believe this literally means water baptism and it is necessary. If you ask them, they may give you this Bible reference in Matthew 3 as one reason. However, they usually have other reasons as well. First and foremost, they believe that water baptism is necessary because it is what their church and many other churches practice. What the church professes does not give legitimacy to a custom; however, it probably has the most influence concerning what people believe. Most churches practice water baptism; therefore, it must be a valid doctrine. Right? There are discussions among various denominations about which type of water baptism is best. Some practice water sprinkling on heads while others practice full immersion.

Church practices are not the only reason to believe. Several Bible verses reference water baptism. For example, we read what John the Baptist did in Luke 3:

> He went into all the country around the Jordan, preaching a baptism of repentance for the forgiveness of sins.- Luke 3:3

There were crowds of people going out to see John the Baptist so he could baptize them. As they arrived, he told them how they should repent of their sins.

Some people believe that repentance (the Greek word is metanoia) is an act of asking God to forgive them of their sins. It includes sorrow and regret. While this definition is correct, it is not complete. In the Biblical definition, repenting means to make a complete change of direction towards God. It is not just asking for forgiveness. It involves a changing of the heart and attitude. So if a person is baptized with an attitude of just forgiveness without changing their attitude, it is not truly an act of repentance. Instead, they are asking for forgiveness but do not plan on changing their life.

Another reason why people believe baptism is important is that Jesus commanded his disciples to baptize in his Great Commission:

> "Therefore go and make disciples of all nations, baptizing them in the name of the Father and of the Son and of the Holy Spirit, and teaching them to obey everything I have commanded you." - Matthew 28:18-19

Finally, we have the water baptism of Jesus Himself. It was a spectacular moment when God spoke and declared that Jesus was His Holy Son. What more Biblical examples do we need to confirm that water baptism is really important, if not mandatory?

Admittedly, these examples make it appear like water baptism is essential, but let's dig a little deeper. Did Jesus himself baptize others with water? From reading John 3, we may think so:

> … Jesus and his disciples went out into the Judean countryside, where he spent some time with them, and baptized. - John 3:22

But then we are not sure Jesus actually baptized because of what is written in John 4:

> Now Jesus learned that the Pharisees had heard that he was gaining and baptizing more disciples than John— 2 although in fact it was not Jesus who baptized, but his disciples. 3 So he left Judea and went back once more to Galilee.- John 4;1-3

So the bottom line is we don't really know whether He ever baptized or not. It seems like it was not Jesus who was baptizing, but it was His disciples. Nevertheless, He could have baptized others, just not at this specific time.

There are other verses in scripture that talk about another type of baptism. First, there was John the Baptist, who said:

"I baptize you with water. But one who is more powerful than I will come, the straps of whose sandals I am not worthy to untie. He [Jesus] will baptize you with the Holy Spirit and fire." - Luke 3:16

It appears that if Jesus were going to baptize, He would not use water. Instead, He would baptize with the Holy Spirit and fire. Whether He did this in the common community is unknown, but He confirmed that this would happen with his disciples shortly before ascending to heaven:

For John baptized with water, but in a few days you will be baptized with the Holy Spirit." - Acts 1:5

This was a different type of baptism, one that may have confused the disciples. What did Jesus mean, and what would this mean for them?

They discovered what it meant, and we learn about it from reading Acts:

2 Suddenly a sound like the blowing of a violent wind came from heaven and filled the whole house where they were sitting. 3 They saw what seemed to be tongues of fire that separated and came to rest on each of them. 4 All of them were filled with the Holy Spirit and began to speak in other tongues as the Spirit enabled them.- Acts 2:2-4

This type of Baptism was not like a typical water baptism we see in churches today. They were enabled by the Holy Spirit to speak in other tongues [languages]. The tongues they were speaking should not be confused with a tongue [singular] that is used when some individuals talk to God. In this incident, the crowd, from many different nationalities, heard the disciples' message in their own language. This is amazing! How could people from different backgrounds hear the message from one person yet, when it reached their ears, they heard it in their own language? This could only happen through the power of the Holy Spirit!

What Did Peter Believe About the Need to Be Baptized with Water?

To understand what Peter believed about water baptism we will continue reading in Acts 2.

After being filled with the Holy Spirit, Peter addresses the crowd. He provides his case for why Jesus was the Messiah. He gives scriptural examples from the prophet Joel and King David as recorded in Psalms. Peter makes his point, and this is where we pick up verses 36 through 41.

> 36 "Therefore let all Israel be assured of this: God has made this Jesus, whom you crucified, both Lord and Messiah." 37 When the people heard this, they were cut to the heart and said to Peter and the other apostles, "Brothers, what shall we do?"
> 38 Peter replied, "Repent and be baptized, every one of you, in the name of Jesus Christ for the forgiveness of your sins. And you will receive the gift of the Holy Spirit. 39 The promise is for you and your children and for all who are far off—for all whom the Lord our God will call." 40 With many other words he warned them; and he pleaded with them, "Save yourselves from this corrupt generation." 41 Those who accepted his message were baptized, and about three thousand were added to their number that day. - Acts 2:36-41

Because the people denied that Jesus was the Messiah, Peter believed that the people should repent and respond with the act of being baptized with water; and they were.

Acts 10 records another event where Peter baptized individuals. He is again giving his testimony about Jesus Christ being the Messiah to the Gentile Cornelius, his family, and friends. As he spoke, the

Gentiles are overcome by the Holy Spirit and began speaking in tongues [other languages]. After Peter and other believers heard this, Peter said in verse 47:

47 "Surely no one can stand in the way of their being baptized with water. They have received the Holy Spirit just as we have." 48 So he ordered that they be baptized in the name of Jesus Christ. - Acts 2:47

In this example, Peter does not ask them to be baptized, but "he orders" them. Other translations use the term "he commands." So for Peter, it was not an option, but it seemed necessary for salvation.

What Did Paul Believe About the Need to Baptize with Water?

So what did Paul believe about water baptism? After his Damascus Road experience, Ananias placed his hands on Paul, and the scales that had kept him blind fell off. After this baptism experience, we would certainly think that he favored water baptism.

And then we read in Acts 19 where Paul himself baptizes others.

> 4 Paul said, "John's baptism was a baptism of repentance. He told the people to believe in the one coming after him, that is, in Jesus." 5 On hearing this, they were baptized in the name of the Lord Jesus. 6 When Paul placed his hands on them, the Holy Spirit came on them, and they spoke in tongues and prophesied. - Acts 19:4-5

From these examples, we can infer that both Peter and Paul both believed in water baptism. However, it is interesting to note that neither one said that it was necessary for salvation. So is it really? If it was essential for salvation, then it seems we would find more examples in the Bible of people being baptized by Peter and Paul. Furthermore, we might also read about their excitement, believing

that they helped to assist the filling of the Kingdom of God.
Instead, we learn that Paul stopped baptizing. If water baptism was
necessary for salvation, then certainly he wouldn't stop this
practice.

So why did Paul quit baptizing others? There are two reasons. One,
it was causing divisions within the church, and there was confusion
about the purpose of baptism.

> 11 My brothers and sisters, some from Chloe's household
> have informed me that there are quarrels among you.
> 12 What I mean is this: One of you says, "I follow Paul";
> another, "I follow Apollos"; another, "I follow
> Cephas[Peter]; still another, "I follow Christ." 13 Is Christ
> divided? Was Paul crucified for you? Were you baptized
> in the name of Paul? 14 I thank God that I did not baptize
> any of you except Crispus and Gaius, 15 so no one can
> say that you were baptized in my name. 1 Corinthians
> 1:11-15

Some followers believed that they should be baptized in the name
of Paul. Paul knew this was wrong, and he wanted to squash any
appearance of people being baptized in his name, nor did he want
any credit given to him.

As we continue reading in 1 Corinthian's 1, we see the fuller
explanation of why Paul did not want to baptize anymore.

> 17 For Christ did not send me to baptize, but to preach the
> gospel—not with wisdom and eloquence, lest the cross of
> Christ be emptied of its power.- 1Corinthians 1:17

At first glance, we may assume that Paul was just rejecting his role
as baptizer; it wasn't his responsibility. However, his reason goes
deeper than this. He did not want to distract from the message of
the cross. He knew that people were saved because of what Christ
had done, not because of anything he had done. Everything
considered, he thought baptism was more of a distraction than
something to be valued. He wanted to make sure that the central

message that Jesus had died for our sins did not get missed. He clarifies this point in verse 18.

> 18 For the message of the cross is foolishness to those who are perishing, but to us who are being saved it is the power of God. - 1 Corinthians 1:18

He realized that baptism didn't really save anybody. We are not saved by anything associated with our own effort. We are 100% saved because of our faith through the Grace of God. After the resurrection of Christ, there was not then, and still is not today, anything more important than this message!

Let's stay on this point of Paul's for a little longer. Did Paul believe that there is anything humanely possible that we can do to save ourselves? In the first six verses of Galatians 5, he writes about the worthless benefit of obeying the law (even if we could). The point of writing these verses is because there were Judaizers who claimed circumcision was necessary for salvation. Paul categorically denies this allegation. He writes only about circumcision, but we could substitute the word "circumcision" with "baptism," or "taking communion," or "tithing to the church," or anything else related to human effort.

> 1 It is for freedom that Christ has set us free. Stand firm, then, and do not let yourselves be burdened again by a yoke of slavery. 2 Mark my words! I, Paul, tell you that if you let yourselves be circumcised, Christ will be of no value to you at all. 3 Again I declare to every man who lets himself be circumcised that he is obligated to obey the whole law. 4 You who are trying to be justified by the law have been alienated from Christ; you have fallen away from grace. 5 For through the Spirit we eagerly await by faith the righteousness for which we hope. 6 For in Christ Jesus neither circumcision nor uncircumcision has any value. The only thing that counts is faith expressing itself through love.- Galatians 5:1-6

Paul claims that anything we do is of little value regarding our salvation. We are saved only by faith through God's Grace. Anything else we do from our flesh that we think makes us acceptable to God is a lie. "The only thing that counts is expressing itself through love." Sure, there are many things we can do that are good. But do not confuse "good and loving" activities as anything that makes us acceptable to God.

It is easy to get these two concepts exchanged in our minds, which is one of Satan's tricks. We think, "Of course Jesus died on the cross, was buried, and then resurrected." Now that I have that clarified in my mind, as a loving person I should go help someone. I should go to church more often. While I am at church, I should take communion. The warning to us is that anytime we think that we "***should do***" something ritualistic, then we have crossed the line. We are then doing things because we think this makes us more acceptable to God. True, we should want to be loving and helpful; that is an appropriate response. But If we are dreading it, but do it anyway because we think it makes us acceptable to God, then we have been deceived. I admit that this may be a fine point, but ask yourself the question, "Why am I doing this? Am I doing this to make me look better in someone else's eyes, i.e., because it is what the church or other church members want me to do?" If the answer is "yes," then the motivation is wrong. Christ has already done it all, and we can't do one thing more to make ourself more eligible to receive the kingdom of God.

What Does Baptism into Water Really Do?

Water baptism, by itself, does nothing except make us wet. Anyone can be baptized in a ceremony, and the fact that someone says "I baptize you in the name of the Father, the Son, and the Holy Ghost" does *not* affect those baptized with their relationship with God. It is strictly symbolic. It does *not*guarantee that they have become part of the body of Christ as 1 Corinthians 12:13 states.

Consider a person who is not sincere about their baptism. He or she can leave the ceremony and continue to lead a very sinful life without the first bit of guilt or remorse. There is no Biblical basis for believing that he/she is in any way affected by the Holy Spirit just because of words they state.

Can an argument be made that a person who takes their faith sincerely is affected by their baptism? It is not likely that the water baptism had an effect, but I would agree that it was the sincerity of their faith that affected them. It is all about their faith, not the ceremony that causes the Holy Spirit to change them (Ephesians 1:13).

If water baptism is relatively unimportant, why do so many people make such a big deal out of it? The significance is what it represents. In Ray Stedman's commentary book on John, "God's loving word", he explains that

> "Water Baptism is a symbol of repentance and an honest admission of need. I have roughly half a century in the ministry and I have observed that the barrier that prevents most people from being born again is their own unwillingness to admit their need. They don't want to admit that they are sinful and helpless and that God must come into them and completely transform them. They cling to the idea that there is some good within them that God ought to accept. They see their lives balanced on a set of scales. If they do more good things than bad things, the scales will tip in their favor and off to heaven they will go!" "But God says no, you need a total renovation. You need to repent. And baptism is a symbolic acknowledgment of the repentance."[15]

---

[15] Stedman, R. C. (1993a). God's Loving Word: Exploring the Gospel of John (p. 90). Our Daily Bread Publishing.

It is not the baptism that saves us; it is the admission that we can't save ourselves. We must rely on the sacrificial and redeeming blood of Jesus. We are broken, and our relationship with God can only be fixed by the One who gave His life for us.

Paul's gospel says that we are saved by faith and not by works. It is our faith that Jesus suffered intently, died, was buried, and raised by the Holy Spirit which saves us. No amount of water can do that. True, we must repent, but it is not necessary to do it in front of a crowd of people. Our attitude of the heart is what is really important. We must acknowledge our sinfulness to God and turn towards Him.

The Apostle John wrote of this critical admission. It is not near as important that we admit our sinfulness to others, but we certainly must admit it to ourselves and God. If we deny it, then we are deceived. He also says that, conversely, if we confess our sins (to God), He will forgive us.

> 8 If we claim to be without sin, we deceive ourselves and the truth is not in us. 9 If we confess our sins, he is faithful and just and will forgive us our sins and purify us from all unrighteousness. -1 John 1:8-9

Some people claim that such confessions must be verbal and performed in front of others. "If you won't confess in front of others, then you really don't believe it." They may site a couple of verses from Romans 8 to reinforce their argument:

> 9 If you declare with your mouth, "Jesus is Lord," and believe in your heart that God raised him from the dead, you will be saved. 10 For it is with your heart that you believe and are justified, and it is with your mouth that you profess your faith and are saved. - Romans 10:9-10

I believe this scripture when taken in its entirety. However, please note that these verses also say that you must also believe in your heart that God raised Jesus from the dead. Why do I emphasize this point? Because public confession does not guarantee honesty. This may or may not happen in front of a crowd of people. And the longer I live, the more I question what a lot of people say compared to the actions they take!

How often have we heard convicted criminals claim in public or before cameras that they are innocent of wrongdoing? The bottom line is that we don't really know what's in a person's heart. Confessions need to be honest and personal. I have witnessed others make confessions, and I know from personal experience that they often make them to please mom, dad, and/or other people. Only God knows our true heart, and He knows precisely what we believe. No matter how hard we try, we cannot fool the Creator who knows our actions and all intent of our actions.

Because baptism indicates the need for repentance, it makes perfect sense why John the Baptist was telling people to repent. He was baptizing others to prepare their hearts for their need of the Messiah. Without this preparatory work, then the Jews of that era would not think they needed saving. They would believe that the animal sacrifices they were making at that time were sufficient. They would be like many people of today, believing that obeying the Ten Commandments makes them acceptable to God. John the Baptist claimed that this wasn't good enough. But now, just like then, many people still don't believe it. They still think they can approach God based on performing a few good deeds. Oh, how wrong they are. Paul's gospel tells us that we must all acknowledge our sin, and recognize that we are only acceptable to God based on what Jesus did for us.

We should not approach water baptism because we think it will do something to us or for us. "Oh, I can't wait to be empowered by the Holy Spirit." Instead, we should approach it with the idea that it is something we want to do; to acknowledge that we are sinners and that we are saved only by God's Grace by accepting and believing that we are saved through the sacrifice of Jesus.

Water Baptism Serves the Church

Some people argue that even though water baptism is only symbolic, there are benefits to the church attendees, and therefore every Christian should do it. Why?

Firstly, there are people sitting in the pew who are on the fence concerning their beliefs. They want to believe that Jesus died for him/her personally, but they are just not sure. Witnessing others' baptism helps them see those who have been moved to the point of confession and salvation. If they knew another person before their baptism and witnessed a change in them, they are encouraged to make a personal decision for their own baptism.

Secondly, there are many people who see themselves as both independent and primarily a product of their own efforts. And while they may admit that they made a few mistakes in their life, they don't generally see much need to acknowledge their sinfulness. Instead, they are more likely to be critical of those who admit they need Christ's blood to pay for their sins. Therefore, they have a reluctance to confess their need. They don't want to be perceived as weak or ridiculed by others. However, when they witness others who are baptized without criticism (by the body of believers), they gain the confidence to do likewise.

Thirdly, churches are filled with people of good intentions, but it is often the experience of seeing a water baptism that inspires its members to go out and witness to the community. They personally know they have confessed their need for Jesus' sacrifice, and they have become a changed person, but they are also too quick to believe that they are "unusual." "There probably aren't that many people who have devoted their life to God, who was a sinner like me." However, when they see the same sort of change take place again and again in others, then they realize they are not "unusual" and develop the will to tell others their personal story. They can more easily confess how they saw their need for God and sought him not because they are "weak," but because they *have been changed* and they are no longer fearful of God's judgment. They do not feel the need to profess that they have become perfect, but instead, openly confess how they aren't.

Why Jesus Was Baptized with Water

If water baptism is used as a method to acknowledge our need for repentance, then the next question is, "Why was it necessary to baptize Jesus?" He was perfect. He didn't need to repent or acknowledge His need for God. He was God's Holy Son. He was put on the earth for our benefit. He is our intercessor between the Father and us. So why did Jesus tell John that he should baptize him?

To find the answer, we must go back to the Old Testament. The first appointed priest of the Jews was Aaron. From then on, it was God's commandments that Aaron's sons and every priest after that had to go through a consecration ceremony to serve as priests. This included a full body washing as well as a cleansing of their clothes. This procedure is documented in Exodus 29:4 and Leviticus 8:6.

While John the Baptist baptized to confirm the people's heart cleansing, the baptism of Jesus was to show others that He was being established as a priest in a similar method to those in the Old Testament. It acknowledged His authority as the intermediary between God and us. Because Jesus always followed the commandments of God to the letter, it should not be a surprise that He would be "washed." And if there was any doubt in the minds of those witnessing this baptizing event was necessary, then God provided two additional signs; He provided His Holy Spirit that landed on Him and He spoke to a crowd in an audible voice:

> 16 As soon as Jesus was baptized, he went up out of the water. At that moment heaven was opened, and he saw the Spirit of God descending like a dove and alighting on him. 17 And a voice from heaven said, "This is my Son, whom I love; with him I am well pleased." – Matthew 3:16-17

This event was amazing! Can you imagine witnessing this symbol of purification, including some kind of physical manifestation of the Spirit of God landing on Jesus and then actually hearing the audible voice of God? This was undoubtedly God's confirmation that Jesus was the chosen Messiah; He was proclaimed as the High Priest who would minister to the Jews in a way that had never happened before and will never happen again. Unfortunately, very few Jews observed the momentous moment. And those who did see it probably didn't recognize Him as the High Priest. He didn't wear the garb that the High Priest of their day did. He didn't talk like other High Priest, merely quoting the law. Instead, He was the High Priest who correctly interpreted and elaborated on scripture in a way like no other person ever explained. He didn't act like He was better than others; instead, he was very humble. During his mock trial, He allowed Himself to be slapped, and even though He was the most powerful man to walk the earth, He humbled Himself and allowed Himself to be hung on a cross (Philippians 2:6-8). Like many other Old Testament events, His baptism didn't make as much sense at the moment it happened as it did years later.

As an aside, some people question whether Jesus was qualified to be a Priest. They argue that He was never a Levite, and it was only Levites, descendants of Aaron, who were supposed to be priests.

Scripture tells us, "Jesus was from the linage of Judah" (Matthew 1:1-6). Therefore, He was not a Levite. However, because His mother and her cousin (Elizabeth) were from the lineage of Aaron (Luke 1:5, 36), then Jesus was also; and the baptism clearly showed that legally, He was qualified to be a high priest. But Jesus was not just like other high priests; He was a high priest after the order of Melchizedek (Hebrews 6:20). (The interpretation of the name Melchizedek means "king of righteousness.") Therefore, His title proved that He should be baptized as the righteous "High Priest."

CHAPTER
14 Paul Writes About a "Different" Baptism

As I was writing the last chapter on baptism, I understood that I was possibly raising the hackles of many people. You were probably thinking, "Who is this guy who says that baptism isn't important. This is one of the seven Holy Sacraments. This is the rite that provides adoption into Christianity.

I should turn this around; baptism is important. The point though, is that it is not water baptism that is important.

There is confusion in some people's minds about what baptism really means. When most people think of baptism, they immediately think about water baptism, but this is not the actual definition. "Baptism" really means being "put into." So one form of baptism is to be put into water. In 1 Corinthians 10, Paul talks about baptism into Moses. This type of baptism means two things. The Jewish people were baptized by following Moses through the Red Sea. They were baptized into the Red Sea, but they weren't submerged; at least not like Pharaoh's army:

> For I do not want you to be ignorant of the fact, brothers and sisters, that our ancestors were all under the cloud and that they all passed through the sea. 2 They were all baptized into Moses in the cloud and in the sea. - 1 Corinthians 10:1,2

Notice, the verses do not say that the ancestors were baptized into Christianity. They couldn't have been. This was 2000 years before Christ. However, the people were considered baptized into Moses because they followed his leadership as God's commander.

In Paul's letters, he doesn't talk much about water baptism; however, he mentions Spiritual baptism several times. For example, he writes in 1 Corinthian's 12 about how, through baptism, we are put into one body.

> Just as a body, though one, has many parts, but all its many parts form one body, so it is with Christ. ¹³For we were all baptized by one Spirit so as to form one body—whether Jews or Gentiles, slave or free—and we were all given the one Spirit to drink. - 1 Corinthians 12:12,13

In this example, we are not undergoing a single ounce of water. It is the Holy Spirit who baptized us to put us into one body, that is, of Christ's. This is where we should set our focus; …but what does being baptized into one body really mean?

There are analogies associated with the body of Christ and a human body. In the human body, we are all joined by muscles, ligaments, nerves, organs, blood vessels, bones, and skin. Therefore, all our elements move as one and behave as one. It would be silly to think of them as all independent. Imagine if our right foot wanted to move right, and our left foot wanted to move left simultaneously. Ouch! We wouldn't get very far. Imagine if we tried to walk across the room, and our muscles said, "okay, let's go," …but our bones said, "no, I don't feel like it." As one body, we move as one. We have a common goal. When we run, all the body parts work together. Likewise, in the body of Christ, we all move together. Christ is the head, but every other body part is essential also. We all look different; we all have different specific functions; nevertheless, we work together and have one main goal; to love and serve together. This type of baptism is far more meaningful than to be baptized by water. Paul uses the same analogy in Galatians 3.

> "… for all of you who were baptized into Christ have clothed yourselves with Christ. ²⁸ There is neither Jew nor Gentile, neither slave nor free, nor is there male and female, for you are all one in Christ Jesus." - Galatians 3:27-28

It makes no difference of our nationality, ethnicity, social-economic status, or gender, if we have been baptized by the Holy Spirit, then we are all one in Christ. We are all different but we should all be motivated with the same desire to love and serve.

In Roman 6:3,4 again Paul speaks of baptism into Christ. However, in these verses he writes that we are baptized into the death of Jesus. Again, this has nothing to do with water baptism, it is strictly spiritual, and that is what is important.

What does it mean to be baptized into His death? It is just as if we have died. We are declared being dead just as Jesus was declared dead. So you are probably asking, "How can this be? I don't feel dead." That is because it is not physical death. That means our old intentions and lifestyle are dead. We no longer have desires like we used to. Our old self was crucified with Him; we no longer desire to live in a competitive world to try to make ourselves better than others. This sounds like a significant change, and it is, but it would be tragic if that's all there is. Paul assures us that there is much more. Just as Christ was raised from the dead, so are we. We are given a new life "Spirit" with new motivation. We were raised up through the glory of the Father and for the glory of His Son. We are given the desire to tell the whole world what God did for us and what Christ sacrificed for us. We have been raised up with a new life, caring about others.

> Or don't you know that all of us who were baptized into Christ Jesus were baptized into his death? 4 We were therefore buried with him through baptism into death in order that, just as Christ was raised from the dead through the glory of the Father, we too may live a new life. - Romans 6:3-4

Just like the example Paul used in his letter to the Romans, he makes the same statement in Colossians 2:12 that references baptism into Christ. We have been buried and raised up with Him through our faith. Our old sinful life has been done away with (killed and buried), and we have a new life with new inspiration. This new life does not make us perfect as Christ was, but it gives us a desire to serve others.

With water baptism, we are literally put in water, and we usually make statements about how we've changed. But in the examples Paul gives, we are baptized into Christ through the Holy Spirit. These are things that can't happen in the physical realm. That which occurs in the Spiritual is always more important than the physical. The physical is only relevant for as long as life exists, but a Spiritual event has eternal significance. It is not temporary; it lasts forever.

Comparing the two types of baptism, the one performed by the Holy Spirit is far more significant. It is by the power of the Holy Spirit that we are united with Christ, joined with other believers to form one body. We are not all the same, but we all have equal value. Through the Holy Spirit we are given the desire to work together with our skills and talents to serve God, not trying to make ourselves acceptable; but instead, our motivation is a result of our gratefulness for what our Savior has already done. By our baptism being Spiritual, then we are assured that our joining with Christ and other believers is eternal and will last well beyond our physical life on earth.

Another point about the difference between water baptism and spiritual baptism is that water baptism originates with human desire and commitment. While this is good, there is no guarantee that we will actually maintain a heart to love others. We may temporarily think it is a good idea, based on community pressure and emotion. But it is only the Holy Spirit that can give us a non-whimsical, perpetual desire.

When is it then that the Holy Spirit Baptizes us? Is it when we make a commitment to follow Jesus? It may be; it all depends. It is probably easier to identify when it doesn't happen. It doesn't happen just because other people gather around and try to encourage us to be baptized. It doesn't happen when a parent, spouse, church leader, or peer try to talk us into water baptism. They may have good intentions, but it just doesn't work that way. Paul tells us in Ephesians 1 when it really happens, and when it does, it is permanent.

> And you also were included in Christ when you heard the message of truth, the gospel of your salvation. When you believed, you were marked in him with a seal, the promised Holy Spirit - Ephesians 1:13

When we believe, (that is the key!), we are marked in him with a seal, one that is unbreakable. This means we have faith in what Jesus has done for us. There is no longer a "maybe" or "I think" question in our minds. It is when we believe it so strongly that we are willing to bet our life on it. It is as confident as you would be as if you were to ride in a jet plane. If you have much doubt before going up in an airplane, thinking the odds are good that it might crash, you would probably not go. However, if you are confident enough to get on the plane, then you have some faith. This is not to say you wouldn't be a little nervous, but at least you have committed to take that scary step of faith.

It is for this reason that no-one can ever determine whether another person is actually saved or not. Only God knows what your faith really is.

There is only one Lord that counts. There is only one faith that matters. There is only one baptism that is meaningful. And it comes from one Spirit, and it puts us in one body.

> There is one body and one Spirit, just as you were called to one hope when you were called; 5 one Lord, one faith, one baptism - Ephesians 4:4,5

**Does the Holy Spirit Indwell Us Immediately When We Are
Baptized and How Do We Know?**

Scripture tells us that the Holy Spirit baptizes all believers into
Christ. Therefore, this baptism is essential. The question is, "When
does it happen?" Some people would say it is when we are
baptized by water. We read in John 1 that when Jesus came out of
the water from his baptism by John (the baptist), a dove landed on
Him immediately, indicating it was the Holy Spirit. Therefore, we
assume that water baptism invokes the Holy Spirit.

Additionally, remember in Acts 2 that after the people repented and
were baptized, they then received the Holy Spirit. Likewise,
remember when Paul baptized in Acts 19, and then the people
received the Holy Spirit?

The connection of water baptism and the receiving of the Holy
Spirit seems to be connected in time and place. However, in Acts
10, we see something a little different. The setting is when Peter is
talking to Cornelius and others.

> 39 "We are witnesses of everything he did in the country
> of the Jews and in Jerusalem. They killed him by hanging
> him on a cross, 40 but God raised him from the dead on
> the third day and caused him to be seen…
>
> 43 All the prophets testify about him that everyone who
> believes in him (Jesus) receives forgiveness of sins
> through his name."
>
> 44 While Peter was still speaking these words, the Holy
> Spirit came on all who heard the message. 45 The
> circumcised believers who had come with Peter were
> astonished that the gift of the Holy Spirit had been
> poured out even on Gentiles. 46 For they heard them
> speaking in tongues and praising God.

Then Peter said, 47 "Surely no one can stand in the way of their being baptized with water. They have received the Holy Spirit just as we have." 48 So he ordered that they be baptized in the name of Jesus Christ. Then they asked Peter to stay with them for a few days. – Acts 10:39- 40, 43-48

So what do we read here? There are two important details. It amazed the other disciples that the Gentiles could also receive the Holy Spirit. They did not believe that this would happen, but sure enough, it did. They became convinced that salvation was not only for Jews but also for Gentiles.

Secondly, when we read closely, we see from verse 45 that the Holy Spirit came over the people *first*. Then, in verse 48 Peter ordered the large crowd of people to be baptized. So we see that it was *not* the baptism that gave people the Holy Spirit; instead, after Peter told them that everyone who believes in Jesus would receive forgiveness, the Holy Spirit came upon them.

Paul explains this phenomenon in Ephesians 1. I know I have used this verse before, but it is worthy of repeating:

13 And you also were included in Christ when you heard the message of truth, the gospel of your salvation. *When you believed*, you were marked in him with a seal, the promised Holy Spirit – Ephesians 1:13

So we see and realize from the writing of Paul that we (Gentiles) *do not* obtain the Holy Spirit by baptism, but instead, it happens when we *believe…*, when we believe the Gospel, that is, that Jesus shed his blood for us, died for us, was put in the grave, and then was raised from the dead. Then we are not only given the Holy Spirit, but the Holy Spirit also seals us until the day when our spirit leaves our bodies (Ephesians 4:30). This is a powerful message. The Holy Spirit indwells us and seals us for eternity despite what happens to our physical body.

What Should We Expect When We Receive the Holy Spirit?

Jesus was the first person observed who, when baptized, the Holy Spirit immediately came on Him. After His baptism, we read about several other baptisms performed by the Apostles. Every time a person was baptized with water, there was noticeable evidence of the Holy Spirit. In most cases, the individual began speaking in a language unknown to him/her. Is this what we should expect? Should we start speaking in a language we have never studied? Or should we expect even more gifts from the Spirit?

Paul wrote in 1 Corinthians 12 about the gifts of the Holy Spirit:

8 To one there is given through the Spirit a message of wisdom, to another a message of knowledge by means of the same Spirit, 9 to another faith by the same Spirit, to another gifts of healing by that one Spirit, 10 to another miraculous powers, to another prophecy, to another distinguishing between spirits, to another speaking in different kinds of tongues, and to still another the interpretation of tongues.- 1 Corinthians 12:8-10

That is quite an impressive list of special gifts. Probably the first thing a person thinks about if they heard or read this scripture and was contemplating being baptized is, "I wonder which gift I will receive when I am baptized?" Or perhaps they may ask other church members, "Who is it in our church that performs healings, has demonstrated miraculous powers, provides prophetic messages, or speaks in tongues?" (How a person answers is usually based on their church culture.)

Quite often, if a church member is asked such a question, he/she feels obligated to respond in some way (even if they don't have an answer) so they may say something like, "In our church, there are several people gifted in wisdom, knowledge, and faith. If pressed about the other gifts, they may say, "There may be people in our church gifted in the ways you asked, but I don't know any of them." Or they may say that it is primarily the Pentecostal churches that focus on the other gifts. In any event, the person asking the question is rarely given a satisfying answer.

For the thinking person, this experience has got to put questions in their minds. Why don't people in our church have these verifiable special gifts? Are they lacking in some way? After all, the gifts are Biblical. Perhaps the problem is that we don't have anyone with enough faith. Heaven forbid, but they may even think that Christianity is nothing but a mixture of a bunch of legends and fabricated stories. If nothing else, the little faith they do have is possibly thrown on the trash heap.

For those of us who aren't so quick to dismiss Biblical scripture, we might wonder silently, "Is the problem really because people just don't have enough faith today? What was the purpose of these gifts in Biblical times? Are they still valid, and should they be petitioned and pursued today? " Some people believe they are both valid and should be observable by some church leaders.

15 The Gifts of the Holy Spirit

As I stated in chapter 2, my dad did not struggle with anything that had been written about Jesus in the Gospels of Matthew, Mark, Luke, or John. He didn't doubt whether Jesus actually lived. He didn't question the parables He told or the miracles He performed. My dad believed Jesus was the Son of God. He believed everything that was written about Jesus in these four books because the writers were eyewitnesses.

However, anything else written in the New Testament was suspect. Were the things written about the disciples true? If it was just that they followed Jesus, then it was true. But to say that they could perform miracles; it was suspect. After all, they were not Deities. Could the Apostle Paul perform a miracle? No way! He was just an ordinary man. Could the disciples have received power from the Holy Spirit?

My dad didn't think so. He said:

"No, that is just more of that hocus pocus people like to talk about. It was only Jesus, the Son of God, who had the Holy Spirit in Him. I have seen those fake faith healers that go around and claim they can heal people. I even saw one lady walking around before a large crowd showed up. She then proceeded backstage, and after everyone had arrived, she came out portrayed as a lame woman. After the faith healer got her up and walking, the crowd went crazy."

My dad grappled with spiritual things. Who or what was the Holy Spirit? How does it relate to our present life? Is there really an afterlife? Was my mom, who had died a few years earlier, nothing more than a pile of bones lying in a crypt?

His answer was, "I don't know…, possibly." My dad expressed his thoughts about how he had heard many different views on the subject. "There are so many different church denominations, and each one has its own particular opinion on the matter." His uncertainty circled back to why there are so many different views about the things written in the Bible. "Aren't they all reading from the same book? Why is there so much disagreement?"

These are good questions, and there is no single answer. But here is another truth that I know is a problem; the differences are divisive and cause many people to question the Bible and their faith. My dad was one of those individuals.

A Broad View of the Holy Spirit

One of the significant differences among all the various denominations is regarding the Holy Spirit (sometimes referred to as the Spirit of God). The groups may be united in that they agree it assists and interacts between God and us, but other than that, there are vast differences about the usefulness and purpose of God's Spirit.

Most people are aware of the Holy Spirit's influence in the New Testament, but references in the Old Testament are not well known. Nevertheless, the references are there. On the first page of the Bible we read that the Holy Spirit has been around since the formation of the world:

> … the Spirit of God was hovering over the waters. - Genesis 1:2

While many people believe that Jesus was the first person filled with the Holy Spirit, the Bible says otherwise. God had given commandments to Moses to set up a tent and to include an altar, the ark of the covenant, and other furnishings. Because Moses didn't have the personal skills to do this work, God chose a man and gave him special skills to build the necessary items. He did this through His Spirit.

> ¹Then the Lord said to Moses, ² "See, I have chosen Bezalel son of Uri, the son of Hur, of the tribe of Judah, ³ and I have filled him with the <u>Spirit of God</u>, with wisdom, with understanding, with knowledge and with all kinds of skills— Exodus 31:1-3

In 2nd Peter, we read something insightful about another purpose of the Holy Spirit. Peter writes that all scripture was written by prophets who did not understand what they wrote, but they wrote by the leading of the Holy Spirit:

> ²⁰ Above all, you must understand that no prophecy of Scripture came about by the prophet's own interpretation of things. ²¹ For prophecy never had its origin in the human will, but prophets, though human, spoke from God as they were carried along by the Holy Spirit. - 2 Peter 1:20-21

Therefore, the Holy Spirit has been active in the lives of prophets and men of God's choosing of both the Old and New Testament. It inspired the prophets of old to write things they didn't understand, and it gave Peter the insight to explain this fact when he wrote his letter.

The Bible has only documented a relatively few number of people who have been given gifts of the Spirit. Some people, me included, believe that the Spirit of God has a personality, and therefore, I refer to the Spirit as "He."

In the example of Exodus, the Holy Spirit gave Bezalel wisdom, understanding, and knowledge. From the example of 2 Peter, we read that Old Testament prophets were not given wisdom, understanding, and knowledge; instead, they simply wrote by inspiration.

This fact is most evident when we read about one of the prophecies written by Isaiah. He wrote that God would choose a virgin to give birth to a boy, and his name would be Immanuel (meaning "God is with us."). I am sure birth from a virgin was just as impossible during the time of Isaiah as it is today; nevertheless, he never let the impossibility of a virgin woman giving birth stop him. Instead, he wrote it by inspiration anyway.

> [14] Therefore the Lord himself will give you a sign: The virgin will conceive and give birth to a son, and will call him Immanuel.- Isaiah 7:14

In the New Testament, we read about how the Holy Spirit was responsible for fulfilling the prophecy made in Isaiah 7.

We read that before Jesus was born, the angel Gabriel came to Mary (the mother of Jesus) to tell her she was the chosen virgin to fulfill Isaiah's prophecy:

> "The Holy Spirit will come on you, and the power of the Most High will overshadow you. So the holy one to be born will be called the Son of God." - Luke 1:35

This was God's greatest gift to mankind, but it was like nothing before. In an earlier dispensation, God had supernaturally freed His people. He had made Abraham wealthy. He had promised His people their own productive land and freedom from Gentile oppression. But this time, it was different. He did not deliver a wealthy king or freedom from oppression. No, a poor, unknown man was not the type of gift that anyone expected God to send.

From the time Christ was a baby until He grew into adolescence, there is no biblical record that He performed any healings or miracles. There is no Biblical evidence that He could speak prophecy or distinguish good spirits from evil spirits before his ministry. We don't even know if He had any special knowledge or wisdom at that time. However, we know that He certainly had a hunger for Old Testament scripture, and He challenged the temple priests.

Just because Jesus had not shown any evidence of the gifts of the Holy Spirit prior to His baptism does not necessarily mean He didn't have them. But what we do know is that when he was baptized, amazing things happened. The Holy Spirit descended on him bodily like a dove, and he was declared by God to be his Son. Subsequently, throughout the Gospels, we read how he had been given all of the gifts of the Spirit that Paul described in 1Corinthian's 12:8-10. There should not be any question in our mind about His attributes. Matthew, Mark, Luke, and John are filled with many examples of exceptional wisdom, knowledge, faith, the gift of healing, miraculous powers, and understanding of future events. Note: I cannot find anywhere in the Bible that Christ was specifically given the ability to speak in tongues, but given all of His other attributes, it certainly wouldn't be a surprise if He did.

Even though God has used His Holy Spirit for multiple purposes, we also realize the most extensive and important uses of Him. He has inspired the prophets to write about the coming Messiah, impregnated Mary supernaturally, and gave Christ superior wisdom, knowledge, and miraculous powers to prove both His Deity and evidence that He was God's special ambassador.

The Holy Spirit's Role After the Baptism of Jesus

When Christ was baptized it signified something significant to the Jews; it proved to all who were witnesses of that miraculous event that Jesus was the Son of God. For those few observers, this also likely meant He was the awaited Messiah. But how was this going to play out? At that moment, no-one knew. They hadn't seen any other evidence of the power of the Holy Spirit. Would this mean that Jesus was immediately going to set up His Kingdom? Would He wave his hand, and instantaneously, everyone would be His subject? Would God generate a virus that would destroy the Roman government? As it turned out, none of these things happened.

However, remember how God required baptism to signify a new High Priest? While many people did not realize it at the time, this was why Christ was baptized. However, this would not be easy to prove because there was already a High Priest in Jerusalem, and the existing religious leaders were indoctrinated into obeying a lot of regimented laws. They were not inclined to believe that this "new kid on the block" was going to be their new High Priest. Furthermore, their hearts were not into it. It was all about their appearance of fervor and religiosity. How would Jesus convince these hard-hearted hypocrites that He should be the new High Priest? For those who never witnessed His baptism, He performed signs, wonders, and miracles, giving proof that He really was the Son of God.

Even though Jesus was filled with the Holy Spirit, and He performed many miracles, He convinced only relatively few Jews that He was the Son of God while He was alive (Romans 9:27). But after Jesus died, things begin to change. Most importantly, He was resurrected, which was a great surprise, even to his loyal followers. We read this fact in John 20:

> "They still did not understand from Scripture that Jesus had to rise from the dead." - John 20:9

When they discovered His resurrection, they gained new confidence. There was still hope that Jesus was going to set up His Kingdom. In fact, His disciples asked him pointedly:

> "Lord, are you at this time going to restore the kingdom to Israel?" - Acts1:6

And although He did not give them a definitive answer, they went out amongst other Jews trying to convince them that Jesus was the Messiah and the Son of God. How would they do this using only their abilities? They couldn't.

Before Jesus died, He promised the disciples that He would send them the Holy Spirit (Advocate). He not only gave them the promise, but He also stated His purpose.

> 8 …He will prove the world to be in the wrong about sin and righteousness and judgment: 9 about sin, because people do not believe in me; 10 about righteousness, because I am going to the Father, where you can see me no longer; 11 and about judgment, because the prince of this world now stands condemned. - John 16:8-11

Sure enough, on Pentecost, 50 days after Jesus' death, the Holy Spirit came mightily on the disciples:

> 1 When the day of Pentecost came, they were all together in one place. 2 Suddenly a sound like the blowing of a violent wind came from heaven and filled the whole house where they were sitting. 3 They saw what seemed to be tongues of fire that separated and came to rest on each of them. 4 All of them were filled with the Holy Spirit and began to speak in other tongues as the Spirit enabled them. - Acts 2:1-4

The result was that they added 3000 believers in one fell swoop (Acts 2:42)!

For several years after Pentecost, we read about how the power of the Holy Spirit was manifest in the disciples. For example, in Acts 3 and 4 we read that Peter and John healed a lame beggar by simply speaking the name of Jesus. They continued to heal others by using the name "Jesus". And because they were speaking with the power of the Holy Spirit, their words were very effective among those living in Jerusalem.

In Acts 8, we read that "an angel of the Lord" commanded the disciple Philip to go to a particular road and meet an Ethiopian eunuch. After Philip explained scripture about Jesus to the eunuch, the Ethiopian was baptized, and the Spirit of the Lord supernaturally took Philip away.

In Acts 10, we read about how Peter spoke to Cornelius and the members of his house. In verse 44, the scripture tells us that the Holy Spirit came on *all* who heard the message.

Even with the aid of the Holy Spirit, it was not easy for these early disciples to persuade other Jews that they could be saved by believing Jesus was both the Son of God and their promised Messiah. We read about times when they had successes individually, but they were not successful in convincing their nation.

The New Convert and New Message

While the disciples were going around preaching the name of Jesus and gathering followers through the power of the Holy Spirit, the Pharisee Saul was busy persecuting those who believed in Jesus. When he was struck blind on the road to Damascus, Saul had a sudden awareness that he was doing the wrong thing. After realizing this, he began to pray. The Lord sent the disciple Ananias to place his hands on him and restore his sight. We read in Acts 9 the result:

> 17 … Placing his hands on Saul, he said, "Brother Saul, the Lord—Jesus, who appeared to you on the road as you were coming here—has sent me so that you may see again and be filled with the <u>Holy Spirit.</u>"
> 18 Immediately, something like scales fell from Saul's eyes, and he could see again. - Acts 9:17-18

So just like all the other examples of the influence of the Holy Spirit, He also greatly affected Saul (who later becomes Paul). Immediately, he was convinced that Jesus is the Messiah and the Son of God. Therefore, he preached the same message as the other disciples in the Jewish synagogues:

… Saul spent several days with the disciples in Damascus. 20 At once he began to preach in the synagogues that Jesus is the Son of God. 21 All those who heard him were astonished and asked, "Isn't he the man who raised havoc in Jerusalem among those who call on this name? And hasn't he come here to take them as prisoners to the chief priests?" 22 Yet Saul grew more and more powerful and baffled the Jews living in Damascus by proving that Jesus is the Messiah. - Acts 9:19-22

After his conversion, Saul/Paul traveled to Arabia and stayed there for three years (Galatians 1:17). It was here he learned a new gospel. Yes, Jesus is the Son of God…, but He was also persecuted for our sins. He died, and on the third day, He was resurrected.

The revelation Jesus provided was on a one-on-one basis. It was certainly much different than what he had believed as a Pharisee. I can imagine it was difficult for Saul to wrap his head around it; therefore, the private disclosure should have afforded him time to wrestle through any unclear points. Jesus would not have sent him to the mission field if He knew that Saul/Paul was unprepared.

Secondly, the revelation occurred after Jesus' death, burial, and resurrection. Before Jesus was put on the cross, the disciples did not expect Him to die (even though Jesus told them - Luke 18:31-34). In the case of Paul, he didn't need to be convinced that Jesus would go to the cross. He had heard about it. More importantly, Jesus revealed to him why He had to die.

As a result of the timing of his personal revelation from Jesus, Paul's understanding was more in-depth than what the original disciples were given. He had learned that Jesus' suffering and bloodshed on the cross paid for our sins. He was also provided the significance of the event. Furthermore, Jesus divulged that it was no longer necessary to make animal sacrifices.

Most scholars generally attribute 13 letters in the Bible to Paul; however, some of them question whether he wrote Hebrews. But I believe he did because of his understanding and wisdom. The author wrote in Hebrews 9, (speaking of High Priests):

12 …he entered the Most Holy Place once for all by his own blood, thus obtaining eternal redemption. 13 The blood of goats and bulls and the ashes of a heifer sprinkled on those who are ceremonially unclean sanctify them so that they are outwardly clean. 14 How much more, then, will the blood of Christ, who through the eternal Spirit offered himself unblemished to God, cleanse our consciences from acts that lead to death, so that we may serve the living God! - Hebrews 9:12-14

As the High Priest, Christ was not like those of the Old Testament. He became our *only* intercessor with God. Old Testament Priests would make animal sacrifices on behalf of the people he served. But this was not the role of Christ. Instead, He had come to bring in a new relationship with God. Sins had to be paid, but instead of mankind making animal sacrifices, He offered Himself as the new sacrifice. He would do it once, and God considered His action to be so complete that it atoned for the sins of everyone once and forever. God showed how much He loved the world by sacrificing His Holy Son.

Furthermore, because Jesus was human, He was able to relate to human weaknesses. He understood our temptation to sin, and He empathizes with us. As our advocate with God the Father, we can have confidence that God knows how difficult it is to be human, and therefore, we can have confidence in His Grace.

14 Therefore, since we have a great high priest who has ascended into heaven, Jesus the Son of God, let us hold firmly to the faith we profess. 15 For we do not have a high priest who is unable to empathize with our weaknesses, but we have one who has been tempted in every way, just as we are—yet he did not sin. 16 Let us then approach God's throne of grace with confidence, so that we may receive mercy and

When God gave the Pharisee named "Saul of Tarsus" the mission to preach to the Gentiles, He realized He could not do this using only his human ability. Therefore, God used his Holy Spirit to indwell Paul. He gave him wisdom, understanding, knowledge, the power to heal, and the ability to speak in tongues. Saul took his responsibility seriously, and he went to the Gentiles, spreading the message of God's Grace.

Yes, Jesus was identified as the Son of God and the Messiah; but He came to earth for more than just those two reasons. At His baptism, He was declared by God as the New High Priest. He was declared the One who would atone for the sins of the world.

His act was more than just paying for our sins; it was redemption. God had lost humanity to sin through the act of Adam, and He repurchased us through the blood of Christ. This was God's great act of Grace.

> [5] For there is one God and one mediator between God and mankind, the man Christ Jesus, [6] who gave himself as a ransom for all people. This has now been witnessed to at the proper time. - 1 Timothy 2:5-6

Therefore, this new relationship with God was complete after the resurrection of Christ. This was entirely different than anything humanity had ever seen before.

God gave the gifts of the Holy Spirit to the Apostle Paul for the purpose of professing and communicating His new and different relationship with mankind. Just as Jesus gave evidence that He was the Son of God through wisdom, knowledge, and miracles, Paul also provided evidence that he was a true Apostle through wisdom, knowledge, and miracles.

Paul had a similar problem to those of the other disciples in that his message was also entirely new. It was like no other promise that had ever been made. There was no way to validate it. There were no books to study it. His letters were sporadically sent to the various churches but it took several years for them to be compiled and widely circulated. His common theme of salvation was not verifiable by each of the other recipients. It was a message that each group of believers had to take strictly on faith. Therefore, the Holy Spirit provided evidence that his theology was true, accurate, and could be relied upon.

The Work of the Holy Spirit in the Disciples

Sometimes when we read verses in the Bible, they have one meaning. However, when we read them later and consider them in light of other verses, we see things we never noticed before. The verses give us a new perspective on their meaning. Let's look again at the verses where Jesus promised that He would send the Holy Spirit to the disciples. Speaking of the Holy Spirit, He said:

> [8] ...He will prove the world to be in the wrong about sin and righteousness and judgment: [9] about sin, because people do not believe in me; [10] about righteousness, because I am going to the Father, where you can see me no longer; [11] and about judgment, because the prince of this world now stands condemned. - John 16:8-11

What do these verses mean? For the disciples, it meant that the Holy Spirit would prove that individuals were not going to be made righteous in God's eyes until they believed Jesus was the Son of God and the Messiah. This was the message Jesus had taught them.

In several places in the book of Acts, we can read that this limited view of Jesus is what the disciples taught. They certainly knew that Jesus had suffered on the cross, died, and was resurrected, but they did not make the connection between these events and salvation. This restricted theology was made evident when we read the details of the Baptism of the Jews in Acts 2:36-38. Peter never said that the Jews were saved by the death, burial, and resurrection of Christ. Instead, his focus was on the more narrow concept that Jesus was the Son of God and the Messiah. The Jewish people needed to repent (turn towards God) and be baptized. Their repentance and baptism was a symbol of their faith. At that time, the disciples were given the Holy Spirit, thereby providing them the confidence and the energy to be strong witnesses and carry this message to others.

This was the same limited view Peter taught when he visited Cornelius in Acts 10:43. The people received forgiveness *not* by the death, burial, and resurrection of Jesus, but instead by acknowledging the name of Jesus. Likewise, in Acts 4:11,12, Peter announced that the Jews rejected Jesus and that people are saved by the "name" of Jesus. He never mentioned that animal sacrifices were no longer necessary, nor did he tell them that obeying God's laws was unnecessary.

The Work of the Holy Spirit in Paul

As we reread John 16:8-11 in light of Paul's ministry, we learn that this verse gives a more complete picture of the Holy Spirit's purpose. We should understand these verses to mean that the Holy Spirit would prove to the world that they had the wrong concept about the reason why God forgives people. It is not because forgiveness is earned by obeying laws, nor is it because they make animal sacrifices. Instead, people are made righteous by believing that Christ suffered for our benefit. He died, was buried, and was raised from the dead by the power of the Holy Spirit.

Many people are confused by the fact that the Holy Spirit was used to communicate two different messages. They say it doesn't make sense. I agree that many of the actions taken by God sometimes seems contradictory and don't make sense from the view of us humans. If it were me, I would never have come up with an idea to have my son pay for the sins of others (I'll bet my sons are glad to hear that). Nor would I have sent the Savior into the world as a babe; I would have instantly translated Him to the earth with a crown on His head and legions of angels surrounding Him.

Nevertheless, I have contemplated why God had two different messages. First, the Jewish people had all the history to look for a Messiah. They had all Old Testament prophecy. It doesn't seem like it should have been that difficult for them to recognize Him for who He claimed to be, but it was. Even when they saw and heard about Jesus performing miracle after miracle, they were still skeptical. They had been steeped into believing it was necessary to obey God's laws and make animal sacrifices for 1500 years. Were they going to be easily convinced that their traditions were unimportant and that they were made acceptable to God strictly by believing in the death, burial, and resurrection of Jesus? No Way!

Conversely, the Gentiles never had the Old Testament. Most of them had never heard about a coming Savior, let alone believe He was coming into the world. They hadn't been steeped in Jewish law and making animal sacrifices. The only mystical "spirit" they understood was idol worship, and they were trying to make all their gods happy. Therefore, it was somewhat easier for them to believe in a new philosophical concept when confirmed by the gifts (knowledge, wisdom, speaking in tongues, miracles, etc.) of the Holy Spirit.

For those who still think that the disciples understood the same message as Paul, but it was not noted in the Bible, I would like to review again some verses written by Peter. Remember: these verses were not written in his early ministry but instead near the end of his life:

> 15 Bear in mind that our Lord's patience means salvation, just as our dear brother Paul also wrote you with the wisdom that God gave him. 16 He writes the same way in all his letters, speaking in them of these matters. His letters contain some things that are hard to understand, which ignorant and unstable people distort, as they do

Peter considers Paul as a brother, a fellow worker in Christ. But he also states that God gave him wisdom. In verse 16, Peter identifies that Paul's letters contain some concepts that are hard to understand. Consequently, ignorant and unstable people were distorting what Paul was teaching. The reason why his concepts were so difficult to interpret was that God had given him extraordinary wisdom. Not only was Paul's teachings on the mark, but he was preeminent. He wrote about things that Peter thought were difficult to comprehend. Peter would not have written these verses if he had easily understood all of Paul's theology.

The Confirming Gifts of the Spirit of the New Message

It is not difficult to see how the gifts of the Holy Spirit played a part in spreading the Gospel during the early developing years of Christianity. Jesus' new message to Paul would have never been accepted had it not been for the power of the Holy Spirit, but what we don't know is why they (the gifts) are not prevalent today. Why do we not see signs, wonders, and miracles? I am not referring to random slow healings or other indications of a loving God. Instead, I am talking about blind people given instantaneous sight, lame people suddenly able to walk, or demons driven out of people. As I write, a verse explaining the extraordinary miracles performed by Paul in Acts 19 comes to mind:

> [11] God did extraordinary miracles through Paul, [12] so that even handkerchiefs and aprons that had touched him were taken to the sick, and their illnesses were cured and the evil spirits left them. - Acts 19:11, 12

We see no miracles in today's time compared to what it was like for Paul or the other disciples.

Why we don't see such signs, wonders, and miracles is an interesting question, and I wish I had a Biblical answer. I would like to direct you to such and such book and verse and say, "See, right here is the answer." Unfortunately, I can't do that. I don't know of any such scripture; therefore, I can only leave you with my speculation.

As stated earlier, I believe the Holy Spirit's primary purpose was to convince the world that we have a new relationship with God. As Jesus said in John 16, we had it wrong about sin, righteousness, and judgment. We didn't understand God's plan for us. We mistakenly thought we were righteous only by obeying the law, and if we messed up, then we should atone for our own mistakes. We believed we would ultimately be acceptable to God by doing more things right than wrong.

As skeptical and forgetful human beings, there are two primary aspects of believing and remembering a person's testimony. One, the message has to be impactful. The best way to do that is to accompany it with a verifiable miracle. When people witness the sudden restoration of a blind man's vision or see some other astounding event, they are convinced of the truthfulness of a person's assertion. The purpose of the Holy Spirit's specific gifts was to give credence and evidence to the Apostles, who provided a different understanding of man's relationship with God. Their words and teachings would not have been very convincing except for their power to perform instantaneous miracles. Secondly, the powerfulness displayed has a lasting effect and causes the witnesses to remember what they learned. This was important for those who had nothing written.

Today we have the written Word. We have the accounts of four different men (Matthew, Mark, Luke, John) to tell us what it was like when Jesus walked the earth. Their messages are not identical but are all similar enough that they complement each other. If we only had one testimony, we would have more doubts about its authenticity. As humans, we need consistency and confirmation to convince us of truth. Dissimilar information causes us to have doubts. We need names, places, events, and concepts from different sources that complement each other.

Although Paul's letters give a message that is different than the disciples, they also provide a much fuller and richer meaning of what Christ has done for mankind. His epistles, which are much different than the Old Testament, complement the concept of blood sacrifice. He expresses his revelations about how Jesus fulfilled Old Testament prophecy. His words explain how we transitioned from being judged by the law to being accepted based strictly on faith and not on works. He explained how we have been enriched spiritually (as opposed to physical).

Except for some very rare cases, I do not see the necessity to pursue the gifts of the Holy Spirit in today's environment. We have much more information through the 66 books of the completed Bible than did the average citizen right around Christ's time. We don't need to see the gifts of the Holy Spirit in action, such as: healings, miracles, prophecies, and speaking of tongues to be convinced of the message of Christ. We have something better. If I were forced to choose between receiving one testimony from an Apostle (including a miracle) compared to receiving a completed Bible, I would take the completed Bible. At least with the Bible, I can read it and study it repeatedly. For me, having the chance to review a deep theological document is more significant than relying on witnessing and remembering a single event.

Now the entire Bible, both Old and New Testament is complete. When I say this, you may be thinking, "How does he know it is complete? Maybe there is more." I base this statement on the words of Paul. He tells the Ephesians in Acts 20:

> "For I have not hesitated to proclaim to you the whole will of God." - Acts 20:27

If he has expressed the whole will of God to the Ephesians, then we can be assured that there is no need for additional books or chapters. God's complete plan has been revealed in its entirety. Therefore, there is no more necessity for prophecy, prophets, or special messengers. The gifts of the Holy Spirit that Paul wrote about in 1Corinthian's 12:8-10, are no longer necessary either.

Does that mean that the gifts of the Holy Spirit are never given out in modern times? I can't say that. The Holy Spirit knows of places in the world where His gifts would prove useful. However, what I can say is that it certainly isn't typical in the United States anymore. As long as we are diligent in our study of the Bible, we will not be deceived by false teachings about how God accepts us. We will not be confused about His will, how to be saved, or how much love and grace He offered when He sent His Son to die for our sins.

Therefore, to keep from being deceived, we should heed Paul's words that he also gave to the Ephesians:

> 11 Put on the full armor of God, so that you can take your stand against the devil's schemes. 12 For our struggle is not against flesh and blood, but against the rulers, against the authorities, against the powers of this dark world and against the spiritual forces of evil in the heavenly realms. 13 Therefore put on the full armor of God, so that when the day of evil comes, you may be able to stand your ground, and after you have done everything, to stand. 14 Stand firm then, with the belt of truth buckled around your waist, with the breastplate of righteousness in place, 15 and with your feet fitted with the readiness that comes from the gospel of peace. 16 In addition to all this, take up the shield of faith, with which you can extinguish all the flaming arrows of the evil one. 17 Take the helmet of salvation and the sword of the Spirit, which is the word of God. - Ephesians 6:11-17

The items of "armor of God" may seem a little cryptic, but once we understand how we can be deceived, it becomes easier to recognize each piece's importance. For example, if someone tries to make a convincing argument that God gives salvation by attending church and trying to be a good person, we need to resist this notion by using the Belt of Truth. Many explanations may sound reasonable, but the writers of the books of the Bible who were inspired by the Holy Spirit give the only real truth.

The breastplate of righteousness covers our heart, which is the center of our emotions and self-worth. It is fragile. It is only when we realize that our righteousness has been obtained by believing Jesus died for us, that we are humbled and protected. When we realize there is nothing we can do to earn righteousness, then all attacks on our heart are meaningless. Our thought will be, "I may not be found worthy by everyone, but I have value to the One who really counts."

We may believe that spreading the gospel is a daunting task, one that is too big for us to accomplish. Yet the shoes of armor protect us and give us strength when we are weary. If a door is closed on our toes, our feet are protected and help us move on.

Satan would like to do what he can to weaken our witness for God. Therefore, as believers in the Gospel, we should expect we will be tempted, insulted, and ridiculed by Satan's advocates (non-believers). It goes with the territory. If we put up the shield of faith, we will see past the earthly attacks and resist whosoever casts them. We will be able to resist unhealthy desires, scorn, mockery, and disparaging remarks.

While the breastplate protects our heart, the helmet of salvation protects our mind. We are easy subjects to doubt God, and Satan knows it. We ask ourselves, "Is God really there?" When we see the evil that we can not explain, then we ask, "Why does God allow it?" If we don't have a helmet, then our mind gets inundated with questions and concerns.

Lastly is the sword of the Spirit, which is the Word of God. The best tool we have ever been given is the Bible. It helps us see truth and helps us understand righteousness; it gives us our faith and reinforces our belief about salvation. It is the ultimate weapon for fighting the attacks of Satan and other non-believers. For those who don't read the Bible or trust it, they are continually swayed by the influence of philosophers. They have no firm rock on which to build their faith. They are defenseless against their oppressors.

CHAPTER

16 Should We Expect the Holy Spirit to Heal?

The concept of modern-day healings became popular with the charismatic movement. It is described by some as the most popular and fastest-growing force among Christians today. According to the www.gotquestions.org website, "The movement traces its roots to 1906, at the Azusa Street Mission in Los Angeles, California, a Methodist-sponsored revival. It was there that people claimed to have been 'baptized by the Holy Spirit' in the manner recorded in Acts chapter 2 during the celebration of Pentecost. People speaking in tongues and miracles of healing roused people to a spiritual frenzy."[16]

Based on Biblical scripture, there are some very good reasons why this movement gained traction:

1. Healings are well documented in the Bible. There are 31 individual healing events recorded that Jesus performed. Besides, several more scriptures point to mass healings He performed. This proves that Jesus was willing to forgive many, many people of their sins. He did not look at their past sins as a qualification for healing. His action showed His love and compassion for everyone. He wanted everyone to know in this age of Grace that God was willing to forgive everyone.

2. Jesus' disciples healed many people, even after He ascended to heaven. In Acts 5:12-16, we read, "…people brought the sick into the streets and laid them on beds and mats so that at least Peter's shadow might fall on some of them as he passed by. Crowds gathered also from the towns around Jerusalem,

---

[16] GotQuestions.org. (2020a, May 21). *What is the Charismatic movement?* https://www.gotquestions.org/Charismatic-movement.html

bringing their sick and those tormented by impure spirits, and *all* of them were healed."

Therefore, the rationale is, "because we are current day disciples, then we should be healing people also."

3. The Apostle Paul healed many people as well. This fact indicates that the power of God can be manifest in anyone who believes.

4. If it's in the Bible and it pertains to our current dispensation, we should see similar events and expect them. After all, even though we live in more modern times, God hasn't changed.

5. We know from our experiences of raising our own children that we don't want them to be sick or discouraged because we love them. Therefore, how much more does our Perfect, Loving Father in heaven want us healed?

6. God wants us to love others, and He wants us to relationally connect with others and heal them using us as His chosen vessels.

7. Healing others serves as being His witnesses to prove His love and His miraculous power. Consequently, when we show others firsthand God's miracles, they will believe, and Christianity will flourish.

While these are all very good reasons, I have saved the best reason for last. True, Jesus, the disciples, and the Apostle Paul all healed many people. We can claim that they were all given miraculous healing abilities to prove that they were given special authority by God to send important messages into the world. However, that does not explain scripture written by the disciple James, the half brother of Jesus. James wrote:

> "14 Is anyone among you sick? Let them call the elders of the church to pray over them and anoint them with oil in the name of the Lord. 15 And the prayer offered in faith

will make the sick person well; the Lord will raise them up. If they have sinned, they will be forgiven. [16] Therefore confess your sins to each other and pray for each other so that you may be healed. The prayer of a righteous person is powerful and effective." - James 5:14-16

James claimed that healings did *not* have to be performed by Jesus, the original 12 disciples, or by Paul. No, the leaders of the church had been anointed with the same power. Go to them, and they can heal you.

With scripture like this, it should not be a surprise that the Charismatic Movement has become quite popular. According to the Pulitzer Center, the number of Pentecostal Christians has grown from 6% in 1980 to 25% in 2013.[17] As more and more people become familiar with their Bible, we might expect to see this percentage to continue to grow.

My question, "Is this healthy?" If, in fact, we see miracles, the answer is a resounding, "Yes!" However, for those expecting to see a miracle and not seeing one, they are, at the very least, greatly disappointed. Initially, they may begin to question their faith. Then they begin to question some of the things written in the Bible. If they have repeated failures, their faith is very much compromised, if not destroyed. Sometimes they become bitter. Their thoughts are, "The power of the Holy Spirit to heal, drive out evil spirits, or to speak in tongues is all nonsense. I see so many people who are dying or are sick."

Those who become the most vulnerable question whether there really is a loving God! If they develop this attitude, it is

[17] *Atlas of Pentecostalism*. (2017, January 5). Pulitzer Center. https://pulitzercenter.org/projects/africa-nigeria-pentecostal-christians-holy-spirit-global-religion-iconography-cartography-data-visualization

unfortunate. God does love us. Jesus and the disciples really did heal people in their day. Why don't we see such Biblical, instantaneous healings today?

Where Are God's Miracles Today?

My dad lived through the depression. As a result of his experiences, he saw a lot of despair and hopelessness. I believe he thought God should intercede and help people. He knew people who were destitute and hopeless. His personal story was that his family had little to eat. Many families were praying for the help of God. Perhaps the Almighty would provide some manna for those going hungry, or maybe He would find jobs for the millions who were unemployed.

My dad also served in World war II. Again people prayed. Maybe God would create a plague to wipe out the Nazi's. Unfortunately, my dad never saw any of this; instead he saw many dead soldiers. I wonder if these events diminished or destroyed his faith in a loving God. He could not comprehend a loving God who would allow millions of Jewish people to be starved, tortured, worked to death, or murdered in mass.

He had heard sermons from the Old Testament and saw how God worked in supernatural ways. He wondered why God hadn't chosen to do likewise during his lifetime.

You might also be asking, "Where's God's blessings today?" Ministers proclaim that God gave His Grace to the Gentiles, yet we still see people go hungry, get cancer and other diseases. Furthermore, we see good people murdered by terrorists and random shooters.

Our observations might also make us ask, "Is God still protecting us? Where are the miracles of God?" Some people might counter that they are everywhere. They might make the argument that His miracles are displayed in created lives.. Only the Almighty God can create humans with complex organs, nervous systems, and powerful brains. After all, even after many years of study, we can't fully understand the body and brain, let alone re-create one. Therefore, the creation of humans must be a miracle.

While I agree that God shows his omnipotence by creating life, there is another side to this argument. Would we also say that all humans are created by His will? If we assume that God is omnipotent, why would He purposely create humans in the womb when He knows that many of them will be aborted? Or, why would He purposely create humans who He knows will be abused for many years, or worse yet, He knows they will be eradicated by Genocide? I can't imagine that He purposely created all the Jews who were murdered in the Nazi death camps! Therefore, my conclusion is that sometimes God allows humans to use His laws of nature despite His objection. He has given us free will to use and abuse His gifts.

Conversely, some good loving husbands and wives have tried to have children but can't. I am not referring to just unbelievers; I am also referring to good Christians who believe that Jesus' atoning sacrifice saves them. Why would God purposely deny His believing children an opportunity a chance for a child? I don't know. My only assumption is that He doesn't try to control all births, but only those for who He has a particular purpose.

Other people say that God sometimes uses His intervening power to save an individual's life. For example, a person is in a horrible car crash and somehow he or she walks away with minor injuries. Again, this certainly seems like it was an act of God. But then there is another side of me that wonders, "Was this really a miracle?" Most people would say it is. After all, they beat the odds.

Would we then say that for a person to win a Powerball or Mega Millions lottery was destined to do so by God's design? The odds of winning either one is about one in 300 million! However, looking at the winning from a little different perspective, the chances are pretty good that a person will win a huge lottery if 300 million tickets are purchased. We might say it was a miracle for that individual, but I doubt that it is God's will that a specific person should win.

So what is my point? Am I saying that God can't provide sudden healings or control specific situations? Absolutely not…; I am sure He can if He wants to. However, as I read my Bible, the verses tell me that Satan has been given pretty much free rein to rule the world.

Who's Really In Control?

Many Christians believe that because God created the world, He is still in control. While this makes sense from a human point of view, the Bible tells us otherwise. Many verses indicate Satan has free will to roam the world and entice us. Often people become unwittingly subject to his schemes. Some people are so attracted by Satan's diversionary tactics that he manipulates them.

He has many names other than Satan, such as "devil," "liar," "god of this age," "prince of this world," "ruler of the kingdom," "evil one." He is subtle; he deceives us. He is so shrewd that we do not realize what he is doing. At times he appears to be a "light," one who seems to be a good person but instead, he has a sinister plan.

Jesus, Paul, and the disciples all gave warnings about the devil. Consider the following few verses.

> When anyone hears the message about the kingdom and does not understand it, the evil one comes and snatches away what was sown in their heart. This is the seed sown along the path. - Matthew 13:19

You belong to your father, the devil, and you want to carry out your father's desires. He was a murderer from the beginning, not holding to the truth, for there is no truth in him. When he lies, he speaks his native language, for he is a liar and the father of lies. - John 8:44

… in order that Satan might not outwit us. For we are not unaware of his schemes. - 2 Corinthians 2:11

The god of this age has blinded the minds of unbelievers, so that they cannot see the light of the gospel that displays the glory of Christ, who is the image of God. - 2 Corinthians 4:4

And no wonder, for Satan himself masquerades as an angel of light. - 2 Corinthians 11:14

But I am afraid that just as Eve was deceived by the serpent's cunning, your minds may somehow be led astray from your sincere and pure devotion to Christ. - 2 Corinthians 11:3

… in which you used to live when you followed the ways of this world and of the ruler of the kingdom of the air, the spirit who is now at work in those who are disobedient. -Ephesians 2:2

Put on the full armor of God, so that you can take your stand against the devil's schemes. - Ephesians 6:11

… and that they will come to their senses and escape from the trap of the devil, who has taken them captive to do his will. -2 Timothy 2:26

Submit yourselves, then, to God. Resist the devil, and he will flee from you. - James 4:7

Be alert and of sober mind. Your enemy the devil prowls
around like a roaring lion looking for someone to devour.
- 1 Peter 5:8

We know that we are children of God, and that the whole
world is under the control of the evil one. -
1 John 5:19

So for whatever reason, God has chosen to let Satan rule the world. Why? No one knows. Has God used this tactic to separate believers from non-believers? Again, no one knows. This is just another mystery of God. We don't know why He gave him control or that He still allows him to deceive and extend his influence. We don't know if we ever directly see him or his agents, however we know Satan has been working wherever we see violence and murder. When we see people get badly hurt or murdered, we ask ourselves, "Where's God?" But even more than this, "the liar" tries to distract us from God. He tries to convince us that God really doesn't love us. It seems that it has been pretty easy for the devil to do his deceptive work from my view point.

In many of those areas where the devil has his influence, we see havoc, devastation, and distraction. But there may be other areas where he has influence, and the outcome does not appear to be bad.

For example, an unbelieving man is asked to attend a church. He reluctantly goes and hears a good message. He is on the fence about becoming a Christian but he is not confident that he is loved by God. He wants to think about it some more. One day he escapes a deadly car crash. People from the church he attended heard about the incident. They tell him that the fact he was unhurt physically is a sign from God. Consequently, he begins developing faith in a loving and caring God. A few days later, he sees a loved one suddenly die. He can't understand it. His loved one had been in good health and was a believer in Jesus. Why would God let the loved one die? Suddenly, the little bit of faith he had is shattered.

He turns away from God and never sets foot in a church again. Was the outcome of his car accident an act of God, or was it from the devil who appeared to be an angel of light?

Some people say that God answers us through our prayers. All we need to do is to ask. The Bible repeats this theme. Jesus said that we should seek and knock. If we ask, it will be given to us (Matthew 7:7,8). James says we do not have because we do not ask (James 4:2); … therefore, we should ask. John says that we should have confidence in approaching God. Whatever we ask according to God's will we will have (1John 5:14,15). Paul says that in every situation we should pray (Philippians 4:6). I would not dispute any of this scripture. It is all good advice. The real question is, what should we expect God's answer to be?

Even when we see answered prayers, we do not see miracles like those performed in Biblical times. We might see an answered prayer of a person pulling through an operation or an answered prayer of a person's cancer going into remission. But if we pray for a blind person, God does not suddenly restore their vision. If we pray for a person who has been lame for many years, God does not restore their legs so that they suddenly jump up and dance around like a person who never had a walking problem. If we know a person who has a large tumor, we do not see it on an x-ray one moment, pray for them, and in the next moment, an x-ray shows the cancer is gone.

We don't see instantaneous healings. We don't see demons driven out. We don't see famines eliminated with a few fish and 1/2 dozen oversized bagels. Why not? This is a very controversial subject, and there are many opinions. The consensus is that God gave Jesus, the disciples, Paul, and others, this remarkable ability in their era, but not during our present day. Why not?

CHAPTER

17 What Kind of Healing Should We Believe In?

Is the reason why we don't see many healings today is because there are not enough people with enough faith? Do you believe that all you need is to have a little bit of faith, and God will heal you and/or provide for your necessities? Consider the following dialog I had with an individual.

I have a friend who has prostate cancer. I asked him, "What is the prognosis by your doctor?"

He said, "Prostate cancer is usually pretty slow-growing."

I followed up with, "So what kind of treatment are you taking?"

"Presently, I am doing a lot of praying."

"But hasn't your doctor recommended cyberknife, external radiation, prostate removal, or radiation implants?"

"He has given me all those options, but for now, I am still just praying."

I did not want to sound discouraging to my friend, but I asked him, "Why do you think God will heal you?"

He responded, "There are several reasons. One, I believe in a loving God. I think he is joyous when his children ask for His help, and He is willing to help when we ask Him. Two, Jesus and His disciples healed many people. I am a disciple also. Three, Jesus said, 'if you have faith as small as a mustard seed, you can say to this mountain, move from here to there and it will move.' And I have more faith than that; just wait-and-see."

I am familiar with the Bible verse from Matthew 17:20, so I started thinking. Okay, so even if I could say to a mountain "move," why would I want to move it? I have never known one to encroach on its own, so it is not like I need it to stop. And it is not like I want to plant a garden, and one was in my way. If that was the case, I should have done a little better planning when I bought my property, and I should have allowed for an extra 20' x 20' plot of ground. So, the bottom line is that I can't come up with a valid reason to move a mountain.

Everything my friend said made sense. I also believe that God loves us immensely. I agree that He wants us to petition Him in prayer. Jesus and His disciples did heal many people; there is no doubt in my mind about it. And, I also agree with the scripture my friend quoted me; we are to have faith.

One day I got a splinter in my finger, and I got a needle from a sewing kit to remove it. I was having difficulty getting it out because I couldn't see that well. I began to think about my friend, who has cancer. So, I put my needle away and decided to give prayer a chance. Would God heal me? I began to pray. I continued praying for another couple of days. The splinter didn't come out, but I noticed inflammation, swelling, and pain. So this made me wonder. Did I not have enough faith to remove this splinter?

If it takes faith the size of a mustard seed to move a mountain, then I should be able to make a proportional relationship. Curing my friend's cancer should take faith the size of 1/10,000 of a mustard seed, and removing my very small splinter should require the faith the size of a couple of molecules of a mustard seed.

As I continued to dwell on this event, I started to ask myself, "What was I trying to prove anyway?" Was I trying to prove to God that I really had faith? Yeah, I was going to show him; …well that's silly. I don't have to prove anything to God. He knows what kind of faith I have. I can't prove anything to Him that He doesn't already know.

Was I testing myself? If I believed that God could answer my prayer by having faith, then possibly it was a test of myself to see if I had as much faith as I believed. Maybe I didn't have as much faith as I thought I had. Perhaps I have just been fooling myself.

Or was the real issue that I wanted to try to convince others what faith will do? Therefore, if I prayed and the splinter came out, I could go around to others and say, "See! I prayed, and God removed the splinter. God can do anything if you have enough faith."

In hindsight, I think I was going for the last option. I think I preferred to be a preacher instead of a teacher. You may ask what the difference is. Technically, a preacher is someone who proclaims the word of God and the teachings of the Bible. But according to my experiences, I envision a preacher as someone who wants to convince us what we should do or how we should behave, and then they use Bible verses to make their point. I suppose I arrived at this conclusion based on years of listening to my dad and several other health and wealth preachers. Using my concept of a preacher, he might take a few verses from the Abrahamic covenant and preach how God wants to make us wealthy. Or he might take a few examples from the many healings performed by Christ and preach how God wants us to be healthy. Or he might try to promote a concept of "tit for tat." "Correct your behavior or suffer the consequences."

On the other hand, a teacher (according to my experiences) uses Bible verses to explain a broader theological concept. For example, a teacher might teach about faith, hope, or love. Or he might explain how great men of the Bible persevered through trials, tribulations, sacrifices, and sufferings. In any event, he would minimize the connection between our behavior and God's response. What a teacher promotes is antithetical to the concept of "tit for tat." For example, a teacher will say, "God gave us Grace even though we don't deserve it."

I realize that my distinctions between preacher and teacher are somewhat skewed; nevertheless, what I was trying to emphasize above about my splinter was that I was establishing a relationship between a cause and an effect. I wanted to "prove" a direct relationship between faith and results *regardless of the request*. If I saw the results I desired, it would be for one of two reasons:
1) I proved to myself how much faith I had.
2) I proved to others how much faith I had.

Now I could understand that I might want to test myself. God is not opposed to this but welcomes it. I am reminded of a few verses taken from the book of James (as he was prompted to write by the Holy Spirit).

> 2 Consider it pure joy, my brothers and sisters, whenever you face trials of many kinds, 3 because you know that the testing of your faith produces perseverance. 4 Let perseverance finish its work so that you may be mature and complete, not lacking anything. - James 1;2-4

It is good that we have our faith tested; it produces perseverance. It causes us not to be complacent. It causes us to be patient and continue striving. Do not take faith for granted. It is not constant; it can change a little from day to day, and over time it can either grow as great oaks or diminish to be next to nothing.

As I continued thinking about my experience, I concluded I wouldn't be happy merely exposing my faith. No, I wanted to promote it. I wanted to show others how God rewards the faithful. I desired to use the preacher scheme instead of the better "teaching" tactic.

I now see how my motives were wrong. God does not need to test our faithfulness. He knows how great or little our faith is, just like

He knew beforehand that Abraham would pass the test by agreeing to sacrifice his son. However, He wanted the experience of Abraham and his son (Genesis 22) documented, so *we* would know that he was faithful. If we could not read about this event in the Bible, what would we end up believing? Would we ever be convinced that Abraham was a man of great faith? I doubt it.

Furthermore, I don't believe God wants us to try to prove to others how much faith we have (and that they don't). To do so would cause disappointment, envy, and strife. We were chosen to be ambassadors, but not special ambassadors like Jesus, the disciples, or the Apostle Paul.

What Was the Real Reason Jesus, Paul, and Other Disciples Could Heal?

Should we question whether Jesus actually healed people? No, not at all. Was the real reason Jesus healed so many people was to show His love and forgiveness to mankind? Was it to prove that God loves everyone and that He would heal both law abiders and sinners? This makes sense, and a lot of people believe it. This is why so many people believe that God heals people today. But let's read scripture. What does it say?

In John 5, Jesus explicitly stated that His purpose for performing miracles was to prove He was from God.

> "… I have a greater witness than John—my teachings and my miracles. The Father gave me these works to accomplish, and they prove that he sent me." - John 5:35

His important message was that He was the Son of God! He wanted everyone to believe in Him, starting with the Jews. He had come to save the world. If the people did not understand this concept, then they were lost. They would not understand

that there was a better life awaiting them. They could have
eternal life! He had told them before that whoever believed in
Him would have eternal life (John 3:16). Jesus states again in
John 14:11 His purpose for performing miracles.

> "Believe me when I say that I am in the Father and
> the Father is in me; or at least believe on the
> evidence of the miracles themselves". - John 14:11

Therefore, his message was clear. If the people doubted that He
was the Son of God, then consider the miracles He performed.
This was what He was proving to the Jewish community.

If you have doubts that this was the purpose of his healings,
consider what He told his disciples in Matthew 10. He had
explicitly given them miraculous powers to prove that the King
had come:

> [1]Jesus called his twelve disciples to him and gave
> them authority to drive out impure spirits and to heal
> every disease and sickness…
> [7] As you go, proclaim this message: 'The kingdom of
> heaven has come near.' [8] Heal the sick, raise the
> dead, cleanse those who have leprosy, drive out
> demons. Freely you have received; freely give." -
> Matthew 10:1,7-8

Their message was essentially the same as Jesus'; to confirm
that He was the long-awaited Savior who had come to set up
His Kingdom. They were appointed messengers to help spread
the news to the rest of the world. They were given the power to
heal to show others that even if they didn't directly witness the
miracles performed by Jesus, they would see the miracles
performed by His appointed disciples.

Jesus continually tried to reveal His true identity to His
disciples. We read about an example of this in Matthew 16.

¹³ When Jesus came to the region of Caesarea Philippi, he asked his disciples, "Who do people say the Son of Man is?"
¹⁴ They replied, "Some say John the Baptist; others say Elijah; and still others, Jeremiah or one of the prophets."
¹⁵ "But what about you?" he asked. "Who do you say I am?"
¹⁶ Simon Peter answered, "You are the Messiah, the Son of the living God."
¹⁷ Jesus replied, "Blessed are you, Simon son of Jonah, for this was not revealed to you by flesh and blood, but by my Father in heaven." - Matthew 16:13-17

What about the Apostle Paul? Do I doubt that he healed people? Again, the answer is no. But apparently, his message seemed pretty outlandish to the Corinthians. They questioned him; they doubted his authority, so he reminded them in his second letter.

When I was with you, I certainly gave you proof that I am an apostle. For I patiently did many signs and wonders and miracles among you. –
2 Corinthians 12:12

So this is why he could perform miracles; it was to prove that he was the equivalent to the twelve handpicked Apostles of Jesus; only he was appointed as God's messenger to the Gentiles while the others had been chosen as God's messengers to the Jews. He confirmed his apostolic message in Galatians 1.

¹⁵ "But even before I was born, God chose me and called me by his marvelous grace. Then it pleased him ¹⁶ to reveal his Son to me so that I would proclaim the Good News about Jesus to the Gentiles." -
Galatians 1;15,16 (NLT)

As I stated earlier, God gave Paul the ability to prove to others that his word was true and the power of the Holy Spirit was the evidence that he was truthful. We may think that his powers were minimal compared to the other disciples, but this was not the case. His powers were great; they proved that God gave him the power to proclaim His important message. It was not just the healing effect from the handkerchiefs and aprons that touched Paul (Acts 19). Consider this amazing example from Acts 20. We read where Paul raised Eutychus from the dead:

> 9...When he [Eutychus] was sound asleep, he fell to the ground from the third story and was picked up dead. 10 Paul went down, threw himself on the young man and put his arms around him. "Don't be alarmed," he said. "He's alive!" ... 12 The people took the young man home alive and were greatly comforted. - Acts 20:9, 10, 12

The Holy Spirit was moving powerfully through Paul. He had done miracles similar to what Jesus had performed. Don't misunderstand; I am not saying that Paul was equal to Jesus; he was not. He did not die and suffer so that we could have eternal life. However, I am emphasizing how powerful the Holy Spirit was in distributing the message about Christ.

Remember, Paul's attestation was not just that Jesus was the Messiah and the Son of God. In addition, he proclaimed that Jesus had come to save us. He had suffered much for us. He died for us, and He was risen by the power of the Holy Spirit. This was the Gospel message that people were to grasp and believe; God gave Paul miraculous power through the Holy Spirit to convince others that his gospel message was true. Paul writes about the authority of his message directly in 1 Thessalonians 2, speaking of himself, Silas, and Timothy:

> ... we speak as those approved by God to be entrusted with the gospel. - 1 Thessalonians 2:4

If we think that the only reason Jesus, the disciples, and Paul healed people was to prove that God loves us unconditionally, we are wrong. True, He loves us, but He has proved something much more significant. Jesus had been sacrificed for us.

The Puzzling Lack of Healing

Even though scripture tells us that Paul was able to perform miraculous healings, it may seem somewhat puzzling why there were times he could not heal. How is it that this man of great faith could not restore the health of others? Let us consider these verses of scripture.

In the first example, we see where Paul could not heal himself. We read in 2 Corinthians 12:

> 7 So to keep me from becoming conceited because of the surpassing greatness of the revelations, a thorn was given me in the flesh, a messenger of Satan to harass me, to keep me from becoming conceited. 8 Three times I pleaded with the Lord about this, that it should leave me. 9 But he said to me, "My grace is sufficient for you, for my power is made perfect in weakness." Therefore I will boast all the more gladly of my weaknesses, so that the power of Christ may rest upon me. - 2 Corinthians 12:7-9 [ESV]

In this example, God had a special purpose, not to heal him; it was to keep him humble and to show that he could still do God's work even with his weakness. However, in the next examples, the reason for his inability to heal is not clear.

In Philippians 2 we read about Paul's friend Epaphroditus.

> 25 "Meanwhile, I thought I should send Epaphroditus back to you. He is a true brother, co-worker, and fellow soldier. And he was your messenger to help me in my need. 26 I am sending him because he has been longing to see you, 27 and he was very distressed that you heard he was ill. And he certainly was ill; in fact, he almost died." - Philippians 2:25-27 (NLT)

Paul does not mention that he tried to heal him, but we would think his friend would not have almost died if he had. This is puzzling that Paul had a friend near death, but he either could not or chose not to heal him. We cannot be sure, but because Epaphroditus was a "true brother, co-worker, and fellow soldier," it does not seem like the problem was lack of faith.

We read Paul's advice to Timothy in his first letter to him:

> "Don't drink only water. You ought to drink a little wine for the sake of your stomach because you are sick so often." – 1 Timothy 5:23

Again, if Paul's young friend who he considered as close to him as a son, was sick, why could he not eliminate this nagging problem? Shouldn't a simple prayer have resolved his ailment? Again, it does not seem that the problem was a lack of faith by Timothy.

In 2 Timothy 4:20 Paul writes,

> "… I left Trophimus sick at Miletus."

So it is unclear why Paul either could not heal these fellow servants of God. They are mysteries to us, and we will not know the definitive answer in this life. However, the one thing we can be reasonably certain of is that the problem was not a lack of faith. They were already believers.

In Timothy's case, someone may argue that the problem was because Paul could not directly lay hands on him. But we see from Acts 19:11-12 (quoted above) that Paul did not apply handkerchiefs and aprons on others directly. Instead, he touched the handkerchiefs and aprons, and someone else laid them on the sick. Therefore, I don't see that "lack of touching" is a valid reason.

Instead, I see two possible explanations of why Paul could not heal his friends:

- Because Paul's healings' primary purpose was to prove that his message about Jesus was true, then for him to heal his friends would not prove anything about Jesus that they did not already know and believe. Perhaps God did not see the necessity for supernatural healing.
- God knows how that, similar to the game of "telephone," words and messages are distorted by being relayed from person to person. The words He wanted to have passed on to others could only be delivered accurately by those who received it directly from Jesus. Consequently, the disciples and Paul wrote God's message (or had scribes write them), and then the immediate healings they performed, through the Power of the Holy Spirit, served as their scripture's authenticity. However, after their letters and books were distributed, instantaneous healings did not seem as prevalent. Possibly the initial phase of God's message and distribution plan was winding down.

Earlier I said that one of the reasons why the present Pentecostal movement had become so popular was because of the words written by James. He said that if any were sick, they should go to the elders of the church where they would anoint with oil, they would pray for them, and the sick person would become well. Why would he say that if it was not true? I believe that at the time he wrote his letter, it was true. According to most theologians, his letter was one of the first writings in the New Testament. So yes, James did see a lot of miracles. But is it still true today? Perhaps on occasion, but not nearly as often or powerful as it did during the first few years after Jesus' resurrection.

Does this mean God won't use His powers to heal people today? No, because God is sovereign. We do not know the mind of God. He may choose to cure a person for a reason only known by Him. Isaiah 55 states:

> "For my thoughts are not your thoughts, neither are your ways my ways," declares the Lord. "As the heavens are higher than the earth, so are my ways higher than your ways and my thoughts than your thoughts." - Isaiah 55:8

When James also wrote, "We do not have because we do not ask," this is true for many people in a lot of situations. However, I am more concerned about the people who have not only asked, but who have poured out their hearts, begging God for a miracle. Their loved ones are at death's door. I have seen many examples of this, and my heart goes out to all of them. Church leaders have promised them that if they have enough faith, God will answer them. However, if their desired miracle does not arrive, then their faith is often diminished or sometimes destroyed. First, they begin having doubts about what is written in the Bible. Next, their interest in reading it disappears. Their interest in attending church dissipates. Finally, they lose faith in believing in spiritual life. I think my dad was one of those people.

As I think about my own experiences, I must admit that I don't know anyone personally who has had an instantaneous, physical healing. One day I mentioned this fact to a fellow believer, hoping he would tell me that he didn't know anyone either. However, my hope was somewhat dashed. He said he did know people who had been healed, although he couldn't swear that it was immediate. With further dialogue, he told me, "Because you don't know anyone who God has healed, you seem pretty determined that God doesn't heal people in today's environment. What makes you so sure He doesn't? After all, there are over 8 billion people in this world, and you know, maybe a couple of hundred. That still leaves a huge number of people that God could have healed and you wouldn't know about it."

I responded, "It's not that I believe God can't heal physical aliments in today's environment. I am certain He can! However, the older I get, I know more and more believers who have ailments, and God has not healed them." Because my friend is about my age, I decided to ask him about prayers for "old people." In Matthew 9:35 is written that Jesus went through towns and villages healing every kind of disease and illness so it seems the elderly would be included. I began with a barrage of questions:

"I have personally known many people who have had Alzheimer's. How many do you know, and how many has God healed? I know of none."

"I had a friend who died from complications of Parkinson's disease. How many people do you know who had this disease, but because people prayed, God instantly healed them?"

"I know many people who wear glasses; many who in recent years had cataract surgery. How many people do you know, who instead of getting cataract surgery or buying glasses, said a prayer, and suddenly their vision became perfect?"

"I know many people who now wear hearing aids. How many people do you know who needed hearing aids at one time but then said a prayer, and instantly God made their hearing perfect?"

My friend admitted he did not know of anyone who has been healed of any of these "old people" afflictions, but he knew of a few people who had an X-ray that showed they had cancer, and after prayer, they had another X-ray, and the mass was gone.

This sounded like a valid point, so I did some research. According to livescience.com, there are 12 million misdiagnosed X-rays in the United States yearly.[18] The research shows that many people have cancer, and doctors fail to catch it in the initial X-ray. Despite that most misdiagnoses indicate a failure to identify cancer in a first X-ray, I will concede that there may be other situations where a second X-ray does not show cancer because of miraculous healing. It is difficult to know the true story.

---

[18] Rettner, R. (2014, April 17). *12 Million Misdiagnoses Occur Yearly in US, Study Finds*. Livescience.Com. https://www.livescience.com/44888-misdiagnosis-doctors-visits.html

I must admit that to satisfy my curiosity completely, it would be nice to see a miraculous, instantaneous healing, but this isn't a necessity for me. I know that for many people it is very important to see a miraculous healing by God. It proves to them that there really is a God and that He loves us. But I don't think we should doubt God's Word just because we don't see a healing. As true believers in the Gospel that Paul revealed, we shouldn't question whether God is punishing us when things go awry. Therefore, referring back to when my mom fell and hurt herself at my brother's house (chapter 1), as a believer, she shouldn't have been questioning why God was punishing her.

Likewise, we shouldn't be wondering whether God loves us if we don't see a miraculous healing. We should trust that Jesus' death, burial, and resurrection should be God's greatest gift proving His love.

If we honestly believe in God and don't see a healing, we shouldn't be wondering whether the problem is due to lack of faith. But here is an important question worth contemplating. Do you need to see a miracle from God to believe the Bible?

I am sure some people would say, "Absolutely not!" I hope you are one of them, and I also hope you are honest when you say it. I hope you have unshakable faith. But let me tell you of an experience.

In the early 1990's, I knew a man who appeared to be a man of great faith. He faithfully attended church, often led Bible studies, and spent time helping other people in his ministry. All was well until he started feeling poorly and then went to the doctor. He was thoroughly checked over and the doctor diagnosed him with stage four cancer. The doctor gave him sixty days to live. One day out of the blue, the man asked, "Do you think all this God stuff is a bunch of crap?" The reality of his terminal condition had sunk in. He had thought that because he had been a good servant, God would reward him with good health. However, when he was about to die, he began to question God. His Helmet of Salvation started to develop holes in it.

Many people prayed for this man. They prayed that God would heal him, yet on the 61st day after he was given his diagnosis, he died. I don't know what he really believed in his last couple of days. This was tragic. Here was a man who had spent a good part of His life believing what he thought was correct theology, and suddenly his faith was shattered. He should never have questioned whether God exists or whether all he had learned was true. I never want to see another person go through this kind of doubt. I have presented many reasons why I believe in God and His plan for salvation. And yes, God may work a miracle in my life, but I have no doubt whether the Bible is true. I don't need to see a miracle to believe it.

Through the experiences of life, we may suddenly develop an incurable, dreaded disease. For no obvious reason, one of our children or grandchildren might suddenly die. We won't know why such bad things happen, and we may question God for some time. But our lack of understanding why shouldn't make us wonder whether Jesus really came to save us of our sins. We should put confidence in the inspired Word of God that He loves us despite our troubles. That was why He sent His Son. If we keep the faith, the Holy Spirit will provide comfort, and God's servants (fellow believers) will help pull us through difficult times.

What we have seen and we continue to see is an increasing fascination with the physical world. The preoccupation or obsession we have with the physical causes us to have a diminished focus on God's Spiritual promises. It is a hard concept to grasp, but the physical is temporary, and the Spiritual is eternal. We should not promote the physical world above the Spiritual world. To do so only makes it harder to grasp and focus on God's Spiritual blessings.

Without realizing it, church leaders may be partially or, in some cases, greatly responsible for a division in what to believe among Christians. One pastor, minister, or priest may put great emphasis on the ability to heal while others don't put much emphasis on it. I have personally been exposed to both sides. In one case, I remember when we were asked as a congregation to stand and put our hands on the person next to us to heal their ailments. Maybe some people would not be too surprised at this request, but I certainly was.

This is not to say that church leaders are evil or are purposefully trying to deceive others. Many are good teachers; however, many in the congregation are confused by what they see. Nevertheless, they perpetuate the beliefs generated by their leaders. They want to see miracles. The result is often a fractured church. Is this what God wants? Certainly not, but this has to put a smile on Satan's face.

Did Biblical Miracles Produce Faith?

One of the arguments I hear about why God answers our prayers for healing today is that it produces faith in others. While there is still a lack of knowledge about Jesus in some parts of the world, I agree that for a humble person to see a miracle by God, a healing might produce evidence that the God of the Bible is the one true God who created the world. An open minded person would perhaps be overwhelmed by the event.

However, seeing a miracle does not always produce the desired results. They did for Jesus and the Apostles, but that is because His miracles were instantaneous. He did not attempt to heal one day, and the results showed up days or weeks later. No, the effects occurred immediately; the blind saw, the lame walked, the deaf heard, and the mutes spoke. He calmed stormy winds, walked on water, fed 5000 men with five loaves of bread and two fish, later fed 4000 men with seven loaves of bread and a few small fish, and cast demons out of people. He healed lepers, stopped the bleeding of a woman who has had this problem for years, and even raised people from the dead. Again, we would have thought that if miracles produce faith, then the people who witnessed the miracles would have put their faith in Him, but for the most part, they did not.

While miracles should instill long-lasting faith, biblically speaking, there is *not* much evidence that this is the case. Astounding miracles often *have not* produced or increased the faith for the majority of witnesses. This is not to say it will never increase anyone's faith because I believe in cases it has; but there are many examples in the Bible where it didn't.

First, let's consider the ten astounding plagues/miracles performed by Moses before Pharaoh so that he would allow the Jewish people to leave Egypt. We would have thought that the Pharaoh would have caved in after one or two plagues; I know I would have, but he just didn't believe that the God of his Hebrew slaves was that powerful, even though God had shown evidence of His power time and time again.

We might say that this was a special case. The only reason Pharaoh did not believe was that God hardened his heart, and he wasn't going to bow down to God.

Okay, then let us consider the Israelites who also knew about the miracles Moses performed, and in addition, they saw Moses part the Red Sea to walk across dry ground. We would have thought that the people would have been very appreciative and would have trusted God, and it seems like they did, but it lasted for only a short while. After God gave the Ten Commandments to the Israelites, they agreed they would obey them (Exodus 19:8). But a relatively short time later, when Moses went back up the mountain to meet with God (for 40 days), the people broke God's commandment by making a golden calf and worshiped it. How could they so quickly break God's commandment? They had just seen evidence through the crossing of the Red Sea that God was a powerful God who could control nature.

Shortly after this incident, Moses sent out 12 scouts to the land promised to them by God, and they discovered that the land was as bountiful as God had promised. Numbers 13:23 states, "they cut down a cluster of grapes so large that it took two of them to carry it on a pole between them!" The promises of God were astounding. He said he would drive out the existing Canaanites. They could have enjoyed a luscious environment as they had never seen before if they would have only trusted God. But they did not, so they sent out scouts to determine whether they could conquer the land under their own power. They concluded they could not do it independently and didn't believe God would do what He said either. The unbelief of the people angered God. We would have thought that the miracles should have given them faith, but they didn't:

> And the LORD said to Moses, "How long will these people reject me? Will they never believe me, <u>even after all the miraculous signs I have done</u> among them? - Numbers 14:11

As a result of their unbelief, God kept them in the desert for 40 years. While they were in the desert, God supernaturally fed them daily and supernaturally did not allow their clothes to wear out. As before, these were astounding miracles and yet they still failed to put their faith in God. We read about this is Hebrews 3:

> [8] " ... don't harden your hearts as Israel did when they rebelled, when they tested me in the wilderness. [9] There your ancestors tested and tried my patience, even though <u>they saw my miracles for forty years</u>." – Hebrews 3:7-9

So the Israelites had experienced God's miracles for 40 years, and yet they did not trust Him!

The religious leaders thought Jesus was an imposter. They thought that if He was really the Messiah, then when they were ready to hang Him on the cross, He would have called legions of angels to save Himself. They reasoned that because he hung out with prostitutes and tax collectors (who at the time extorted money from the local people), certainly, He must not be a man sent by God. So we must ask, "If miracles alone really convinced the masses that God is drawing others to Him, would the religious leaders been so eager to have Jesus hung on the cross?"

We would think that witnessing such miracles would have convinced the Jews that Jesus was really the Son of God. However, after Jesus sent out the twelve disciples and gave them authority to cast out evil spirits and to heal every kind of disease and illness so that others would believe He was the Messiah, did the Jews believe them? No, most of His disciples were also persecuted and eventually murdered.

In Luke 16, Jesus tells a story about a rich man, and a poor man named Lazarus (not to be confused with the Lazarus whom He raised from the dead). We are not sure whether it was a parable or a real story, but the point of the story is unmistakable.

Jesus tells of a rich man who, day after day, ignored a poor beggar who laid at his gate. The beggar dies and is carried to be with Abraham. The rich man also dies and goes to hades(hell). The rich man begs Abraham that the beggar be allowed to come to him and give him water (it is hot in hades). Abraham reminds him of his life on earth and how he had ignored the beggar. The rich man pleads not for his sake but the sake of his 5 brothers. He does not want them to make the same mistake he made. Again, Abraham denies his request. The rich man continues to argue:

Just like the other examples, if a person has their heart closed to God, even if they see a supernatural miracle such as someone raised from the dead, they won't be convinced by His Word either!

I believe miracles can cause some people to believe that God loves them and wants to draw others to Him, but I would say that it won't affect the masses. The Apostle Paul said essentially the same thing in 1 Corinthians:

Statistically, there are billions of Christians in the world. But if the numbers are really this large, then it is not because of signs, miracles, or special wisdom. Instead, it is because they realize that salvation resides in Jesus' death and resurrection.

Should churches emphasize to the congregation the importance of miracles? Again, please take this in context. I am not saying that God does not perform miracles; I am just saying to put it in proper perspective. Paul did not write in his letters about all the miracles he performed. He did not say that miracles produced believers. Instead, he wrote that Christ was crucified. This was the real takeaway. Jesus died on the cross for our sins. He died and was raised from the dead. This is what we really need to know to have eternal life.

I have never witnessed an instantaneous healing of a person similar to what Jesus or the Apostles performed. Maybe you have. However, if you haven't, it does not mean that you should abandon any thought of praying for healing. After all, who knows, maybe God will heal someone based on a prayer or many prayers. I have changed my approach to praying for a person to be healed. The first thing I pray for is that God opens their heart to believe in Him. After all, the person's eternal soul is far more important than the next few months or years of their physical life. I want the person to know and believe that God has provided grace no matter what a person has done so that they may have eternal life. All they must do is accept that they are a fallen person who does not meet God's requirements for perfection. They must have the Savior.

Secondly, I do not want others to lose faith in the promises of God just because they are not healed. I have seen others question their faith, and it shouldn't be because they were not healed. Instead, they should be encouraged how Jesus came to this earth, was tortured and crucified for his/her sins, and was resurrected through great power. If a person believes this, then they too will have eternal life.

After I pray for an open heart to be receptive to God's promises, I pray that the person recognizes God's comfort. In the face of extreme adversity, if we realize that God loves us and He will never leave us or abandon us, then we may still be somewhat fearful of the immediate unknown, but we will still be comforted by knowing that what we are going through is only temporary. We will have eternal life, and we will be given a new body that will not deteriorate as our present one will (1 Thessalonians 4:13, 1 Corinthians 15:42-49, Philippians 3:20,21). After I have prayed for these two things, then I will pray for a healing if it is His will. By the time I get to this part of the prayer, the healing seems to be somewhat insignificant. After all, if they realize that God loves them and wants to comfort them, then maybe physical death and eternal spiritual life would be seen as preferable compared to living with chronic or extreme pain and dying a slow death.

One of the most important things for us to realize is that God loves us regardless of whether we experience a miraculous healing. I don't want anyone to believe the lie that God does not love us or listen to us or care about us just because He doesn't instantaneously heal us like Christ did when He laid hands on others.

I don't know anyone who claims to have the power of healing, but I will implore them to go to hospitals and empty them if I meet such a person. I can only imagine how a person near death would feel to have their life extended pain-free. Or imagine that a person was brought into an emergency room with a severe laceration, and suddenly they are healed. Hopefully, the person would feel grateful, and possibly that person would be one of the rare ones who would see the miracle and draw closer to God.

Fewer Healings Should Not Equate to Diminished Faith

The emphasis on "faith healings" can be destructive to the church in several ways. The first one I have already mentioned is a fractured church. Another devastating result is that it can cause people to focus too much on the physical aspects of Christianity and too little on the other Spiritual aspects.

It can cause some people to conclude that they don't have "enough" faith to appropriate the gifts of the Spirit. They may lose faith in the more essential elements of Christianity and doubt the authenticity of Biblical scripture. It is tragic when people give up on beliefs about verses in the Bible just because they don't seem appropriate in today's time.

At the end of the book of John, we read some amazing verses about the importance of faith. The disciples were to believe in

Jesus as well as His message. It is just as significant that He gave them more evidence to believe in Him than He has given us. But why is this? It is because they did not have the completed New Testament. They didn't have the complete story as we do today. They needed the miracles, and they needed the proof.

The backdrop of these verses takes place after Jesus' resurrection, and He shows Himself to his disciples. When He presented himself to the "doubting" disciple Thomas, He told him to put his finger in His pierced hand. This is what we read:

> 27 Then he said to Thomas, "Put your finger here; see my hands. Reach out your hand and put it into my side. Stop doubting and believe."
> 28 Thomas said to him, "My Lord and my God!"
> 29 Then Jesus told him, "Because you have seen me, you have believed; blessed are those who have not seen and yet have believed."
> 30 Jesus performed many other signs in the presence of his disciples, which are not recorded in this book. 31 But these are written that you may believe that Jesus is the Messiah, the Son of God, and that by believing you may have life in his name. -
> John 20:27-31

Jesus provided evidence of His resurrection. He told Thomas to quit doubting and believe. He also knew that there would be many others who never had the opportunity to see what the disciples had seen. But we are given more. We have the testimonies of Matthew, Mark, Luke, and John. Notice how John ends his manuscript. "Jesus performed many other signs in the presence of His disciples, which are not recorded in this book. We got the minimalist version of the story of Jesus. But these were written so that we may believe that *Jesus is the Messiah, the Son of God, and that by believing we may have life in His name.*"

If We See Miracles from Jesus Again, Should We Believe It Is Him?

I have seen lots of good magic tricks, but I have never seen a true miracle. I am guessing this is true for a lot of people. What would you think if you ever saw what you believed was a true miracle? First, I would be dumbfounded. I wouldn't know whether to believe it or not. If you saw several miracles performed by the same person and they claimed to get their power from God, then what would you believe?

I have made the point that Jesus, the disciples, and Paul were all given special wisdom and power through the Holy Spirit as verification that their testimony about Jesus was valid. Therefore, if you saw similar miracles today, wouldn't you tend to believe the same thing? Would you perhaps think it might be Jesus, especially if He said He was? His miracles would be proof that He really was who He claimed to be.

Jesus is expected to return to earth in the same manner that He left it (Acts 1:11). If we don't personally see it, then we could perhaps believe that it is Jesus. We all look forward to that day, but beware! If someone says they are Jesus, it will not be Him. Instead it will be an imposter. How do we know this? Because Jesus warns us that this will happen when He is about to return:

> 21 "Then if anyone tells you, 'Look, here is the Messiah,' or 'There he is,' don't believe it. 22 For false messiahs and false prophets will rise up and perform signs and wonders so as to deceive, if possible, even God's chosen ones. 23 Watch out! I have warned you about this ahead of time! - Mark 13:21-23

Similar words are used in Matthew 24:23-25. But these prophecies of a false Messiah are just not recorded in these two verses. The warnings are also issued in 2 Peter, 1 John, 1 Timothy, Revelation, and 2 Thessalonians.

[1] But there were also false prophets in Israel, just as there will be false teachers among you. They will cleverly teach destructive heresies and even deny the Master who bought them. In this way, they will bring sudden destruction on themselves. [2] Many will follow their evil teaching and shameful immorality. And because of these teachers, the way of truth will be slandered. [3] In their greed they will make up clever lies to get hold of your money. - 2 Peter 2:1-3

[1] Dear friends, do not believe everyone who claims to speak by the Spirit. You must test them to see if the spirit they have comes from God. For there are many false prophets in the world. [2] This is how we know if they have the Spirit of God: If a person claiming to be a prophet acknowledges that Jesus Christ came in a real body, that person has the Spirit of God. [3] But if someone claims to be a prophet and does not acknowledge the truth about Jesus, that person is not from God. Such a person has the spirit of the Antichrist, which you heard is coming into the world and indeed is already here. - 1 John 4:1-3

[3] For a time is coming when people will no longer listen to sound and wholesome teaching. They will follow their own desires and will look for teachers who will tell them whatever their itching ears want to hear. [4] They will reject the truth and chase after myths. - 1 Timothy 4:3,4

[20] And the beast was captured, and with him the false prophet who did mighty miracles on behalf of the beast—miracles that deceived all who had accepted the mark of the beast and who worshiped his statue. - Revelation 19:20

[9] This man will come to do the work of Satan with counterfeit power and signs and miracles. [10] He will use every kind of evil deception to fool those on their way to destruction, because they refuse to love and accept the

truth that would save them. ¹¹ So God will cause them to
be greatly deceived, and they will believe these lies.
¹² Then they will be condemned for enjoying evil rather
than believing the truth. - 2 Thessalonians 2:9-12

These verses beg the question, "If a false Messiah shows up, then
how will we know when it is really Him?" I personally believe that
those who have accepted that Jesus died for their sins, was buried,
and rose from the dead will be taken away; we will be raptured.
We will be removed from the earth, and in the twinkling of an eye,
we will be with Him. This theme is documented in 1 Thessalonians
4:13-18. Therefore, because we will be gone, we won't have to
know whether He is real or not. But for the nonbelievers, this is a
warning…, don't be misled!

There are others who believe that the rapture will happen only at
the end of the prophesied tribulation, after the earth is nearly
destroyed. If this is what really takes place, then we will all need to
be on our guard. We will need to watch for the other signs as
spoken by Jesus and documented in Matthew 24 and Mark 13.

CHAPTER
18 The Effects of the Spirit

How Do We Really Know if the Holy Spirit Is In Us?

Paul writes that when we believe that Christ is our Savior, then the Holy Spirit enters us. But having the Holy Spirit live within us is a hard concept to grasp. What does it mean? Can we hear Him talk? No. At the moment we believe, should we feel emotional? Possibly, but probably not. Should we feel goosebumps or something equivalent? No. Does our mind instantly turn away from sin? No. If we have an addiction problem, are we immediately freed from it? No.

For typical people who decide to accept Jesus, they do not notice any immediate emotional or attitude change. At least that was my experience and the experience of many others I talked with after they became a believer. If we don't experience any notable gifts (ability to speak in tongues, interpret tongues, perform healings, etc.), how can we be assured that He enters us? Do we have tangible evidence? No.

The only way we know for sure the Spirit is in us is to take it on faith. It is the same way we know that Jesus died on the cross for our sins. All of Paul's writings lead us to this truth. He is consistent. He was chosen by God to teach us. If we believe in the Biblical God, then we should accept this Biblical truth.

Without Gifts, Is the Holy Spirit No Longer of Value?

If the Holy Spirit does not give us extraordinary abilities like those of the Apostles, is He now useless and of no value in this world? No, He is a part of God that still helps us with many things.

But first, let us acknowledge one important point. Some people try to convince us that if we are not given a special gift as described by Paul in 1 Corinthian's 12, then the problem is either immaturity or not having enough faith. Someone might tell us if we are an immature Christian, "If you can't speak in tongues or heal others or predict the future, don't worry about it for now. It will come in due time."

Unfortunately, this false teaching has many people reaching and continually striving for more faith (in miracles), believing themselves as inadequate. If they hear of others who claim to have such extraordinary power, it further reinforces their perception of deficiency. Consequently, they go to great lengths to obtain something that they never receive. They spend more time in prayer (not expressing thanks for what God has given them but instead asking for more gifts of power). They give away more money to the church (hoping that God will provide them with a special blessing). They try not to miss church services (anticipating that God may reward them for their dedication). Essentially, they try to "work" their way into receiving special gifts.

When church leaders emphasize the gifts of the Holy Spirit, we see another unfortunate outcome; it causes people to focus on using prayer to create a supernatural physical manifestation of God's power. It makes people believe that God will answer prayers in unusual ways. For example, if people pray for the country's unity, they look for God to take control and make people more amenable. If they pray diligently for God to stop wars, they expect that the loving God will provide peace on earth. If they pray that God will give them a new job, they anticipate that the God who loves them will have someone call and offer a better job. If they pray that God will restore their marriage relationship, they expect that God will cause their spouse to become loving and submissive. Ministers and other believers say prayers in public that imply that if people plead with God using heartfelt emotion, He will respond favorably.

I cannot affirm that God never answers these types of requests; however, I can't find Biblical evidence that suggests that prayer will cause God to change the minds and will of those who do not ask to be changed, especially if the other person is an unbeliever.

In 1 John 5, John writes of the promises of God:

> 14 This is the confidence we have in approaching God: that if we ask anything according to his will, he hears us. 15 And if we know that he hears us—whatever we ask—we know that we have what we asked of him. - 1 John 5:14,15

As an immature Christian, this verse confused me. My thought was, "So if I ask God for something that is His will (desire), then will He provide it?" My confusion increased when I read in 2 Peter:

> 9 The Lord is not slow in keeping his promise, as some understand slowness. Instead he is patient with you, not wanting anyone to perish, but everyone to come to repentance. - 2 Peter 3:9

So if God wants everyone to repent and be saved, then everyone will be saved. Right? There is no exception…, it will happen! But it is apparent that not everyone is saved. Many people have rejected God's saving Grace. Therefore, the two sections of Scripture seem contradictory to what we know is true. God does not save everyone.

The answer is that God saves only those who ask to be saved. He wants everyone to repent and turn their hearts to Him; if they do, He will respond. But the problem is that not everyone will ask. They just don't want to humble themselves.

The Biblical God is a Deity who has provided free will. He allows us as individuals or as a nation to do evil and destructive things to ourselves and others.

What are some of the other verses of Scripture that show that God doesn't use His power to try to control people and situations?

Consider the Biblical event where God promised He would give Abraham's descendants a very productive land (Exodus 3:17). This area was called the land of milk and honey. We read in Deuteronomy 1 Moses commandment to the people:

> ..."You have reached the hill country of the Amorites, which the Lord our God is giving us. [21] See, the Lord your God has given you the land. Go up and take possession of it as the Lord, the God of your ancestors, told you. Do not be afraid; do not be discouraged."- Deuteronomy 1:20,21

But the people were afraid and wanted to first send scouts to the land and spy on the existing inhabitants. After spying out the land, only Joshua and Caleb agreed that they could actually overtake the land. The other scouts had said that the people living there were too big. They didn't believe God would send a hornet to drive out the people (Exodus 23:28 or give them the power to overcome the existing Canaanites (Numbers 13, 14). Do we think Joshua and Caleb could have prayed to God to change the minds of the other ten scouts, and God would have changed them? Had they asked, God would have turned them down. God saw that the other scouts did not have faith. He does not intervene in the free will of others. Once He makes a promise, He expects us to have faith to believe Him.

God could have brought the people together, or He could have driven them into the promised land, but He did not. Instead, He became angry and forced them to live in the desert for 40 years (Numbers 32:13, Hebrews 3:17-19).

In another example, we should contemplate when Jesus was ministering to the Jews. God gave Jesus power to perform every miracle imaginable to convince the people that He was truly the Son of God, but He would not change the minds of the other Jews. God has always given us free will. He will not change unbelievers' minds to become believers, nor will He miraculously change people's nature to become compassionate and loving individuals.

It is just as inappropriate today to ask God to control a situation as it was two thousand years ago. If we want God to move people, then all we can do is to pray that the Holy Spirit convicts others. And the only thing the Holy Spirit will do is to try to push people in accordance with the fruits of the Spirit. He wants to change people to be more loving, joyful, patient, gentle, kind, good, self-controlled, or faithful, but there are two caveats. One, the Spirit only affects believers, and two, He only tries to *influence* others; it is still up to them to be submissive. God does not control people and situations unless it is to serve His purpose, not ours.

Today, people of the world believe in using God to serve their purpose quite regularly. This is not to say that their motive is strictly self-serving; in some cases, their motive may be altruistic. They may want God to intervene in the life of another person. However, their focus is to get God to take control of people and situations.

Instead, we should set our minds on how the Spirit was given for the purpose of personal spiritual renewal. He is there to provide us with new ambitions, attitudes, and desires. He wants us to understand the important things in life.

The Holy Spirit tries to renew our minds. He tries to overcome our old sinful nature, giving us the desire to do the things God wants us to do. Does this mean we will become perfect? Oh no, we will still sin because we are people with raw emotions that sometimes cause us to react at the spur of the moment and fall back into sinful ways.

Notice that Paul tells us in verse 22 how we were taught "to put off our old self, which is being corrupted by its deceitful desires". We might imagine that Paul is talking about non-believers, but he never writes to non-believers. No, he is writing to believers. He also tells us to put on our new self, which is created to be righteous and holy. Therefore, the Spirit is trying to renew us. In other words, it doesn't happen automatically. We are not instantly changed and never turn back. The Spirit wants to change us; He tries to influence our attitudes; however, it is up to us to allow it to happen. We should not fight it or deliberately move in the direction of sinful behavior.

Before we believe, we are like a book that is initially leaning away from God and decidedly in the direction of sin. But after we accept what Jesus did, then the Spirit gives us a new attitude, and He causes us to lean towards righteousness. We are given the desire to move in the opposite direction, but we can resist it and continue to desire to sin. That is why Paul continues in verses 25-30 of the same chapter warning us of many ways that we can resist the Holy Spirit. If we don't do what He tells us to do or we do the things He tells us not to do, then we are resisting the Holy Spirit.

29 Do not let any unwholesome talk come out of your mouths, but only what is helpful for building others up according to their needs, that it may benefit those who listen. 30 And do not grieve the Holy Spirit of God, with whom you were sealed for the day of redemption. 31 Get rid of all bitterness, rage and anger, brawling and slander, along with every form of malice. 32 Be kind and compassionate to one another, forgiving each other, just as in Christ God forgave you. – Ephesians 4:25-32

From my vantage point, I cannot recall that the Holy Spirit has ever directly spoken to me. However, I have noticed that my desires have changed. I don't desire to sin, but if someone is driving recklessly and cuts me off while driving, I still get perturbed. The anger does not last as long as it used to, but I still get upset. So just like everyone else, I am a work in progress. I notice changes in my thoughts and attitudes, but I admit that I still have a long way to go on a moment to moment basis.

What Are the Most Important Things In Your Life?

In the early 1970s, states created lotteries to be a source of extra income to fund schools. Initially, the payouts were relatively small (compared to today's standards). But the distributions were widely publicized and led to lotto drawings that grew and grew. I remember people asking, "So what would you do if you won a few million dollars?" I remember discussing with friends about what we would do if we won a large stash of cash. One guy wanted a new Lamborghini. Someone else wanted a big mansion. Another person wanted a winter home. And another friend wanted a collection of motorcycles.

As we grow older, our conversations about what is really important usually change quite a bit. Except for possibly the destitute, none of us now think that money is the most important thing to have. Call it maturity (or more likely "old age"); we tend to think more about the importance of having good health more than anything else. I suppose this is because we take good health for granted, or at least until it starts to fail. Then it becomes very important.

Knowing how my views have changed over the years, I thought it might be interesting to search for the opinions of others. What do they find most important, of course ignoring the obvious, such as water, food, and air? Naturally, we need these essentials, but I want to know what people consider to be of foremost importance. In my quest, I went to where everyone now looks to get answers, the internet.

Like everything else searched for, we can find many different answers, especially if it regards people's opinions. Therefore, there is no guaranteed single right or wrong answer, but only opinions. So I typed, "What do people think are the most important things in life". The problem with the internet is that you can find so many answers by so many people of different backgrounds, religious groups, ethnic groups, ages, etc. it is difficult to get a common answer, so I had to make a judgement. What sounds reasonable? What are the things that sounds representative of thoughtful people, representative of mature people. Here is one list I found that I considered to be pretty reasonable.

1. Health.
2. Family.
3. Friends.
4. Purpose.
5. Freedom.
6. Peace.
7. Self-Development.
8. Love.

Maybe it was just because health was the first item on the list that I tended to believe this was an excellent list. As I continued looking at all eight items, I wondered who could argue with them? This list sounds like it was generated by individuals who have lived long enough to recognize that the most important things in life aren't a new Lamborghini and a large home. No, these are thoughtful responses from those who have probably experienced troubles and learned some life lessons through the school of hard knocks. The important things in life aren't "things" at all!

We can't deny that these are good goals and virtues for which to strive. And while I agree with the list, as I contemplated it, I realized that many of these items are not easily attainable. For example, consider good health. Good health in our 30s and 40s is relatively easy to obtain; therefore, it may not seem that important. But by the time we get into our 60s, 70s, and into our 80s, we really recognize its importance. And good health, while somewhat attainable, is pretty rare. Old age is fraught with heart or circulatory problems, diabetes, cancer, and dementia. I can try to eat right, I can exercise, but I am also subject to the "gene factor." I can't control that aspect that makes me somewhat dispositioned to a specific illness.

Likewise, I considered the possibilities of having a "good" family. Cohesive families come from people who can put aside youthful jealousies, past releases of prior frustrations, and decades of criticisms and arguments. But we are either born into a family or adopted into one and can't choose who our family will be. It is terrific to have loving members, but it is not common to find a group of people who have lived together for decades who can put away years of insecurities and confrontations and leave them in the past. A friend once told me many years ago that he remembers a brother who went after his sister with a carving knife at a family reunion. So recreating a good family is not always that easy to do.

In a like manner, good friends are often hard to find. Oh, you can find people who are willing to sit down and share a fine glass of wine. But it is a lot more challenging to find those who are not critical, ready to accept others' flaws, and stand by your side through thick and thin. Quite often, friends stay friends for a few months or possibly a few years, but it is rare for a group of people, even a small group, to be lifelong friends.

Having a purpose is undoubtedly a valuable life quality, but insufficient time cuts into our intentions of doing meaningful things of real value. It seems that a person needs to be retired to obtain this asset.

Freedom is something worth striving for, but most of us are overworked and spend too much time running here and there, which usually prevents us from feeling free. Likewise, peace, self-development, and love are all worth striving for, but how often does a person actually achieve these life qualities? What we learn is, "It is the difficulty of obtaining such goals that make them seem so valuable."

How Often Do You Consider the Things Given by God As the Most Important Things In Life?

Similar to good health, we rarely think about the things we already have. Instead, our focus is mostly about what we had and lost, or we think about what our neighbors or friends have, and we don't. For example, think about the ability to see. How often do you think about your sight? We usually take it for granted. Now imagine if you suddenly went blind and had no hope of seeing again. No more sunsets, no more viewing mountain tops, no more seeing white, sandy beaches. All paintings and many more forms of art would seem worthless. Imagine that you could never see any of your loved ones again. Then eyesight would become extremely important.

Or, consider losing your hearing; never to hear the sound of your significant other (which some may think is a blessing). But regardless, imagine that you could never hear a bird or cricket chirp, a frog croak, or a dog bark. There are so many things for which we use hearing, whether it is to determine the time it takes for a thunderstorm to pass, listening for a needed emergency vehicle, watching television, listening to a concert, learning from a lecture, or communicating with others. It would be devastating to have once had the ability to hear and then lose it.

Like all pleasures in life, we genuinely enjoy many things because of our senses, regardless of whether it is our sight, hearing, smell, taste, or touch. Without any senses, we might likely develop a feeling that life is not worth living. So while at one level, we believe that our health, family, friends, having purpose, freedom, peace, self-development, and love are the most important things in life, I think they're secondary to what God has already given us. The problem is we can't realize it because most of us have had them since we were born, and we continue through life day by day, taking them for granted.

I find that as I have become, shall I say, "more mature," the list of earthly desires (as people identify on the internet) is somewhat lacking. The problem is that they are merely human and lack the realm of the Spiritual. When I say Spiritual, some people might think I mean emotional or psychological well being. While I am referring to the non-physical, I am also referring to human attributes we obtain through human development. You may be asking, "What does he mean by 'attributes we obtain through human development.'"

The Simplistic Version of Who We Are

We are born with specific genes, and this controls much of our initial makeup. According to the Human Genome Project, we have somewhere between 20,000 to 25,000 genes. Our genes, given to us by our mother and father's lineage, determine much of our physical attributes, such as eye, skin, hair color, and some of our predisposition to specific health conditions (both good and bad). The nourishment we receive, both inside and outside the womb, further develops and "controls" our physical attributes. I do not mean to imply that we (self, parents, physicians, etc.) necessarily know exactly how we are affecting our physical development. I am simply saying that human "effort" affects us beyond the factors provided by our genes. The food, liquids, and the air we consume (healthy and toxic), the exercise we perform (or lack of it) all affect us physically. Granted, no one knows for sure precisely how all this works. In fact, the medical profession seems to change their opinion about how the environment has caused and affected human development quite a bit over the years. Should we eat eggs or not? How much salt should we consume? At what levels of air and water toxins are safe for us to ingest? Scientists and doctors can only approximate how human "effort/action" causes physical development; much appears to be learned and relearned over decades and centuries.

We develop emotionally and psychologically in a similar way. The interaction of our genes initially create our personality traits. While we may not think much about how physical sustenance affects us emotionally and psychologically, it most certainly does. Likewise, physical exercise (or the lack of it) also has an effect on us emotionally and psychologically. How much do we need? How much does frequency and intensity of exercise affect our emotions?

How much does social interaction (or lack of it) affect us emotionally and psychologically? How much does spending long hours on the internet or playing violent video games affect people of various ages? All of these questions are up in the air. My point is that, even though the outcomes are unknown, we are affecting the emotional well-being of our children and ourselves as a result of our everyday activities.

Adding in to the mix are other life experiences. Some children interact with their parents quite a bit while others interact more with a television, a smartphone, or other internet connected devices. When some children cry, their parents pick them up or try to distract them. Others parents put their children in an isolated room. As a result of these experiences, some children view the world as a safe place while others are less secure. What was going on in the mind of the child while they were developing? No-one knows for certain. Then children go to school and are exposed to other adults and other kids. Some who they meet are friendly; some have had a bad day; some are frustrated; some are bullies. All experiences in a person's life affect their emotional and psychological development.

While we grow, we have many impactful experiences. One woman told me how she was greatly affected by her fourth grade teacher. She remembers her like a mother figure; she was very caring. Someone else will say that a particular book, such as "Origin of Species" by Charles Darwin or "The Rights of Man" by Thomas Paine has had a significant effect on their thinking and life. Another woman will state that going to church for many years and finally being baptized has been life-changing. Yes, all of these life experiences affect us.

The whole kit and caboodle determine who we are as humans. Some of us grow up caring and nurturing, some of us remain alone and isolated, while others become rebellious and violent.

The goals we would like to achieve in life, (like those listed in the Internet survey) are extremely difficult to obtain if we haven't had the "proper" developmental experiences. Yet most Christians believe that they can be achieved through the Grace of God. Mostly what we need to do is to pray for them. Pray for good health, a good family, good friends, a sense of purpose, freedom, peace, enlightenment that results in self development, and an opportunity to experience love. Because the things we ask for are not materialistic and because God is a loving God, He will provide them.

Yes, it certainly seems this way, but is it true? Will God help us to obtain these life goals? It is true that God loves us and He wants us to have fulfilling lives, but we cannot find Scripture that confirms that He wants us to have them, or that He will provide the things mentioned above. I know that many religious leaders teach such concepts. I don't totally disagree but I should clarify. I do believe God wants for us several of these same attributes and feelings but not in the way that much of society defines them.

For example, He wants us to have good relationships with family, but our family is fellow believers. These are our family members, regardless whether they are blood relatives or not. After all, these are the people with which we will be spending eternity.

God wants us to have friends, but not just friends in the way society defines them. Many people want to have friends so that they have a feeling of unity and acceptance by others. They want friends so they can feel good about themselves. From a standpoint of other believers, it is great to associate with people who have the same values as us, but we should not desire unbelieving friends for the purpose of being accepted by them. Instead, we are to be friendly to non-believers in hope that we can attract them to God.

Likewise, God wants us to have a sense of purpose, but the goal is not how much of society defines it. Most of society identifies purpose as doing something of personal value, enjoying our work. Quite often it results in recognition. But it is not the desire of God that we develop a fondness for how we make a living or enhancing our pride. Instead, He has a purpose for us that consists of helping lift others up; to serve them.

God wants us to have peace, but the peace is not necessarily the type of peace people desire. Most individuals want lack of strife with others. They want world peace and peace with their neighbors. They don't want stress from an illness. God doesn't want us to have stress either, but He doesn't promise peace by removing all strife or curing all diseases. After all, Satan continues to raise havoc globally, and we can only eliminate all strife by leaving the world.

God wants love in the world but He doesn't promise to give us love as we would like it. Many people are looking for a soul mate; someone with whom they can share their life and is compatible. But God only tells His servants to be helpful, caring, and supportive of others.

I don't doubt God will help those with a troubled heart; however, I am skeptical He will answer any prayers that will cause us to:

- Be drawn away from Him or His Spirit
- Be attracted to worldly desires
- Be pulled away from interacting with other believers
- Satisfy desires that generate pride or complacency

God loves us too much to *cause* these things to happen. Instead, He wants us to be continually drawn to Him. He wants us to know Him as we would know any really good friend. He wants us to understand how much He loves us and others. He wants us to serve Him, but not for His benefit or ours; instead, it is for the benefit of those who don't know Him. It is for these reasons that He has given us his Holy Spirit. His Spirit will provide us all we need and a fulfilling life if we let Him.

This is not to say God won't allow us to obtain primarily self-fulfilling life goals without His help. We absolutely can. And when we do, I believe we satisfy our own desires (and that of Satan), not necessarily the desires of God. Consider that the more contented and proud we are of ourselves, the less we find a need to be drawn towards God. He wants us attracted to Himself, which is eternal, not to the things of the world which are temporary. But God allows free will, so if we choose to be captivated by self-fulfilling rewards, He allows us to do so. The optimum goal is finding a job or activity, which is both self-fulfilling and helpful to others.

The bottom line is that God did not prompt any of the Apostles to write that He would provide for the life goals that humans find desirable. Instead, He has provided for everything we need, that is, those things which are spiritual and eternal. I am speaking of blessings, or more specifically, fruit that are given by God's Holy Spirit. These are human attributes that either most people take for granted or don't realize the value of what they have been given. They are free attributes from God and are valuable not just because they provide us a more fulfilling life. They also enrich the lives of those with whom we interact; children, relatives, friends, neighbors, co-workers, and strangers.

Paul writes of these blessings/fruit in Galatians 5, but before I elaborate on them, I want to point out something about fruit.

For the most part, the fruit that grows on a tree is a result of the nature of God. As an example, several years ago, I planted three apple trees. I staked them and watered them when I initially planted them, but I have done nothing since. As a result of God's nature, the trees are pollinated every year; and they receive adequate sun and water. So, by my estimation, other than desiring them initially, all the fruit that has been produced has been free. Over many years, by God's nature, He has produced thousands, or perhaps tens of thousands of apples. By no means do I want to trivialize His provisions; I just want to acknowledge that God's provision of tangible apples helps me understand the fruit of His Spirit. We do not have to do anything to earn it; it is His free gift that continually produces.

Jesus is the greatest gift to mankind in that He saved us and provided a way for eternal life. The Holy Spirit is the second greatest gift to mankind in that He continually provides for a fulfilling life. He is in us and continuously works to mold us and shape us according to the fruit God wants to produce.

Furthermore, this type of fruit is guaranteed only for those who believe that Jesus suffered, died, was buried, and rose from the dead. It is for those who turn their heart over to God. For these individuals, they are affected by more than their genes and life experiences. They are not left alone searching for happiness wherever they can find it. Instead, the Holy Spirit gives them desires and an attitude that is beneficial and rewarding. He helps them build relationships and helps them realize their value to God and to others.

CHAPTER
19 Spiritual Fruit Part 1

Fruit of the Spirit

There are many things the Spirit provides, some of which are in the heavenly realm and some of which are earthly benefits. Let's first look at the earthly benefits and what I mean are those "things" given by the "fruit of the Spirit." Paul writes in Galatians:

> 22 But the fruit of the Spirit is love, joy, peace, patience, kindness, goodness, faithfulness, 23 gentleness and self-control. - Galatians 5:22,23

Love

While the love provided by the fruit of the Spirit sounds like the desires expressed by people from the internet survey of "important things in life," love supplied by the Spirit is different. The "love" on the internet survey list likely refers to worldly love, that is, a romantic love of interpersonal affection and pleasure, such as being together and sharing life experiences. It involves finding and communicating common goals and activities. The result is a feeling of love.

But the love that comes from the Spirit is a benevolent, charitable characteristic. It is called agape love and is defined as "seeking another person's highest good." It involves trying to help another person in a way that is good for them. I will admit this is not always easy to do. In fact, I have told people that quite often, it can be challenging and difficult to help others. How do you help people who are poor, and their work ethic is very weak? How do you help those that struggle financially, and part of their problem is that they continually overspend? How do you help those with poor

244

health who do not care about how unhealthy their food is, nor do they want to exercise? How do you help those who are addicted and destroying themselves by their lifestyle but don't have a strong enough desire to change? No, it is often very challenging to help many people.

We may be indwelled with the love that comes from the Spirit, but we should not indiscriminately give others whatever they want. Nor should we give someone advice just to make them feel good but is not true. In other words, you wouldn't want to tell a friend who's spouse cheated on them that you believe their spouse will return with loving arms just because your friend is distraught and without their partner. Likewise, you wouldn't tell a friend who is abused by their spouse that you believe their mate will someday quit mistreating them if they simply show them some love. These untruths would simply give your friends false hope.

Agape love is not a self-fulfilling love, nor does it cause a person to fabricate a false narrative. It does not encourage others to be malicious. In fact, any thought or emotion that is expressed with the intent of generating or encouraging anger, hatred, discord, jealousy, dissension, spitefulness, factions, vengeance, immorality, impurity, debauchery, selfish ambition, degradation, or wickedness (Galatians 5:19-21) is not from the Spirit. Doing such things might make an individual feel good temporarily (as a matter of revenge or as a release valve), but these are not traits that God wants anyone to embrace.

The fruit of the Spirit produces a love which is encouraging and helpful. It is the type of love described by Paul in 1 Corinthians 13:

> 4 Love is patient, love is kind. It does not envy, it does not boast, it is not proud. 5 It does not dishonor others, it is not self-seeking, it is not easily angered, it keeps no record of wrongs. 6 Love does not delight in evil but rejoices with the truth. 7 It always protects, always trusts, always hopes, always perseveres.8 Love never fails. - 1 Corinthians 13:4-8

While it may seem like expressing love is straightforward, it is not always. Giving love for another person's betterment is sometimes very difficult for the provider because it doesn't always look like love. For example, when rearing children, love sometimes includes discipline. From an outsider's view, it may look like the opposite of love. It may appear to be punishment as a result of vengeance, tiredness, and/or frustration. And if it is done for any of these reasons, it is *not* a result of the Spirit's prompting. However, if the discipline teaches right from wrong or teaches how a person should control his/her emotion, it is likely to be done from the Spirit's prompting. Love prompted by the Spirit always produces that which is ultimately good.

Communicating love can be further complicated by a desire to dominate or prove self-righteousness. An authority figure may express this type of attitude. A spouse may be thinking, "My mate can't control their spending; therefore, I'm going to put my foot down and cut up their credit card." A parent may think, "My child is out of control. I am going to prevent them from dating." A police officer may think, "This guy is out of control. I need to put him in an uncomfortable choke hold until he calms down." Some of these behaviors may seem legitimate, but the Spirit should be trying to guide us. What are our true motives? Are our intentions for the other person's good, or are we simply frustrated and trying to impose a severe discipline on the other person? Are we thinking, "I'm going to show him or her!" If the Holy Spirit does not guide us, our action will likely be guided by frustration or a desire to control another person. If we have the Holy Spirit in us, we should pray for wisdom about handling difficult situations and complex relationships.

When we try to implement love for our own benefit, it is not love directed by the Spirit. But giving instruction or discipline for the benefit of another is a prompting inspired by the "fruit of the Spirit."

Joy

Too often, we mistakenly misuse the word "joy." In our society, we tend to think of joy and happiness as the same characteristic, but they are not from a Biblical perspective. Happiness comes from things going well, such as getting a good health report from the doctor, securing a raise from your boss, having a lot of money in the bank, having a beautiful home, receiving a compliment from another person, etc. It is a matter of circumstances.

However, "joy" is a fruit of the Spirit. It is not a result of something we experience based on a particular circumstance, but it is a God-given characteristic, despite our circumstance. It is more stable than happiness. For example, we have unspeakable joy because we have eternal life. We know that we have many promises made by God. Just consider this one promise:

> 9 … as it is written:
> "What no eye has seen, what no ear has heard,
> and what no human mind has conceived"—
> the things God has prepared for those who love him—
> 10 these are the things God has revealed to us by his
> Spirit. - 1Corinthians 2:9,10

By knowing and trusting this promise by God, we should have great joy. We don't know what God's "preparations" are exactly, but because He made them, we should believe Him. However, we should also remember that having joy does not necessarily mean that we are always happy. Things can still go wrong in our lives. We can get a bad report from our doctor, lose our job, and be short on money. When things are going awry, it's pretty hard to be happy, but we can still have joy. We can still rejoice.

You may question my wisdom in those last several sentences. You may say that it is impossible to be joyful when things are going badly. However, let's look at some Bible verses in Philippians that show how this worked for Paul. Remember that Paul wrote this letter while he was in jail. His contemporaries were ridiculing him. Other religious leaders were teaching out of selfish ambition. Paul was teaching his Gospel because Jesus personally revealed it to him. He writes:

17 The former preach Christ out of selfish ambition, not sincerely, supposing that they can stir up trouble for me while I am in chains. 18 But what does it matter? The important thing is that in every way, whether from false motives or true, Christ is preached. And because of this I rejoice. Yes, and I will continue to rejoice" - Philippians 1:17,18

Obviously, Paul was not happy; in fact, he was probably frustrated, but he was joyful. He had great joy, just preaching about Christ…, and he was rejoicing. A few verses later, he writes about joy again. Here he writes about two alternatives: either death and being with Christ, … or living and continuing to teach about Christ.

21 For to me, to live is Christ and to die is gain. 22 If I am to go on living in the body, this will mean fruitful labor for me. Yet what shall I choose? I do not know! 23 I am torn between the two: I desire to depart and be with Christ, which is better by far; 24 but it is more necessary for you that I remain in the body. 25 Convinced of this, I know that I will remain, and I will continue with all of you for your progress and joy in the faith, 26 so that through my being with you again your boasting in Christ Jesus will abound on account of me. Philippians 1:21-25

These verses provide a perfect example showing the difference between happiness and joy. He writes that he would rather depart this world and be with Christ (personal happiness) but instead, he will remain so that he will share in the joy that comes from faith. This was his way of showing love to others. Happiness is similar to "eros" love (where we get the word erotic). It is fulfilling to us personally. However, in this example, Paul intimated "agape" love (serving others) so that others could experience joy.

In Philippians 2, again, Paul mentions that his joy does not come from self-serving happiness but instead, it comes from being like-minded with one spirit thinking of others' interest.

> 2 … make my joy complete by being like-minded, having the same love, being one in spirit and of one mind. 3 Do nothing out of selfish ambition or vain conceit. Rather, in humility value others above yourselves, 4 not looking to your own interests but each of you to the interests of the others. - Philippians 2:2-4

Again in Chapter 2, Paul mentions his situation. He is in a dark, dank prison. If he were like any non-believer, he would be grumbling and arguing. But this is not Paul. Even though his environment is terrible and his position is dreadful, Paul is still rejoicing. And he tells the Philippians to rejoice with him.

> 14 Do everything without grumbling or arguing, 15 so that you may become blameless and pure, "children of God without fault in a warped and crooked generation."…
> 17 But even if I am being poured out like a drink offering on the sacrifice and service coming from your faith, I am glad and <u>rejoice</u> with all of you. 18 So you too should be glad and <u>rejoice</u> with me. - Philippians 2:14-18

When we think about the pressure Paul was under, we have to consider his attitude as remarkable. Some people might even think he was crazy. He was continually being persecuted for the sake of the gospel. Imagine for a moment if we were under a similar situation. Someone knocks on our door, and we are arrested for being a Christian. Or worse yet, imagine you are on vacation in a foreign country, and you decide to visit a Christian church. A terrorist shows up and decides to slit your throat because he identifies you as "one who believes Christ is your savior." We have no idea how fortunate we are that we live in a country with great freedom.

Paul was under constant persecution, and yet he was full of joy. Yet, in our world, most of us do not experience anywhere near his level of joy. We worry too much about the things of this world. If we lose our job, we become very concerned. Will we lose our house or our car? How long can we continue to pay our bills and still feed our family? If we get an abnormal report from the doctor, we worry and fret; an unexpected mass, blood components out of range, or an unexplained pain in the chest.

If your world started to fall apart, could you be just as joyful as Paul? I doubt I could; I am too worldly. I am not saying that the Holy Spirit will automatically make us as joyful as Paul, because there are two components to all aspects of the fruit of the Spirit. There is the Spirit's part, which is the giving, and there is the receiving part, which takes personal acceptance. All we know for sure is that for everyone who has confidence (believes) that they have eternal life, they also have been given serenity and joy. And having fellowship with other believers does for us as it did for Paul; it adds to our joy.

I do not want to be misleading. You can't make yourself joyful. You can't do this by chanting a mantra, "I am joyful. I am joyful. I am joyful." You can't talk yourself into it. No, this attribute can only be given to us by the work of the Holy Spirit.

In Philippians 3:1, Paul tells the people to rejoice regardless of what happens. He doesn't really know about his future, but if something terrible does happen to him, they shouldn't feel despondent and give up on their faith. The message should be the same for us. Regardless of what happens to other believers or us in the physical world, don't let the situation get us down. Don't be misled into thinking that the end of our natural life is the complete end. We still have a spiritual life. After death is an even better life. Be joyful anyway.

Whatever happens, my dear brothers and sisters, <u>rejoice</u> in the Lord. I never get tired of telling you these things, and I do it to safeguard your faith. - Philippians 3:1 (NLT)

In Philippians 4, Paul again commands the people to be joyful and rejoice:

Always be full of joy in the Lord. I say it again—<u>rejoice</u>! - Philippians 4:4

We are not to let adversity and our temporary troubles get the best of us. Always rejoice because we can proclaim what Christ has done for the world. We will have eternal glory. That is where we should put our focus. This is what Paul did. He states it plainly in 2Corinthians 4:

[16] Therefore we do not lose heart. Though outwardly we are wasting away, yet inwardly we are being renewed day by day. [17] For our light and momentary troubles are achieving for us an eternal glory that far outweighs them all. [18] So we fix our eyes not on what is seen, but on what is unseen, since what is seen is temporary, but what is unseen is eternal. - 2Corinthians 4:16-18

Peace

Peace from the "fruit of the Spirit" is another attribute that might seem similar to the peace identified on the "Internet important life" list, but it is definitely different. Peace from the Internet list is more likely a feeling derived from a lack of strife with family members, friends, neighbors, and coworkers. And while the peace from the fruit of the Spirit can include being at peace with others, it also consists of tranquility of the soul regardless of whether there is a notable physical peace or not. The predominant peace given by the Holy Spirit is peace with God.

Romans 5:1 stipulates this peace. It is not earned; we receive it by his Grace. We are given it through faith.

> Therefore, since we have been justified through faith, we
> have <u>peace</u> with God through our Lord Jesus Christ -
> Romans 5:1

This verse does not mean we will never be anxious or never have any problems in our life. That's what many people want to think it means, but that is not true. Just like what I acknowledged while describing joy, we will have storms throughout our entire life.

How does a person react when he or she hears the words cancer, divorce, or pandemic. While such comments will generate concern and anxiety, it is only the Holy Spirit that can help put human life in perspective to eternal life. It is only the Holy Spirit that allows us to understand that God loves us despite our physical condition. He is still concerned, and He will guide His servants to serve and comfort believers who suffer. True servants of God will try to encourage, make whole, and add tranquility to the situation. However, the storm will still be there. Given a choice between trusting God or not trusting God, I would much rather go through life knowing that He is in my corner. We do not have to be fearful that He will zap us or disown us. We can all have peace if we have faith in His unfailing love.

When we are at peace with God, then we have no fear of retribution. Conversely, imagine what it would be like for a person to believe that they always need to please God. Try to comprehend how a person would feel if they believed God would punish them every time they stepped out of line. For them, there would never be any peace.

Paul's words provide a great example of the peace he felt by the work of the Spirit. As mentioned earlier, in Philippians, he is in a cold, damp jail because of his teachings about Jesus. In Philippians 1, he writes about what has happened as a result of his imprisonment:

> 12 Now I want you to know, brothers and sisters, that what
> has happened to me has actually served to advance the

gospel. 13 As a result, it has become clear throughout the whole palace guard and to everyone else that I am in chains for Christ. 14 And because of my chains, most of the brothers and sisters have become confident in the Lord and dare all the more to proclaim the gospel without fear. - Philippians 1:12-14

How many people could be imprisoned, chained to a guard, and speak with that kind of attitude? He is not concerned about his personal well-being. But because he is in jail, he has given other believers confidence to proclaim the gospel without fear. His faith and peace have become contagious. As impressive as this sounds, he continues expressing his lack of fear of death. I wrote about this earlier, but it is worthy of repeating.

21 For to me, to live is Christ and to die is gain. 22 If I am to go on living in the body, this will mean fruitful labor for me. Yet what shall I choose? I do not know! 23 I am torn between the two: I desire to depart and be with Christ, which is better by far; 24 but it is more necessary for you that I remain in the body. 25 Convinced of this, I know that I will remain, and I will continue with all of you for your progress and joy in the faith, 26 so that through my being with you again your boasting in Christ Jesus will abound on account of me.

Can you imagine having such peace that you had thoughts of how wonderful physical death was going to be? And Paul is talking about comparing death to a jail sentence. I am sure many people would prefer a jail sentence, but not this guy. This just shows what kind of faith he had; his faith was as solid as a rock. Yes, the peace he experienced was truly a calmness and confidence that can only be obtained and known through the fruit of the Spirit.

The peace that comes from a lack of strife with family, friends, workers, and enemies is barely attainable from a human perspective. But the peace that transcends our situation or despite our situation is a peace from the Spirit of God.

Hopefully, we see the difference between human desired peace, and God's peace. Whatever peace we obtain from life's experience, God Spirit provides more. His is more complete, more valuable, and more enduring.

Paul tells us in Philippians 4 what this peace looks like:

> [6] Do not be anxious about anything, but in every situation, by prayer and petition, with thanksgiving, present your requests to God. [7] And the peace of God, which transcends all understanding, will guard your hearts and your minds in Christ Jesus. - Philippians 4:6-7

Imagine not being anxious about anything! When Paul says, "Do not be anxious about anything," I interpret that to mean "anything"!! He means, "Do not let any storm of life affect your focus on what God has promised." When bad news comes, we cannot help but feel some anxiety, but the peace of God will allow us to keep our focus on how much Jesus did for us. His Spirit will remind us that Christ's suffering paid for our account 100%. We are justified! Therefore, keep "storms," even bad "storms" in perspective. Look towards the future. The Spirit should help us keep our focus on the fact that we have eternal life.

Granted, there are some situations where we have a limited ability to resolve our problems. We can try to keep a positive attitude; we can read scripture; we can surround ourselves with uplifting friends. We can pray; but when we do, we are to present our request to God "with Thanksgiving." Be thankful that God is there and is listening. Thank him personally.

Do not assume what some people believe, and that is, that God will answer all our problems as we request. Nothing in Scripture says this. Instead, when we make a request of Him, we are never sure if He will say "yes," "no," or "wait." But Philippians 4:7 is always an affirmative response to our prayer. He will always give us His peace in Christ Jesus.

Do not take this verse lightly. Do not think that this came strictly from the mind of Paul. No, he was inspired to write it. It came from the Spirit of God. And for that reason, it also says that the peace "transcends all understanding." That means we can't explain it. We don't know the mechanism of how it works, but it is a promise from Him, and we should believe it!

I had a friend who was about to die from cancer. In his last days, he could have been moaning in his suffering, but he wasn't. When I saw him, I wasn't really sure what to say, but he broke the ice. He had a smile on his face, and I thought that perhaps he was making a recovery. So I asked him if he was feeling better. He said, "No! But I am excited."

"Why!" I asked.

"I have read in my Bible about Jesus many times. But in a few days, I am going to meet him face-to-face. I've been waiting a long time for this!"

20 Spiritual Fruit Part 2

Patience, Gentleness, Kindness

Jesus' exhibition of many signs, wonders, miracles, Spiritual knowledge, and superior wisdom were all attributes that captured the Jewish people's interests. But these were characteristics that primarily drew curiosity, not necessarily a desire to know Him personally. Instead, it was His qualities of patience, gentleness, and kindness, which attracted others to Him personally.

These three attributes often work together. In other words, a patient person often exercises restraint. Sometimes patience is also called long-suffering or forbearance. A patient person is usually gentle and kind. Likewise, a gentle person is often patient and kind. And a kind person is frequently patient and gentle. These human characteristics work together to help in establishing relationships. They set an attitude of friendliness as we relate to neighbors, friends, families, and coworkers. Granted, they won't help us with everyone because, to be quite honest…, some people are difficult "to deal with" a good deal of time. They put a hefty tax on our patience.

For me, having good relationships with others is personally very rewarding. And while I think this is a reward from the Holy Spirit, I don't believe it is the only reason why the Holy Spirit tries to enhance these personality traits. It is not strictly for our benefit; God instills these qualities in us to be His witnesses to others.

Some people may read these words and are skeptical. They may not see how these qualities have much to do with being good witnesses. They may be trying to compare themselves to Jesus's disciples and reflect on the times when Jesus specifically called them to be His witnesses. For example, in Acts 1, the disciples met with the resurrected Jesus, and they wanted to know if "now" was the time that He was going to set up his kingdom on earth. His response was:

> 7 … "It is not for you to know the times or dates the Father has set by his own authority. 8 But you will receive power when the Holy Spirit comes on you; and <u>you will be my witnesses</u> in Jerusalem, and in all Judea and Samaria, and to the ends of the earth." - Acts 1:7,8

This promise was a reiteration of His commandment for them to go among the nations and make disciples (Matthew 28:18-20). Many people think that's fine for those disciples, but they were given the power of the Holy Spirit. "They lived with Jesus and were given special knowledge and wisdom. He gave them the power to perform miracles and healings. I don't have any of those gifts. Nor can I be anything like Billy or Franklin Graham. I don't have that kind of talent. How can I be a witness and make others disciples?"

We may feel inadequate. We may think that the disciples were effective witnesses because they had a special power. But, also remember that we have been given the complete word of God, and they didn't have it. They were given the gifts of the Holy Spirit, but we have also been given attributes to be patient, gentle, and kind. We may not know our Bible through and through with intricate detail, but our personalities have been altered by the Holy Spirit to be a witness showing others that the God we believe in is a patient, gentle, and good God (2Peter 3:9).

Few believers are called to be preachers; but *we are all* called to be witnesses. Our witnessing is going to be much different than that of the disciples. They proved their testimony through miracles. But keep in mind that their miracles often had the same results as Jesus's miracles. They drew curiosity but not necessarily relationships.

Our mission is to expose our faith, but not argue our faith. We never convince anyone of God's love by being aggressive, overbearing, or argumentative. Such behaviors come across as "mostly vinegar" and "little honey." We simply need to exhibit patience, gentleness, and kindness as we tell our reason for believing God.

Some people believe it is their job to be able to defend the Bible. I know, because I have been one of them. I can't help it; I believe it is the truth. With that being said, as I have matured, I've come to believe that the Holy Spirit will do the defending. What I try to do is to have people look at me and say, "His faith appears to be working for him. He appears to be concerned about others. He mentioned that he had some problems but he seems to be holding up well. He appears to be somewhat joyful. He seems to have a peace about him." My sole intention is for them to ask themself, "How does he do it? I would like to have a similar peace." This is a more realistic view of what it means to be a witness for God.

Now, this does not mean I exclude all other conversations about God from my speech. Of course, I mention God when appropriate. However, I have found that confronting a stranger with my belief about God is usually not effective. We need to develop a relationship with others first and then expose our faith. We need to let our Holy Spirit attributes shine through.

One person who has inspired me personally, as well as hundreds of thousands of others, is Alex Trebek. Here was a man who had been struggling with stage 4 pancreatic cancer for well over a year. Typically, someone with stage 4 pancreatic cancer doesn't live too long, but he seemed to do moderately well. He said that the drugs sometimes gave him great depression, but his feelings were only temporary. He claimed that the secret to doing as well as he had was because of his faith and prayer. He talked about his condition with gentleness and kindness.

Anyone who knew of his situation would probably like to know more of the specifics of what he believed, but regardless, he is an excellent draw to his faith. I don't know what he believed, so I can't say unequivocally that I agree with everything he believed in.

Nevertheless, he has become an inspiration to many people and a great witness for the power of his belief.

Paul wrote quite a bit about patience, gentleness, and kindness. It wasn't the main point of his writing, but the Holy Spirit guided him to include verses in his letters.

Regarding patience, Paul writes about two types of patience. One is patience while waiting for what we hope for but do not have. For example, we are to be patient while we are suffering. Paul writes not to give up, but persevere. This does not mean that we will necessarily get what we want or that God will end our suffering, but just pray and be patient. Perhaps God will answer us favorably.

> But if we hope for what we do not yet have, we wait for it patiently. -Romans 8:25

> Be joyful in hope, patient in affliction, faithful in prayer. -Romans 12:12

Paul also writes that we should be patient for what we already have assured to us but has not yet come to fruition, i.e., our salvation. Once we are saved, it is in the bag; there is no need to hope for it. We may want something besides salvation; we may be praying for it; it probably won't be answered immediately, but do not be anxious; instead, be steadfastly patient.

The Holy Spirit gives us patience while loving others. I will admit that sometimes it doesn't feel like it, but like all attributes of the Spirit, He tries to give it to us. Will we listen to the Spirit?

> Love is patient, love is kind…-1 Corinthians 13:4

> Be completely humble and gentle; be patient, bearing with one another in love. -Ephesians 4:2

> And we urge you, brothers and sisters, warn those who are idle and disruptive, encourage the disheartened, help

Christ was very patient, gentle, and kind to everyone. Well…, He
did lose his patience with the Pharisees and the money changers at
the temple, but these were the exception to how He treated others,
not His normal reaction. Considering Jesus' normal behavior,
people may want to know why He lost his patience and gentleness
with them? What was it that angered Him so much? Was it because
the Pharisees were liars and cheaters? This was an issue, but this
was not the primary source of His wrath. No, if they were regular
Jews, it would not be as upsetting. After all, we are not surprised
when we see such behaviors from "worldly people." But these
were religious leaders, and they were representing God. They were
lying, cheating, and putting on facades under the auspices that they
were under the influence of God. Their behavior was not just a
disgrace, but it had reached the level of abomination.

As Paul was ministering to Gentiles, he was often a spectacle to
the crowds. He said some things that were not easy to grasp, but he
backed up his theology with signs, wonders, and miracles. But
being a great speaker and a wizard did not draw others to want to
know him personally. Instead, it was the same qualities that drew
others to Jesus, i.e., patience, gentleness, and kindness that
attracted others to Him. This is the way it is. We can develop
admiration of a charismatic person, but we will not desire to
engage with them personally if they are not gentile, kind, and
patient.

As a result of his friendly demeanor, Paul acquired many friends.
He was a great witness for God. Therefore, he gave advice to us to
do likewise. This is another way to develop good relationships
with others and, at the same time, show others grace. Here are
some Bible verses where the Holy Spirit inspired Paul to write of
patience, gentleness, and kindness.

By the <u>humility and gentleness</u> of Christ, I appeal to you…- 2 Corinthians 10:1

Be completely <u>humble and gentle; be patient</u>, bearing with one another in love. - Ephesians 4:2

Let your <u>gentleness</u> be evident to all. The Lord is near. - Philippians 4:5

Therefore, as God's chosen people, holy and dearly loved, clothe yourselves with compassion, <u>kindness, humility, gentleness and patience</u>. -Colossians 3:12

[1] Remind the people to be subject to rulers and authorities, to be obedient, to be ready to do whatever is good, [2] to slander no one, to be peaceable and considerate, and always to <u>be gentle toward everyone</u>. - Titus 3:1,2

CHAPTER
21 Spiritual Fruit Part 3

Goodness

There are many things in life we say are good. But when we use the term "goodness," it is a virtue; it results from someone doing something right. Some of these things are obvious, i.e., being kind, gentle, generous, hospitable, friendly, etc. But as soon as I say these things, I can suddenly think of several activities that throw our motives into question. For example, if we tell our child that we refuse to do something, "No, I am not going to do this or that, are we doing good?" Or, if we tell a friend, "No, I will not help you. I will not give you more money.", are we being mean, antagonistic? The correct answer is, "It depends." We are to be kind and generous, but if we are too willing to bend or too accommodating to help those who won't push themselves, we become enablers. For those who we are trying to create discipline, it is a very tricky situation. Will we make them angry, bitter, or frustrated? We do not want to do this, but sometimes it just happens. If our action causes a person to ultimately come out better on the other side of their temporary situation, then we did well. But we often do not know this when we say "No!" Sometimes, as the granter of a desire, the answer to say "Yes" or "No" is obvious, but there are a fair amount of other times when we are uncertain in knowing what is ultimately good for a person. Therefore, as humans, we are going to make mistakes.

What the Holy Spirit does is give us the desire to do good. It is to love others, to be considerate, friendly, and kind, but will we always succeed? No, there will be times we fail. What the Holy Spirit does is that it gives us the heart, the desire to do good. It does not give us the ability to know the outcome. Therefore, while most of our efforts may result in something that is godly, there are times when we fail. Fortunately, God does not look at actual results but instead sees our desire and intent.

Consider, for example, if we donate time or money without caring whether it actually does good. We might do this because either we think it is expected of us or because we are trying to look good in the eyes of others. If we do such things, then our motivation is not through the Holy Spirit. However, if we truly try to help others and hope to see a positive outcome, we are being motivated by the Spirit.

Only God knows our true motivations:

> All a person's ways seem pure to them, but motives are weighed by the Lord. - Proverbs 16:2

> "… The Lord does not look at the things people look at. People look at the outward appearance, but the Lord looks at the heart." - 1 Samual 16:7

Paul tells us in many verses to do good. The rewards are great, not only for us but also for the ones we serve. Read and dwell on these verses; they speak volumes more than I could ever say.

> To those who by persistence in <u>doing good</u> seek glory, honor and immortality, he will give eternal life. - Romans 2:7

> [9] There will be trouble and distress for every human being who does evil: first for the Jew, then for the Gentile; [10] but glory, honor and peace for everyone who <u>does good…</u> - Romans 2:9,10

> Very rarely will anyone die for a righteous person, though for a <u>good person</u> someone might possibly dare to die. - Romans 5:7

Love must be sincere. Hate what is evil; cling to what is good. - Romans 12:9

Do not be overcome by evil, but overcome evil with good. - Romans 12:21

Therefore do not let what you know is good be spoken of as evil. - Romans 14:16

Each of us should please our neighbors for their good, to build them up. - Romans 15:2

… I want you to be wise about what is good, and innocent about what is evil. - Romans 16:19

Your boasting is not good. Don't you know that a little yeast leavens the whole batch of dough? - 1 Corinthians 5:6

No one should seek their own good, but the good of others. - 1 Corinthians 10:24

And God is able to bless you abundantly, so that in all things at all times, having all that you need, you will abound in every good work. - 2 Corinthians 9:8

It is fine to be zealous, provided the purpose is good…- Galatians 4:18

Let us not become weary in doing good, for at the proper time we will reap a harvest if we do not give up. - Galatians 6:9

Therefore, as we have opportunity, let us do good to all people, especially to those who belong to the family of believers. - Galatians 6:10

For we are God's handiwork, <u>created in Christ Jesus to do good works</u>, which God prepared in advance for us to do. - Ephesians 2:10

…because you know that the <u>Lord will reward each one for whatever good they do</u>, whether they are slave or free. - Ephesians 6:8

9 We continually ask God to fill you with the knowledge of his will through all the wisdom and understanding that the Spirit gives, 10 so that you may live a life worthy of the Lord and please him in every way: <u>bearing fruit in every good work</u>, growing in the knowledge of God. - Colossians 1:9,10

Make sure that nobody pays back wrong for wrong, but always <u>strive to do what is good for each other</u> and for everyone else. - 1 Thessalonians 5:15

With this in mind, we constantly pray for you, that our God may make you worthy of his calling, and that <u>by his power he may bring to fruition your every desire for goodness</u> and your every deed prompted by faith. - 2 Thessalonians 1:11

May our Lord Jesus Christ himself and God our Father, who loved us and by his grace gave us eternal encouragement and good hope, 17 encourage your hearts and <u>strengthen you in every good deed and word</u>. - 2 Thessalonians 2:17

And as for you, brothers and sisters, <u>never tire of doing what is good.</u> - 2 Thessalonians 3:13

Self-control

The Greek word, self-control, used in Galatians 5:23 is "egkrateia," meaning "strong, having mastery, able to control one's thoughts and actions. It is another attribute of the Holy Spirit, meaning that there is no guarantee that we will actually develop self-control, but the Spirit gives us the desire or inclination to be self-controlled. Like all promptings by the Spirit, we choose whether to abide by Him or to ignore Him.

The scripture concerning the fruit of the Spirit was given to us by Paul, but Peter wrote something similar by inspiration of the Spirit:

> "...make every effort to add to your faith goodness; and to goodness, knowledge; 6 and to knowledge, self-control; and to self-control, perseverance; and to perseverance, godliness; 7 and to godliness, mutual affection; and to mutual affection, love." - 2 Peter 1:5-7

Then in verse 8 he tells us why we should try to abide by the Spirit:

> For if you possess these qualities in increasing measure, they will keep you from being ineffective and unproductive in your knowledge of our Lord Jesus Christ. - 2 Peter 1:8

Paul provides us with similar advice, except he writes that self-control is part of a sanctification process. Synonyms for sanctification include purification, being set apart for a special purpose, anointed, consecrated. It refers to making ourselves usable by God. We are to be God's witnesses, and people only consider us credible when we behave in a godly way. Here are some of the verses given to us by Paul:

> 3 It is God's will that you should be sanctified: that you should avoid sexual immorality; 4 that each of you should learn to control your own body in a way that is holy and honorable - 1 Thessalonians 4:3-4

> 2 Now the overseer [church elders] is to be above reproach, faithful to his wife, temperate, self-controlled,

respectable, hospitable, able to teach, 3 not given to drunkenness, not violent but gentle, not quarrelsome, not a lover of money. - 1 Timothy 3:2, 3

1 But mark this: There will be terrible times in the last days. 2 People will be lovers of themselves, lovers of money, boastful, proud, abusive, disobedient to their parents, ungrateful, unholy, 3 without love, unforgiving, slanderous, without self-control, brutal, not lovers of the good, 4 treacherous, rash, conceited, lovers of pleasure rather than lovers of God— 5 having a form of godliness but denying its power. Have nothing to do with such people. - 2 Timothy 3:1-5

He [church elders] must be hospitable, one who loves what is good, who is self-controlled, upright, holy and disciplined. - Titus 1:8

In Titus 2, Paul tells Titus to teach self-control. He then summarizes in verses eleven and twelve:

11 For the grace of God has appeared that offers salvation to all people. 12 It teaches us to say "No" to ungodliness and worldly passions, and to live self-controlled, upright and godly lives in this present age. - Titus 2:11,12

It makes no difference whether it is Peter or Paul's writings; they both tell us to be self-controlled, not necessarily because it is good for us. Instead, it is because we are God's representatives and witnesses. Just as we can attract people by exuding patience, gentleness, and kindness, we can push others away by being wild and out of control.

22 Spiritual Fruit Part 4

Faithfulness

A Pew study revealed that 80% of all Americans believe in God.[19] Some people probably see this as something good, something of which to be proud. Isn't it great that so many people in our country believe in God?

While this fact may sound like good news, unfortunately, this statistic by itself doesn't mean much. Saying you believe in God is non-descriptive. What kind of God do you believe in? Some people simply believe in a higher power. They believe that the universe is too big and too diverse to have materialized on its own; therefore, God must have created it. Some people believe in God when they see a newborn baby. Certainly, only an all-powerful God could create a remarkable, beautiful child. Other people say they believe in God whenever they see a beautiful sunrise or sunset. How could anything that beautiful be created by something other than an Almighty God?

The diverse opinions about what God is like today is not much different than the opinions of those who lived back in the day of the Apostle Paul. In Acts 17, he was visiting Athens and was invited to speak:

> 22 Paul then stood up in the meeting of the Areopagus and said: "People of Athens! I see that in

---

19 Research Center Religion and Public Life, "When Americans Say They Believe in God, What Do They Mean?," https://www.pewforum.org/2018/04/25/when-americans-say-they-believe-in-god-what-do-they-mean/04-25-18_beliefingod-00-01/ (Pew April 23, 2018)

every way you are very religious. 23 For as I walked around and looked carefully at your objects of worship, I even found an altar with this inscription: TO AN UNKNOWN GOD. So you are ignorant of the very thing you worship— and this is what I am going to proclaim to you.- Acts 17:22,23

What was the problem with these people? Were they not religious? No, they were very religious. They believed in many gods. They had many statues. Although they never realized it, their minds were split among many philosophies. This is every bit as true today, if not more so. Most of us do not believe in many gods, but we do seem to have many varied ideas about who God is and what He is like. If we haven't read from Scripture about who He is and hear someone else's thoughts, we likely take a little of it and accept it as either truth or perhaps partial truth. What do we trust? What we hear! And if what we hear is from Satan, the liar, and master deceiver, then that is what we believe.

It is required of us to have faith, but what must we have faith in? Some people have faith in a God who wants them healthy and wealthy. Is this really true? Can they show scripture from the current dispensation to prove what they believe? If not, on what do they base their opinion?

Are we required to have faith in an omniscient, omnipotent, personal God who does not want us to suffer in order for us to obtain eternal salvation? No. Must we be able to look at all tragedies of life and believe that God has a purpose for them? Heaven's no! We do not need to be able to answer all life's difficult questions to obtain everlasting life with Jesus and loved ones. Let me be clear. True, we must believe "in" God; but this is just the starting point.

Instead of believing "in" God, we are asked to believe God. So what's the difference between believing in God and believing God? Aren't they the same thing? No, to believe "in" God does not necessarily mean that we have to do anything. We may simply say,

"I believe" and that is all that happens. It does not really even require any kind of specific faith. To what degree do we believe? That is what many people do today. They believe in God, but it does not give them anything or guarantee anything for them in the physical or spiritual world.

However, when we say we believe God, that means we believe God told us something. In Abraham's time, that meant he believed God either told him something verbally or revealed something to him in a dream. In modern times we shouldn't rely on God's voice or special revelation. God revealed everything we need to know (but not necessarily everything we want to know) in the Bible. All the books of the Bible were written 1900 or more years ago. They reveal how God created and interacted with early man, how He interacts with us in the present, how the world will come to an end, and how to obtain eternal life. Although it might be nice to have an appendix to fill in more details, it is not essential. It is complete. There is no more we need to know.

There is much scripture written in the Old Testament describing God and His interaction with humans. There are a significant number of prophecies written that describe future events. The writers could not have possibly known what was going to happen many years later if it wasn't through God's inspiration.

Before Jesus started His ministry, Peter may have wondered how the prophets wrote the things they had written. He may not have even believed it all. However, after he hung around Jesus, he probably started to have more confidence in the prophets' writings. But it wasn't until Jesus opened his mind that Peter fully believed it all and accepted it as God's Holy Word. This revelation event took place after Jesus' resurrection. He was alone with the disciples:

> **Then he opened their minds so they could understand the Scriptures. - Luke 24:45**

Certainly, Peter then realized that the Holy Spirit inspired all the prophets to write Scripture, so we too would read it and believe it.

The Apostle Paul concluded the same thing Peter had said. He knew all Scripture came from God, and therefore, he also wrote why Scripture is useful:

"All Scripture is God-breathed and is useful for teaching, rebuking, correcting and training in righteousness" - 2 Timothy 3:16

Paul understood that all Old Testament scripture is to be read and believed. Of course, why wouldn't he believe this? Jesus, the fulfiller of much of the Old Testament revealed Himself to Paul and assigned him the task of carrying the message of Grace to the Gentiles.

It was not good enough for Peter and Paul to believe "in" God, but they also needed to believe God; to believe that Biblical scripture was inspired by God. Therefore, they led their lives, believing God's words were true.

What did Abraham believe, the father of the Jews? Did he only believe "in" God? No, he also believed God when he was told to make his son a sacrifice. This Scripture tells us that simply believing in God is not enough. We must also believe what God says.

"…Abraham believed God, and it was credited to him as righteousness." – Romans 4:-3

Abraham was considered righteous, but it was not *just* because he believed "in" God. No, it was because he believed God.

What does this mean for us? Just like Abraham, we should certainly believe all Scripture. We should believe all that Jesus said. Yes, Jesus is the Messiah and the Son of God. But we must also believe all that Paul said about Jesus.

Now, brothers and sisters, I want to remind you of the gospel I preached to you, which you received and on which you have taken your stand. 2 By this gospel you

are saved, if you hold firmly to the word I preached to you. Otherwise, you have believed in vain.
- 1 Corinthians 15:1-2

These are the verses to which we are held accountable. Paul tells us in verse 2 that it is by *his* gospel that we are saved.

God has never been happy when we believe in gods who are not real. The Bible says he is a jealous God. Does that mean He has an ego so big that He just can't stand to have others believe in something else? Of course not! However, let us look at an analogy. We want our children to trust and believe in us. Our egos are much more fragile. But the Creator of the world and everything in it does not need our approval. He is jealous because He wants us to believe in the real truth. He doesn't want us to be misled. He knows that ultimately we would be hurt, … just like we know that it is very dangerous for our children to associate with a drug dealer. We want truth for our children, and God wants truth for His children.

Here is a defining point in your life. Either you are going to believe what is in the Bible or what people in society tell you. Do you believe what some people claim is the inspired word of God without reading it yourself?

If we are to have faith, we should take God at His Word. We should believe it from cover to cover. Some people will take this to mean, "If I believe the whole Bible, then I should believe in all of God's commandments and do as He said." The problem with this concept is that we need to remember the differences in the dispensations. God gave His commandments to the Jews for a specific time. They were not given to the Gentiles.

So, for example, Leviticus Chapter 5 states that "anyone who has touched something unclean" should give a female sheep or goat to the priest for him to make a sin offering on his behalf. I know of no one who actually believes that it is a sin in today's world and, therefore, does what Scripture says. No, we don't do that.

The Bible is for us to learn, but not all of it was written for us to obey. We need to keep separate the various dispensations. We are Gentiles who are living in the time of God's Grace. We need to read, understand, and abide by what the Apostle Paul wrote and passed on to us.

Do you believe that Jesus shed his blood and died for your sins, or were these just the thoughts of Paul? According to the Gospel of Paul, this is the only way we are saved.

Saved By Faith and Faith Alone

Do we need to believe in present-day miracles in order to have enough faith required for eternal life? Not at all. What Jesus said about the importance of having the faith as small as a mustard seed (Matthew 17:20) was not regarding believing in modern miracles. The primary focus of believing in miracles in Jesus' day was to believe that He is the Son of God and the Messiah.

The Apostle Paul tells us that we must have "another" faith; it is the faith that gives eternal life.

> 23 for all have sinned and fall short of the glory of God, 24 and all are justified freely by his grace through the redemption that came by Christ Jesus. 25 God presented Christ as a sacrifice of atonement, through the shedding of his blood—<u>to be received by faith</u>. He did this to demonstrate his righteousness, because in his forbearance he had left the sins committed beforehand unpunished— 26 he did it to demonstrate his righteousness at the present time, so as to be just and the one who <u>justifies those who have faith in Jesus</u>. 27 Where, then, is boasting? It is excluded. Because of what law? The law that requires works? No, because of the law that requires faith. 28 <u>For we maintain that a person is justified by faith apart from the works of the law</u>.
> - Romans 3:23-28

These verses clearly state that we are not justified by obeying the law, nor are we justified by believing in miracles. Instead, we are justified by believing (having faith) that the Holy Jesus was tortured and sacrificed for us.

> For in the gospel the righteousness of God is revealed—<u>a righteousness that is by faith</u> from first to last, just as it is written: "The righteous will live by faith."- Romans 1:17

The verse says that we are made righteous by faith. If we are righteous, does this mean we will live perfectly? No, instead, it means we live believing the gospel. It means we know we will never be good enough to approach God based on our own works. This is the truth that will keep us both humble and appreciative of all we have. The following verses describe how that faith makes us righteous and how we are saved through faith.

> However, to the one who does not work but trusts God who justifies the ungodly, <u>their faith is credited as righteousness</u>. - Romans 4:5

> [13] And you also were included in Christ when you heard the message of truth, the gospel of your salvation. <u>When you believed</u>, you were marked in him with a seal, the promised Holy Spirit. - Ephesians 1:13

> For it is by grace you have been saved, <u>through faith</u>—and this is not from yourselves, it is the gift of God - Ephesians 2:8

> For <u>we live by faith</u>, not by sight. - 2 Corinthians 5:7

> And <u>without faith it is impossible to please God</u> - Hebrews 11:6

> [11] Clearly no one who relies on the law is justified before God, because "<u>the righteous will live by faith</u>. [12] The law is not based on faith; on the contrary, it says, "The person who does these things will live by them." [13] Christ

redeemed us from the curse of the law by becoming a
curse for us, for it is written: "Cursed is everyone who is
hung on a pole." 14 He redeemed us in order that the
blessing given to Abraham might come to the Gentiles
through Christ Jesus, so that <u>by faith we might receive
the promise of the Spirit</u>. - Galatians 3:11-14

What this Scripture doesn't say is probably just as important as
what it does say. What it doesn't say is that we can earn
righteousness by the things we do. Here is a question every person
should ask themself. "Do I think I earn righteousness by going to
church, taking communion, being baptized, tithing, or anything
else? Or do I do such things because there are others around me
watching what I do?" These are certainly not the reason to do such
things. Instead, we should only do such things because we have
faith, but we should never do them thinking it proves our faith.

Do We Receive the Fruit of the Spirit as Soon As We Become Believers?

I would be misleading if I said that the fruit of the Spirit is
something we obtain as soon as we become believers.
Unfortunately, this is not the case. We are not guaranteed these
wonderful attributes at any particular time. In fact, they are
attributes we may only partially accept. We must recognize that the
Spirit is simply trying to give us these characteristics.
Unfortunately, we can become so attracted to the physical world;
we become numb to the Holy Spirit's leadings. We fail to see what
He is trying to do. We can be as blind as those who aren't believers.
For this reason, Paul gives us several good tips in Galatians 5:

13 You, my brothers and sisters, were called to be free.
But do not use your freedom to indulge the flesh; rather,
serve one another humbly in love. 14 For the entire law is
fulfilled in keeping this one command: "Love your
neighbor as yourself." 15 If you bite and devour each

other, watch out or you will be destroyed by each other. 16 So I say, walk by the Spirit, and you will not gratify the desires of the flesh. 17 For the flesh desires what is contrary to the Spirit, and the Spirit what is contrary to the flesh. They are in conflict with each other, so that you are not to do whatever you want. Galatians 5:13-17

As we read verse 15, "If you bite and devour each other…", you might think he is talking to non-believers. It seems hard to comprehend that believers would be biting and devouring one another, but it is true. Just because we are believers does *not* mean we always follow the leadings of the Holy Spirit. If we are sincere, the Spirit is in us, but we don't have to listen to the instinct He provides. And just like other matters concerning relationships with other humans, if we disregard when someone is trying to tell us something once, then it becomes easier to ignore the impulse again and again. When this happens, then we have not matured enough to be truly free. We are still under the control of the flesh and holding on to nature, obsessions, and habits.

18 But if you are led by the Spirit, you are not under the law. 19 The acts of the flesh are obvious: sexual immorality, impurity and debauchery; 20 idolatry and witchcraft; hatred, discord, jealousy, fits of rage, selfish ambition, dissensions, factions 21 and envy; drunkenness, orgies, and the like. I warn you, as I did before, that those who live like this will not inherit the kingdom of God. - Ephesians 5:18-21

Notably, we humans identify the important goals of life as desires, which seem to make life meaningful. We believe we need to make ourselves feel worthy, useful, loved, purposeful.

Conversely, the attributes produced by the "fruit of the Spirit" would not generally be viewed by the secular world as things that seem significant. However, these are things that God desires for us. He wants us to express love to others. He wants us to be at peace in all we do, and in all that happens to us. He knows that we will experience pain and suffering in this world, yet we need to charge on. Do not let life's tragedies steal our joy. Do not be impatient and restless. Instead, be patient and express kindness, goodness, gentleness to everyone and in every situation. Be faithful. Know what you believe and why you believe it. And once you do, then stick by it. Don't waiver. Use your faith to produce good works. Be a person of self-control. Do not fly off the handle towards others. Do not be over-indulgent in what you eat, drink, or do. Do not feel like you need to grab the spotlight or be the center of attention. Set a fine example for everyone regardless of age, race, creed, color, or sex.

CHAPTER

23 Can the Holy Spirit Solve Most of Societies Problems?

The Holy Spirit is mighty and can be very transformational. We might wonder if there are any limits to His power. Can He change anyone? Can He cure all forms of mental health and personality disorders?

The NIMH (National Institute of Mental Health) has seen large increases in all types of mental disorders in recent years. The type and amount of surge vary by age group and for several reasons. Overall, these mental illnesses affect tens of millions of people each year.[20]

The important question to answer is, "What is the cause of the surge in mental health problems?" There could be several factors, but results taken from the National Survey on Drug Use and Health could explain a significant part of the reason.

Data from the survey was analyzed by Jean Twenge, Ph.D., author of the book "iGen" and psychology professor at San Diego State University. She and her co-authors took responses from more than 200,000 adolescents aged 12 to 17 from 2005 to 2017, and almost 400,000 adults aged 18 and over from 2008 to 2017. Over the time frame studied, the results showed that major depression increased an astounding 52% among adolescents and 63% among young adults age 18 to 25. Also, "The rate of young adults with suicidal thoughts or other suicide-related outcomes increased 47 percent from 2008 to 2017."

---

[20] *NIMH » Mental Illness*. (2019, February 1). Merikangas KR. https://www.nimh.nih.gov/health/statistics/mental-illness.shtml

The results of their study were published in the *Journal of Abnormal Psychology*. The conclusion:

> "Cultural trends in the last 10 years may have had a larger effect on mood disorders and suicide-related outcomes among younger generations compared with older generations," said Twenge, who believes this trend may be partially due to increased use of electronic communication and digital media, which may have changed modes of social interaction enough to affect mood disorders. She also noted research shows that young people are not sleeping as much as they did in previous generations.[21]

It would be interesting to know how many people from the National Survey on Drug Use and Health survey were believers in the gospel. We don't know, but, what we do know is that those who use electronic media a great deal of time can become focused on the physical world more than the spiritual world. Worldly focus is the cause of many of societies problems. Some people become overly concerned with what others think. It may start with a simple expression of concern but continued conversation through email and texting can cause a person to obsess with being understood and respected. It is only after they set their mind on Spiritual things that their mind gets rid of worldly obsessions and earthly problems begin to diminish.

Therefore, won't praying help? We just turn the problem over to God and let Him handle it. While theoretically this seems true, my reading of scripture does not cause me to come to this conclusion. I cannot find anywhere where Jesus or any of the Apostles prayed for a person's mental state. The closest example we see to Jesus

---

[21] Mental health issues increased significantly in young adults over last decade: Shift may be due in part to rise of digital media, study suggests. (2019). ScienceDaily. https://www.sciencedaily.com/releases/2019/03/190315110908.htm

curing a mental problem is when he cast out a demon. But we cannot assume that all mental problems are a result of demons.

Nevertheless, many people of faith who believe that an effective method of reducing these disorders is to pray. They would assert that the powerful Holy Spirit can directly heal a person.

As long as the individual who needs help is a true believer in the gospel described by Paul, then I agree. However, if the person is not a believer, I am skeptical that praying will do much good. Why do I say such a thing? Do I not believe in the power of the Holy Spirit? No, I absolutely do believe He can help, but He provides His help by being *in* the person; He does not do it by controlling the world around a person. And the only way He can be *in* someone is through their personal faith.

I can't find any example in the Bible where the Holy Spirit has helped an unbeliever with what I would call a "worldly" problem. "Worldly" would be anything that is not spiritual. For example, this would include matters of finance, relationships, addictions, demeanor, temper, lack of patience, etc. Before a person becomes a believer, the Holy Spirit convicts a person of their need for God. He tries to persuade him/her that they are inadequate to save themself. The benefits of the Spirit only comes after they believe in the atoning work of Jesus, and they submit to the leadings of the Spirit.

Some mental disorders are linked to heredity, but I believe that the cure for mental depression, distress, and disorders not related to genes must start from the inside. It must start with a personal desire to change. Limited benefits can be obtained by counseling that focuses only on worldly issues. True, this is the only kind of help available for non-believers, but if Spiritual help is an option, it should be used. Keep in mind that I do not have a degree in psychology, nor have I attended college to become a counselor. I am sharing my ideas only as a person who studies the Bible.

Can a rational explanation of Spiritual help convince a person to believe in saving Grace? Let us consider the study just mentioned. Let us assume that the conclusion is correct. Increased use of communication and digital media are responsible for most of the increases in major depression and thoughts of suicide among adolescents and young adults. If you were the parent and your son was an unbeliever, and he was one who was having major depression, could you convince him to cut back on his cell phone usage to relieve his anguish? Unless you have an unusual son, I can almost guarantee that he will not take your advice. So could you forcibly take his phone away and expect him to get better? From my experience, you will likely run into stiff opposition, and a fight will ensue. Why is this? Part of the answer is because they are young, impulsive, and don't want to submit to a parent. But the Bible says he has a rebellious sin nature (from Adam). He does not want to honor the instruction of his father or mother.

Let us assume you are convinced that if he becomes a believer in the gospel, he will become respectful of your wishes. Therefore, you try to convince him of the plan of salvation, i.e., Jesus suffered for our sins; he was crucified, buried, and resurrected.

Without the power of the Holy Spirit within him, he likely will not listen to you. Here is my biblical reason for saying this:

> The person without the Spirit does not accept the things that come from the Spirit of God but considers them foolishness, and cannot understand them because they are discerned only through the Spirit. - 1 Corinthians 2:14

It is a vicious circle. Pushing an agenda does not help. Therefore, take whatever measures necessary to reduce your teenager's time on electronic media. This may be painful. But supplement your action with prayer; not prayer that God will take away his desire to minimize time on social media; but prayer that the Spirit continues to convict and show him his need for Jesus. His change in motivation and attitude towards God is the only effective and permanent cure.

I am confident that by now there are people who take me as a fanatic. I am a person who thinks there is only one solution. My first response is that I do not believe there is only one solution. However, I am saying there is one solution that will work far better than any other. It is one that works from the inside. It works by the power of God. It is not temporary, but it is permanent.

To some, I appear narrow minded. I am sorry, but I can't argue with that. You are correct. Therefore, let me spoon out a little food for thought. Answer this question honestly, "Why did Jesus come into this world? Did He come to bring peace?" Most people answer, "Of course!"

While this sounds correct, it is not. He was an exclusivist. Jesus said:

> 34 "Do not suppose that I have come to bring peace to the earth. I did not come to bring peace, but a sword. 35 For I have come to turn 'a man against his father, a daughter against her mother, a daughter-in-law against her mother-in-law— 36 a man's enemies will be the members of his own household.'
> 37 "Anyone who loves their father or mother more than me is not worthy of me; anyone who loves their son or daughter more than me is not worthy of me. 38 Whoever does not take up their cross and follow me is not worthy of me. 39 Whoever finds their life will lose it, and whoever loses their life for my sake will find it. - Matthew 10:34-39

You may think that perhaps He was being arrogant. You may think He was trying to tear families apart literally. No, this was not the case. But what He was saying was that His words and His ways were uncompromising. Either you believed Him (and in Him), or you didn't. There is no middle of the road. There would be many people who would disagree with Him. (This was obvious because they put Him on a cross). But the same type of disagreements would also occur in the family. Some will agree with Him, and some will not.

So if you think I am a crackpot, then I am in good company. I believe that obtaining the Holy Spirit and listening to Him is the answer to all our worldly and spiritual problems. With that being said, I am a realist. I know that this change will not take place until Jesus returns to rule on earth again.

We would all benefit by experiencing the fruit of the Spirit and submitting ourselves to the changes the Holy Spirit would try to make in us. We would all be better off being more Spiritually focused and less worldly focused. Therefore, do I think the Holy Spirit can solve the problems of the world? Theoretically, the answer is yes. He has the ability. But He won't interfere with the free will of man. He will not give us the attributes associated with the Holy Spirit until we acknowledge our need.

My dad never exhibited any signs of any mental disorder. But because he was without the Spirit, he could not understand the things of the Spirit. He did not believe he needed to accept that Jesus died for his sins. He was fine on his own. He thought God was going to forgive him because he was not such a horrible person. No, he wasn't perfect, but he thought he was good enough. He believed God would accept him based on his own merits.

The Holy Spirit convicts us of our inability to approach God based on our own works. We are inadequate. Therefore, we need a savior. That savior is Jesus, and He died for us. Furthermore, we must be convinced that He was buried and raised by the Holy Spirit. Once we accept the gospel, then we are saved. After we are saved, then the Holy Spirit tries to give us a new perspective and purpose for our life. It is only after we give in to the Spirit and submit ourselves to His will that we are changed. So the problems of this world are not a failure of the Spirit, it is because of humanity's failure to accept the need for Jesus and to acknowledge the Holy Spirit's power.

Personal and Eternal Benefits From the Spirit

As mentioned in previous chapters, the Spirit affects us in many ways. He affects our ability to love, experience joy and peace. He encourage us to be patient, gentle, kind, good, and self-controlled. He increases our faith. Because He give us these attributes, you could call them gifts. (However, I want to be clear that these are not the physical manifestations from the Spirit as defined In 1Corinthian's 12:8-10). Instead, these are attributes that are recognizable in our personality and character. They affect our witness for God.

As good as these benefits are, the Holy Spirit affords us even more advantages. These additional endowments are often overlooked by believers but are described as heavenly benefits.

One of these benefits is that when Jesus died, we also died. You may ask, "How is that a benefit?" After all, if we have died once, we will have to die again anyway, so it's not like we escape physical death. This is true, but Paul tells us in Romans 6 that we were not only baptized into Jesus' death, but we were also given new life. Keep in mind that this baptism is a baptism by the Holy Spirit, not water baptism.

> 3 Or don't you know that all of us who were baptized into Christ Jesus were baptized into his death? 4 We were therefore buried with him through baptism into death in order that, just as Christ was raised from the dead through the glory of the Father, we too may live a new life. 5 For if we have been united with him in a death like his, we will certainly also be united with him in a resurrection like his. 6 For we know that our old self was crucified with him so that the body ruled by sin might be done away with, that we should no longer be slaves to sin - Romans 6:3-6

In verse 6 we read that our old self was crucified with Jesus. This crucifixion is obviously not physical but spiritual. Just like when Jesus paid for all sins, our body is no longer ruled by sin. This does not mean we will never sin again because we will. The difference is that it will not be intentional sin. If we were 100% spiritual, then we would never sin, but because we still have a human element to us, we become emotional and are subject to sin.

Secondly, in verse 5, we see that when Jesus was raised from the dead, He was given a new life. Likewise, when we believed that Jesus' death purchased our salvation, we also were given a new life; a new attitude. Our old desires for self-gratification become diminished. Paul also writes about this in Ephesians 2:

> [1] As for you, you were dead in your transgressions and sins, [2] in which you used to live when you followed the ways of this world and of the ruler of the kingdom of the air, the spirit who is now at work in those who are disobedient. [3] All of us also lived among them at one time, gratifying the cravings of our flesh and following its desires and thoughts. Like the rest, we were by nature deserving of wrath. [4] But because of his great love for us, God, who is rich in mercy, [5] made us alive with Christ even when we were dead in transgressions—it is by grace you have been saved. - Ephesians 2:1-5

By our faith, the Spirit has made us dead to the spirit of disobedience. But now we are made alive in Christ, given a new Spirit, one that has been raised up with Christ, to do good works, i.e., to help and love others.

If we are trying to help a believer, they too are influenced by the Spirit, and it is not usually difficult to help them. Their values are more focused on Spiritual things. Their immediate problems result from living in the world, not from a desire to strive for worldly things.

The real difficulty is trying to help a person who has chosen to be mainly in the world (a non-believer). They don't see problems the same as believers. They are still in the mode of trying to control people and situations using worldly tactics. For example, they will use means like threat, intimidation, and power to improve their situation. They have a different view of money. They put a higher priority on things they want; therefore, they are more likely to spend beyond their means. To fix their financial problem, they try to persuade others to "give them a break," or they out-and-out try to defraud others.

Our new desire given by the Holy Spirit causes us to see people and their predicaments differently. We struggle to help others but should not lose sight of the end goal. Paul was willing to put his life on the line to spread his gospel message. The result? Others would hear his message, and ultimately they would accept Jesus as their savior. He states his view in 2 Corinthians 4:

> 11 Yes, we live under constant danger of death because we serve Jesus, so that the life of Jesus will be evident in our dying bodies. 12 So we live in the face of death, but this has resulted in eternal life for you. - 2 Corinthians 4:11, 12 [NLT]

Paul's commitment to serving others came from having a new life and attitude, as described above in Romans 6.

> I have been crucified with Christ and I no longer live, but Christ lives in me. The life I now live in the body, I live by faith in the Son of God, who loved me and gave himself for me. - Galatians 2:20

Paul had become a much different person after he believed in the atoning blood of Jesus. His spirit had become much more like the spirit of Jesus. In fact, it was so close to being like Jesus that he said he wasn't even being himself. It was the will, the ambition, and the desires of Jesus living in him. This new attitude gave him the confidence to write in Timothy 2 that his motivation was evidence that he would reign with Jesus one day.

> ¹¹ Here is a trustworthy saying:
> If we died with him, we will also live with him;
> ¹² if we endure, we will also reign with him.
> If we disown him, he will also disown us; - 2 Timothy 2:11,12

Paul wrote that we not only died when Jesus died but conversely, when Jesus was raised, we were raised. Because of our Spiritual connection with Jesus, we have an attitude that transcends the physical realm. Some people recognize this better than others. In the case of Paul, he evaluated the positives and negatives. He was able to look beyond all of his present sufferings; he could look towards the future. He tells us what it will be like:

> ⁶ And God raised us up with Christ and seated us with him in the heavenly realms in Christ Jesus, ⁷ in order that in the coming ages he might show the incomparable riches of his grace, expressed in his kindness to us in Christ Jesus. - Ephesians 2:6, 7

> ¹ Since, then, you have been raised with Christ, set your hearts on things above, where Christ is, seated at the right hand of God. ² Set your minds on things above, not on earthly things. ³ For you died, and your life is now hidden with Christ in God. ⁴ When Christ, who is your life, appears, then you also will appear with him in glory. - Colossians 3:1-4

He assures us that if we have changed, then it was because of the Holy Spirit. Consequently, we are guaranteed eternal life with Jesus.

By the Spirit We Are Adopted As Children of God

When a person says that God has blessed them, they almost always mean that they have been blessed in some physical way, e.g., health, financial well being, life is made easier, improved relationships, etc. And while this may be true, Paul writes about spiritual blessings. What does this mean? It means our relationship with God. He means that as a result of Jesus' sacrifice, we have become blameless and justified. When we are justified, God views us just as if we had never sinned. As a result, we have become adopted as his child.

> 3 Praise be to the God and Father of our Lord Jesus Christ, who has blessed us in the heavenly realms with every spiritual blessing in Christ. 4 For he chose us in him before the creation of the world to be holy and <u>blameless</u> in his sight. In love 5 he predestined us for adoption to sonship through Jesus Christ, in accordance with his pleasure and will— 6 to the praise of his glorious grace, which he has freely given us in the One he loves. - Ephesians 1:3-6

We have become a child of God through Spiritual baptism. In Galatians, Paul continues and expands on what it means to become adopted as a child of God.

> 6 Because you are his sons, God sent the Spirit of his Son into our hearts, the Spirit who calls out, *"Abba, Father."* 7 So you are no longer a slave, but God's child; and since you are his child, God has made you also an heir. Galatians 4:6,7

Likewise, Paul says the same thing in Romans. Through the Spirit we have become an heir; someone who is entitled to something (even if we don't know exactly what that something is).

> 14 For those who are led by the Spirit of God are the children of God. 15 The Spirit you received does not make you slaves, so that you live in fear again; rather, the Spirit you received brought about your adoption to sonship. And by him we cry, *"Abba,* Father." 16 The Spirit himself testifies with our spirit that we are God's children. 17 Now if we are children, then we are heirs—heirs of God and

co-heirs with Christ, if indeed we share in his sufferings in order that we may also share in his glory. – Romans 8:14-17

It's difficult to imagine what it means to be adopted as a child of God. In both Galatians and Romans, Paul uses the language of "Abba, Father." "Abba" is a term of endearment. It means a child-like intimate affection for one's personal father. Some Christian literature has translated it to mean "daddy." Just imagine that your relationship is so close to God that you would refer to him as "daddy." (Try using that in your prayers). Picture yourself as a 5 year old and your daddy wants the best for you. He loves you and wants to interact with you.

Paul prompts our imagination of what it means to have a deep relationship with God, but he stretches it even further when he tells in Romans 8:17 that we are co-heirs with Christ. I look at this personally, as I think we all should. If God is my daddy, and I am a co-heir with Christ, then Jesus is my brother. He is the brother I would have hoped for but never had. He is not the one which I argued, fussed, and fought with. No, he was the one with whom: I rode a bike; I played one-on-one soccer; I went swimming. He was the more mature one, telling me stories and reading to me. When we went to the ice cream store, he would give me his spare change so I could add that extra scoop of cookie crunch.

When I was in my late teens, I did some bad things and then lied about it to avoid being punished. My brother, Jesus, stepped in to intercede. He took on the wrath from those who wanted to punish me for what I had done. It wasn't just verbal punishment, but the scene became violent. My loving Brother was beaten to a pulp. I looked at Him and realized His bloody condition was because He protected me. He did this knowing that I had learned my lesson, and He didn't want me to suffer again for my mistakes. And when His suffering was too great for Him to bear, He died. When I finally get to heaven, my Brother Jesus, the one true High Priest, is there, sharing all He has with me and all other brothers.

Verse 17 makes it seem that our heirship is dependent on suffering. So what if we don't suffer as Jesus did? After all, we will not likely be physically crucified, and few people could tolerate the pain even if they were. This type of death would be gruesome. No, I don't think our suffering has to be physical, but we should suffer emotionally when we see so many people reject the great sacrifice Christ made for them. We should want to help them if we can. It is unfortunate and painful when we see others turn away; this is our shared suffering.

Paul tells us by inspiration of the Holy Spirit how God views those of faith. We are blameless. We are God's adopted children. We are joint heirs. Spiritually, we are on equal status with Christ. You may find that hard to believe (as most people do), but this is how God sees us. We have been both justified and glorified (Romans 8:30).

Which Is More Important, Physical or Spiritual life?

What should the blessings of God mean to the believer? One, it should mean we are more focused on spiritual life and less on our physical life. Yes, our physical life is important, and the younger we are, then the more important it seems. But our spiritual life is more important. If we are a believer, then we should think about our eternity. It should also cause us to think about the eternity of others. I will reiterate Colossians 3:

> [1] Since, then, you have been raised with Christ, set your hearts on things above, where Christ is, seated at the right hand of God. [2] Set your minds on things above, not on earthly things. [3] For you died, and your life is now hidden with Christ in God. [4] When Christ, who is your life, appears, then you also will appear with him in glory. - Colossians 3:1-4

Yes, we should set our minds on heavenly things. We will spend eternity with Jesus. But, as we think about heaven, we realize that it is just not for our personal benefit. We expect to see loved ones there as well, but will we? In the case of my dad, I don't expect to see him there. This thought greatly saddens me, but I think about others I will know rather than dwelling on it.

I think about others who I may be able to have some effect on presently. I think about how I should treat individuals. Additional verses from Colossians 3 come to mind:

> 12 Therefore, as God's chosen people, holy and dearly loved, clothe yourselves with compassion, kindness, humility, gentleness and patience. 13 Bear with each other and forgive one another if any of you has a grievance against someone. Forgive as the Lord forgave you. 14 And over all these virtues put on love, which binds them all together in perfect unity.
>
> 15 Let the peace of Christ rule in your hearts, since as members of one body you were called to peace. And be thankful. 16 Let the message of Christ dwell among you richly as you teach and admonish one another with all wisdom through psalms, hymns, and songs from the Spirit, singing to God with gratitude in your hearts. 17 And whatever you do, whether in word or deed, do it all in the name of the Lord Jesus, giving thanks to God the Father through him.- Colossians 3:12-17

With all the benefits God has provided through His Spirit, many of us are distracted. We tend to focus on either what we can obtain by our own effort or even the miracles we might receive from God. We focus more on the "Gifts of the Spirit" (which He promised to a few to promote His new relationship with us) than we do the other Spiritual benefits (which He promised to everyone to demonstrate His love for us.)

24 What Kind of Disciple Should the Spirit Lead Us to Be?

Leaders of churches often ask their congregations to be disciples of Jesus. How could you argue this? Jesus was a righteous man who obeyed all God's laws. He was not one to condemn but always tried to lift others up from their downtrodden, oppressed lives. He did not show anger even when others persecuted Him. Even on the cross, He said, "Father forgive them for they do not know what they are doing." (Luke 23:24). He was not arrogant or critical with the sinners with whom He interacted. Instead, He loved and served others. When asked who is the greatest in heaven, He answered, "… whoever humbles himself like this child is the greatest in the kingdom of heaven." (Matthew 18:4). How could we disagree with the ways of Jesus?

Yet, can we really follow Jesus? Stay with me while I explain the difficulties of trying to be a follower of Jesus. Certainly, Jesus was a righteous man; we cannot begin to be an example like Him. He did many, many great things. In the last verse of the book of John we read, "And there are also many other things that Jesus did, which if they were written one by one, I suppose that even the world itself could not contain the books that would be written." (John 21:25). Even though this is hyperbole, it says quite a bit! So should we try to be the type of disciples like those who walked with Jesus? Let's look closer at these disciples and review what they did.

After Jesus ascended back to heaven, the disciples continued to try to win converts. But remember that their primary message was that Jesus was the Messiah and the Son of God. Peter specifically told the people that they should repent and be baptized, but they needed to repent because they rejected Jesus as the Messiah (Acts 2:36-38).

Is this supposed to be our message? True, we have all sinned and we need to acknowledge our sinfulness. Should we tell others that they need to repent and be baptized so they can be saved? According to Paul, acknowledgement of a sinful life is only a first step. We are not saved by this action alone.

Jesus' disciples continued to perform many healings as proof that they were God's messengers. They laid their hands on others, and they were instantaneously healed. I contemplate what would happen to a person's faith if I lay my hands on someone, and they aren't healed. If it doesn't happen immediately, do I tell them to just wait awhile? How do I explain that it happened for Jesus' disciples immediately, but it takes awhile for my healings to take effect? I haven't healed one person in my entire life, let alone hundreds. I can't perform any miracles. Peter walked on water, … at least, a little bit. Should we try to do likewise?

Jesus told people that they should obey all God's commandments. Knowing that I am a sinner, I can't fathom me telling others that they should obey God's commandments. I get angry when others cut me off in traffic. I get upset when others tell me I'm wrong. I am not as loving or as forgiving as I should be (just ask my wife). I work on Sundays. Others would look at me and say, "You hypocrite!" And they would be right!

Remember that the disciples were teaching that everyone should obey all God's commandments, including the requirement that their converts become circumcised. It wasn't until Paul had a serious conversation with them in Acts 15:5-11 that they conceded that this procedure was necessary for Gentiles.

In Matthew 28, Jesus gave the disciples the "Great Commission," which was to make disciples of people throughout the whole world. Yet God's commandment was that it was unlawful to interact with Gentiles, so they did *not* go to them. Should I be held to the same standard and try to reach Jews only? Or conversely, because I am a Gentile, should I be trying to reach Gentiles only? In either case, this would be prejudice. This isn't what God wants in the current dispensation.

Therefore, when I contemplate being like one of Jesus' disciples, it doesn't seem appropriate. Instead, I think about Paul and how he ministered to others. Yes, he did perform healings; but this was not the focus of his ministry. His healing of others was to prove he had authority from God. God had given him the ability to prove that his doctrine and message about His Grace was true. God showed justification for believing in Paul.

Paul preached and interacted with many Gentiles, and some Jews would come and listen to him. His doctrine was plain and simple; we are saved not by works, baptism, circumcision, going to church, or tithing. We are not saved by trying to obey all of God's commandments. Instead, we are saved by accepting and knowing that Jesus paid for our sins by His suffering on the cross. Jesus died a horrible death, but on the third day, he arose. I know I referred to this scripture before, but it does not hurt to repeat.

> [1] Moreover, brethren, I declare to you the gospel which I preached to you, which also you received and in which you stand, [2] by which also you are saved, if you hold fast that word which I preached to you—unless you believed in vain.
> [3] For I delivered to you first of all that which I also received: that Christ died for our sins according to the Scriptures, [4] and that He was buried, and that He rose again the third day according to the Scriptures -   1 Corinthians 15:1-4

His message was straightforward and clear. There are no two ways about it. It is a message we should read repeatedly. It is the message that we should spread around the world. If we are not the kind of disciple that spreads this message, we have missed our calling. This should be the essential message for all Christians.

If you are doubting what I am saying, then don't listen to me. Instead, read what scripture says. Paul told his beloved co-worker Timothy that he should imitate *his* message.

> What you <u>heard from me, keep as the pattern of sound teaching</u>, with faith and love in Christ Jesus. -
> 2 Timothy 1:13

I asked earlier, "Should we tell others that they need to repent and be baptized so that they can receive the Holy Spirit?" According to Paul, we do not receive the Holy Spirit when we repent and are baptized. No, we receive the Holy Spirit when we accept what Jesus did for us.

> When you believed, you were marked in him with a seal, the promised Holy Spirit, - Ephesians 1:13

This message was different than what the other disciples were teaching. They were still trying to convince the Jews that Jesus was the Messiah and the Son of God. Paul was preaching that when Jesus died on the cross to pay for our sins, this was God's Grace.

Not only does Paul give a different message than the other disciples, but he also explains to the Corinthians what he is doing:

> [10] By the grace God has given me, I laid a foundation as a wise builder, and someone else is building on it. But each one should build with care. [11] For no one can lay any foundation other than the one already laid, which is Jesus Christ. -1Corinthians 3:10-11

Paul was given first-hand knowledge about Jesus' mission as a revelation directly from Him and from no one else (Galatians 1:11,12). What Paul realized was that salvation is impossible without Christ's sacrifice. It cannot be obtained by any works or obeying some or all of God's laws. His knowledge was much more complete, and he expressed it in his letters. He certainly did not try to replace the foundation Jesus laid, but he put another layer on top of it.

Because Jesus was perfect, we cannot follow Him even closely. We are too imperfect. However, because Paul was imperfect, we can follow him. We can keep spreading his word to whoever listens. We can tell others how Jesus sacrificed himself for us.

You may be thinking that I am out in left field somewhere; that we should try to be like Jesus or one of His disciples. You may think that Paul never told his churches how that they should be imitating him. But Paul *did* tell them and in several places in his letters. Here are a few examples:

> 16 Therefore I urge you to *imitate me.* 17 For this reason I have sent to you Timothy, my son whom I love, who is faithful in the Lord. He will remind you of my way of life in Christ Jesus, which agrees with what I teach everywhere in every church. - 1 Corinthians 4:16,17

> 1 And you should *imitate me, just as I imitate Christ.* 2 I am so glad that you always keep me in your thoughts, and that you are following the teachings I passed on to you. - 1 Corinthians 11:1,2 (NLT)

> <u>Join together in following my example</u>, brothers and sisters, and just as *you have us as a model*, keep your eyes on those who live as we do. - Philippians 3:17

Similarly, Paul commends the Thessalonians for their willingness to imitate him.

> 6 You became *imitators of us* and of the Lord, for you welcomed the message in the midst of severe suffering with the joy given by the Holy Spirit. 7 And so you

So while many well-intended people try to teach us to be disciples of Jesus, this is only a partial truth. Yes, we should be kind to others. Yes, we should try to love and serve others. We should be forgiving. We should recognize that what the disciples said is true; Jesus is the Messiah and the Son of God.

But we should also be convicted by the truth of what Paul said also. The revelations by Jesus led him. His message is more complete than what Jesus taught (Jesus couldn't teach about the importance of His death when He hadn't died yet. And had He taught about His future death, the Romans and religious leaders would have let Him rot in jail rather than crucify Him). So Paul's message that Jesus Christ died and through His suffering, He paid for our sins is a more complete message. Just as significant was his message that by the power of the Holy Spirit, He rose from the dead. This is proof that we, who have the Holy Spirit in us, will also rise again to have eternal life.

By What Gospel Are We Held Accountable?

Just like in present times, there were other people during Paul's time who were proclaiming a different message about how we are accepted by God. Paul was very adamant that his assertion was the only correct one. To many people of today, this type of proclamation seems very arrogant. In our present world of political correctness, some people are offended by his claims.

Paul was upset that some people were teaching a false gospel, but there was nothing he could do to stop them. Instead, he just continued to preach his gospel and emphasize the importance of it. Let us take this one step at a time and review what he wrote about his true gospel:

1. This was the definition of his gospel:

[3] ... that Christ died for our sins according to the Scriptures, [4] that he was buried, that he was raised on the third day according to the Scriptures - 1 Corinthians 15:3,4

2. There are several places where Paul states our accountability to his gospel. This is how we are saved (have eternal life). One of those occurrences are the 2 verses just preceding where he defines his gospel, that is, 1 Corinthians 15:1,2

[1] Now, brothers and sisters, I want to remind you of the gospel I preached to you, which you received and on which you have taken your stand. [2] *By this gospel you are saved, if you hold firmly to the word I preached to you.* Otherwise, you have believed in vain.

Definitively, we are saved by following his gospel, not by the claim of anyone else's. He states this fact again in Romans 1; we are saved by understanding, believing, and following his gospel. All that is required of us is that we believe it. He doesn't say it is one gospel or one of many gospels that brings salvation. No, it is *his* gospel. This was a point he was unwavering, and for this reason, he was not ashamed of telling it to everyone. Was he conceited? No, he was stating the truth.

For I am not ashamed of the gospel, because it is the power of God that *brings salvation to everyone who believes*: - Romans 1:16

Near the end of his life, he states this is what he lives for; to proclaim his gospel (good news) so that others might be saved.

... I consider my life worth nothing to me; my only aim is to finish the race and complete the task the Lord Jesus has given me—the task of *testifying to the good news of God's grace.* - Acts 20:24

3. Was there any uncertainty in the back of his mind? Could there have been another gospel that maybe was true? Absolutely not! In fact, this is what else he writes in Galatians 1. Let me warn you; he uses strong language! (I can picture hellfire and brimstone coming from his pen).

> 6 I am astonished that you are so quickly deserting the one who called you to live in the grace of Christ and are turning to a different gospel— 7 which is really no gospel at all. Evidently some people are throwing you into confusion and are trying to pervert the gospel of Christ. 8 But even if we or an angel from heaven should preach a gospel other than the one we preached to you, let them be under God's curse! 9 As we have already said, so now I say again: If anybody is preaching to you a gospel other than what you accepted, let them be under God's curse! - Galatians 1:6-9

4. Paul's gospel message was not known about before him, nor was it known by anyone else other than him (until he taught it to others). He makes this proclamation in Romans 16. He says it was a "mystery hidden for long ages past." That means it was hidden from the beginning until it was revealed to him.

> Now to him who is able to establish you in accordance with *my gospel*, the message I proclaim about Jesus Christ, in keeping with the revelation of the mystery hidden for long ages past - Romans 16:25

To emphasize this mystery, I will state again what Peter said in his second letter:

> 15 ...consider *that* the long suffering of our Lord *is* salvation—as also our beloved brother Paul, according to the wisdom given to him, has written to you, 16 as also in all his epistles, speaking in them of these things, in which are some things hard to understand, which untaught and

unstable *people* twist to their own destruction, as *they do* also the rest of the Scriptures.- 2 Peter 3:15,16

There are two important points to take from the writing of Peter. One, he states that some of the things Paul writes in his epistles are hard to understand. Why would Peter, who lived with Jesus for three years, say that anything Paul wrote was difficult to understand? It was because it was a concept that no-one else taught. Secondly, Peter is testifying to the gospel taught by Paul. He is comparing it to other Scriptures. He is holding him up as the gold standard.

5. Paul was given special wisdom, a revelation. He stated this fact about himself not only in Romans 16:25 but also in Galatians 1:

> 11 But I make known to you, brethren, that the gospel which was preached by me is not according to man.
> 12 For I neither received it from man, nor was I taught *it, but it came through the revelation of Jesus Christ.* - Galatians 1:11,12

Paul claimed that his gospel was not something he manufactured, nor was it taught to him by some other human (like a disciple). Instead, it was given to him directly by Jesus Christ.

You may be thinking, "I can't minister to others as Paul did. People believed him because of the healings he performed." Granted, Paul was exceptional in many ways. We are not the person Paul was. However, it is a fallacy to think that we can not effectively witness his gospel. All believers have been endowed with the fruit of the Spirit.

Regarding healing others, remember that Paul was no longer healing others near the end of his life. All he had left was his message, which is the same message we also have.

CHAPTER
25 How Should the Spirit Lead Us to Pray?

Spiritual life is more important than physical life, yet that doesn't mean we won't spend time thinking about our physical life. Spiritual life and physical life are intertwined. A person's spiritual life should affect the actions of their personal life. It is not just a matter of avoiding a sinful lifestyle. It should affect things such as prayer life, interactions with others, administering resources, etc.

Many books have been written describing various prayer techniques. There are multiple ways to begin and close prayer. Some people advocate the Lord's Prayer as a model. There are many ways to handle the "Yes," "No," and "Maybe slow" answers.

As you might guess, I have taken a different approach. My focus is not a lesson in how to pray or how to respond when God doesn't respond as we desire. Instead, I use Scripture to describe how the Holy Spirit should be affecting the things for which we pray.

Before I show Scripture, I need to confess that I am not a prayer warrior like some Christians. I know I should pray more often than I do. The Apostle Paul wrote that we should pray about all things, yet, I don't even come close. I suppose part of the reason is because of my upbringing. As a child, my parents taught me some basic prayers. "Now I lay me down to sleep; I pray the Lord my soul to keep. If I should die before I wake, I pray the Lord my soul to take." This prayer was somewhat fearful. Should I be concerned that someone will enter my bedroom and kill me in the middle of the night?

Likewise, as a child, my father prayed before meals. I remember my dad thanking God for our food, and he requested that God make us into the type of person acceptable to Him. As I reflect on this prayer, it is no wonder that my dad was always trying to work his way into heaven. Never did he thank Jesus for his sacrifice for our sins.

As a young adult, I said prayers asking God for things. Sometimes I asked him to change people. I asked that He stop wars. I never asked for a new car, but I did ask that He help me establish relationships. If we take Paul literally at his word, then my prayers fell into the category of "all things." It was also scriptural that I ask because James said, "You do not have because you do not ask God." (James 4:2) If I didn't receive God's blessing, then it was my own dang fault! (It is ironic that I won a new car in a raffle.)

At about my mid-century mark, my prayers took another turn. I started to see people with more ailments and other health problems. I prayed for God's miraculous healing powers. I asked that He heal those who have broken limbs, defective hearts, or Alzheimer's Disease. I discovered that those with broken limbs eventually recovered. Those who had heart ailments got better with time and medicine, and those with Alzheimer's never got any better.

I prayed for friends who were about to get divorced because of "irreconcilable differences" to understand their own motivations and those of their spouses. I prayed that God would change the hardness of their hearts. What usually happened was that the couples divorced anyway.

In summary, over the years, God has not positively answered many of my prayers. Yet what I repeatedly hear from some church leaders is how God wants us to come to Him in prayer. He wants to heal us. He cares for our needs. It's no wonder that I have not become a prayer warrior.

Despite that not many of my prayers have been answered as I requested them, I have not stopped praying. I still pray, but my prayers have continued to evolve. Now, I often say prayers of thankfulness. My wife and I feel incredibly fortunate to be in the position we are in. When we compare our relationships, as well as our health and financial situation to those of others we know, our lives are phenomenal.

But moving past our personal position of well-being, I am thankful for God's Word. Where would I be if I did not have the Bible? I would not have any faith in the goodness of God. I would not understand the sacrifices of Jesus. I would not have any confidence in eternal life. I would believe that when I died, then it was all over. I am a changed man because of all that the Bible proclaims.

In addition to being thankful for the Bible, I am grateful for my family and friends. I believe the Holy Spirit has affected all my relationships and my entire personality and attitude. Yes, I have much that I am thankful for.

In recent years, I find myself praying more often for others. Sometimes it is because of prayer requests, and sometimes it's because I feel a need within myself; I pray for my children, grandchildren, friends, authority figures, and first responders. Occasionally I am asked by friends to pray for their friends and relatives. These are people I may have met once or twice, or in some cases, these are people I don't even know. It has been the request for prayers by others, which has caused me to think deeper about this topic.

How Should We Pray for Others?

If we profess to be a believer in God, we will undoubtedly be asked to pray for others. We should be evaluating the things of which we are asked to pray. Should we always pray for the things that others request? Does it make a difference whether the request is for a believer or an unbeliever?

What troubles me most is the type of requests I receive. 85% of them are for someone's health, an operation they are about to undergo, or for a follow-up CT or x-ray scan (but maybe the large quantity shouldn't be a surprise seeing how I know so many older people). 10% of the requests come in the form of helping someone overcome an addiction, find a job, or reconcile a relationship. Finally, there are another 5% of miscellaneous requests.

Granted, we should pray for others, but these are only requests to resolve immediate physical needs. They usually come across via email or text only when a situation becomes dire. Part of the reason for this is because most people don't want to bother others. They think they can handle it themself... until they can't; then they need more support.

Although people usually only request things of dire nature, they, like all humans, have other needs as well. We all need strength, comfort, hope, understanding, encouragement, wisdom, enlightenment, discernment, etc. Unfortunately, we rarely hear about those needs. We all have them; we just don't talk about them much.

Paul, who was inspired by the Holy Spirit, knew how great the needs of the faithful are. Consequently, he prayed often for believers. He desired God's power to help them. In a few cases, he asked for prayers for himself, but they were usually for him in his ministry to others.

Paul's ministry message, as well as his prayers, should serve as an example of our message and our prayers. Listed below are several of his prayers. It would be difficult to remember them using the same words that he used, but when we pray in the Spirit, we should be praying for the same kinds of things. Those general items are what we should remember.

Notice not only the things for which he prayed but also that he thanks and praises God.

- Thanking God for the faith of others

First, I thank my God through Jesus Christ for all of you, because
your faith is being reported all over the world. - Romans 1:8

- Unity

May the God who gives endurance and encouragement give you a
spirit of unity among yourselves as you follow Christ Jesus, so that
with one heart and mouth you may glorify the God and Father of
our Lord Jesus Christ. - Romans 15:5–6

- Hope

May the God of hope fill you with all joy and peace as you trust in
Him, so that you may overflow with hope by the power of the Holy
Spirit. - Romans 15:13

- Ability to comfort as we have been comforted

Praise be to the God and Father of our Lord Jesus Christ, the
Father of compassion and the God of all comfort, who comforts us
in all our troubles, so that we can comfort those in any trouble with
the comfort we ourselves receive from God. - 2 Corinthians 1:3–4

- Praising God for adoption to sonship

Praise be to the God and Father of our Lord Jesus Christ, who has
blessed us in the heavenly realms with every spiritual blessing in
Christ. For He chose us in Him before the creation of the world to
be holy and blameless in His sight. In love He predestined us for
adoption to sonship through Jesus Christ, in accordance with His
pleasure and will— - Ephesians 1:3-5

- Spiritual wisdom, and revelation to know God better

I have not stopped giving thanks for you, remembering you in my
prayers. I keep asking that the God of our Lord Jesus Christ, the
glorious Father, may give you the Spirit of wisdom and revelation,
so that you may know Him better. - Ephesians 1:15–17

- To know the width, length, height, and depth of Christ's love.

… I pray that you, being rooted and established in love, may have
power, together with all the saints, to grasp how wide and long and

high and deep is the love of Christ, and to know this love that surpasses knowledge—that you may be filled to the measure of all the fullness of God. - Ephesians 3:17–19

•   Asking prayers so we can fearlessly give the gospel
Pray also for me, that whenever I open my mouth, words may be given me so that I will fearlessly make known the mystery of the gospel, for which I am an ambassador in chains. Pray that I may declare it fearlessly, as I should. - Ephesians 6:19–20

•   Thank God He will complete a good work in others
I thank my God every time I remember you. In all my prayers for all of you, I always pray with joy because of your partnership in the gospel from the first day until now, being confident of this, that He who began a good work in you will carry it on to completion until the day of Christ Jesus. - Philippians 1:3–6

•   Abound in love, knowledge, and insight to discern what is best
And this is my prayer: that your love may abound more and more in knowledge and depth of insight, so that you may be able to discern what is best and may be pure and blameless until the day of Christ - Philippians 1:9–10

•   Knowledge of God's will to live a worthy life and bearing fruit.
…We continually ask God to fill you with the knowledge of His will through all the wisdom and understanding that the Spirit gives, so that you may live a life worthy of the Lord and please Him in every way: bearing fruit in every good work, growing in the knowledge of God, being strengthened with all power according to His glorious might so that you may have great endurance and patience - Colossians 9-11

•   God open a door for our testimony
…And pray for us, too, that God may open a door for our message, so that we may proclaim the mystery of Christ, for which I am in chains. Pray that I may proclaim it clearly, as I should. - Colossians 4:2–4

- That God make your love increase and overflow for each other

May the Lord make your love increase and overflow for each other and for everyone else, just as ours does for you. May He strengthen your hearts so that you will be blameless and holy in the presence of our God and Father when our Lord Jesus comes with all His holy ones. - 1 Thessalonians 3:11–13

- That God make your whole spirit, soul, and body blameless

May God Himself, the God of peace, sanctify you through and through. May your whole spirit, soul and body be kept blameless at the coming of our Lord Jesus Christ. The one who calls you is faithful and He will do it. - 1 Thessalonians 5:23–24

- That Jesus may be glorified in you

We pray this so that the name of our Lord Jesus may be glorified in you, and you in him, according to the grace of our God and the Lord Jesus Christ. -
2 Thessalonians 1:12

- That God encourage your heart and strengthens you in every good deed and word

May our Lord Jesus Christ Himself and God our Father, who loved us and by His grace gave us eternal encouragement and good hope, encourage your hearts and strengthen you in every good deed and word. - 2 Thessalonians 2:16–17

- Deliverance from evil people and spirits

And pray that we may be delivered from wicked and evil men, for not everyone has faith. But the Lord is faithful, and He will strengthen and protect you from the evil one. - 2
Thessalonians 3:2–3

- Prayer for those in authority so we may live peaceful lives

I urge, then, first of all, that requests, prayers, intercession and thanksgiving be made for all people—for kings and all those in authority, that we may live peaceful and quiet lives in all godliness and holiness. - 1 Timothy 2:1-2

As we read through this list, it may not be apparent, but Paul wrote every one of these prayers to believers. He does not ask for Spiritual wisdom, glorification, sanctification, hope, unity, encouragement, or deliverance for unbelievers. Instead, he is asking for such things for believers in an unbelieving world. It is to help them relate to worldly people and treat others with love and respect. He wants them to have wisdom and discernment. He also wants them to understand the promptings of the Holy Spirit.

How Do We Help Unbelievers?

We see Paul's prayer request for believers, but how should we pray for unbelievers? They have concerns about their health, job, family, friends, peace, love, etc. However, they are not promised any help from the Holy Spirit. The Holy Spirit only helps people once He enters them. The only thing He does in the meantime is to try to convince others of their need. Therefore, what is the best way to pray for them?

Can we simply pray to God that they become convicted by the Holy Spirit, and it will happen? It is not that simple. Unbelievers must reach a point in their life where they feel they are no longer in control, or they have a need that cannot be fulfilled on their own. They cannot be stubborn and obstinate. They must be willing to open their heart to the possibilities of the existence of a loving God.

In Romans 1, Paul wrote:

For since the creation of the world God's invisible qualities—his eternal power and divine nature—have been clearly seen, being understood from what has been made, so that people are without excuse. - Romans 1:20

People may not believe in the God of the Bible, but scripture tells us that there is enough evidence to convince anyone and everyone that the earth and universe did not materialize on its own. If a person doesn't believe in at least a powerful Deity, they are truly lost, and there is not much we can do for them. We can pray for them and be friendly towards them, but I cannot think of any Bible verse that indicates God will try to influence a person who does not have any confidence in His existence.

A person must have at least a small amount of faith before the Spirit can begin to convict them. Therefore, if they indicate even a small amount of faith, we should pray that God helps them see their need for Him. We can pray that they begin to relinquish their will. I must admit that some people are a long way from salvation, but no one who had even a little amount of faith should be considered "hopeless" or beyond the help of God's Grace. God may help them.

There are two reasons for believing this. Firstly, although we may sometimes believe that God is indifferent, let me assure you he is not. God values everyone. He wants us to come to Him and trust in Him so that everyone will be saved. He assures us of this with scripture, one from the Apostle Peter and one from the Apostle Paul:

The Lord is not slow in keeping his promise, as some understand slowness. Instead he is patient with you, not wanting anyone to perish, but everyone to come to repentance. - 2 Peter 3:9

Secondly, the Holy Spirit is always trying to convict people, to open their hearts so that they will accept God and know of His love and the purpose of His Son Jesus. We read an example of this in Acts 16 where a woman named Lydia had her heart opened by the Holy Spirit.

In the case of Lydia, she already believed in God, but she had not come to the belief that Jesus died for her sins. She was probably like a lot of people in today's world. They believe in God. They may have a Bible lying around. Perhaps they have even read part of it, but they still have doubts about what Jesus accomplished. However, if we pray for someone, then when the time is right, perhaps the person will be convicted by the Holy Spirit, as it was for Lydia.

We never know when or how the Holy Spirit will work. It may take a long time to convict someone. I know of one lady who prayed that the Holy Spirit open the heart of her husband. It took seventeen years of praying, but it eventually happened. He is now the leader of a home Bible study group, so anything is possible.

Because I believe that the unspecified need is just as important or often more essential than the written request, does that mean I ignore what is written? No, but it would be helpful to know whether the need is for a believer or a doubter. Unfortunately, that information is rarely provided. Someone might ask, "So what difference does it make? Don't you believe in helping everyone?" And if I were asked, I would say, "Yes, I do believe in helping everyone, but the reason I want to know is that it affects the specifics of my prayer."

For example, if a person wants prayer for an operation who is a doubter, then praying for them to turn their heart over to God is the most important and immediate need. After all, what good is it for them to pull through an operation, and they eventually die as an unsaved person. If this is the situation, then what good have I done? If I asked God to extend their physical life another 5, 10, or 15 years, yet their spirit is lost for eternity; then, it is not very satisfying.

Let's say we pray for a doubter who has an addiction problem, and God is gracious enough to give them the strength to stop for a while. If the person never turns their heart over to God, then again, we have only asked God to fix a temporary problem. The more critical eternal problem remains unresolved.

Instead, we should look at the long term and lasting view. If a doubter is about to undergo a risky operation, we should pray first that the Holy Spirit convicts them to turn their heart over to God. We want them to know that their greatest need is God, not the operation. If they develop the belief in the atoning work of Jesus, then the Holy Spirit will give them peace and comfort, regardless of their health problem. They will have an assurance that God has accepted them. Regardless of any physical situation, they will have comfort knowing God is with them. They will be forever changed. Not only will the Spirit work on changing their personality, but they will have been baptized into the death of Jesus and raised with a new life. They will be given a new attitude and a new purpose for living.

If a doubter needs a new job, then I find me asking myself, "Why do they need a new job? Were they unproductive in their last job? Do they have a drinking problem?" Maybe the underlying cause of why they need a new job is a more significant issue. If I am asking

God for a miracle, then I want to pray appropriately. I don't want to ask God to find them a good or a better job if they have a destructive addiction. If this were the case, I don't believe God would answer such a request anyway.

I am not trying to be judgmental; I just want to get at the core issue. In any event, if a person doubts whether Jesus died for their sins, I will pray for the Holy Spirit to convict them of their unbelief. When they become a believer, then they too will have a new attitude and purpose. They may not keep the next job very long, but I can take solace knowing that they will have eternal life. And what if they don't become a believer? Then I am still convinced that I have done what is best for them.

If doubters need their marriage reconciled, then I could pray for them to attend counseling, but because they are people of the world, their interest is mostly self-serving. The problem may appear to be uncontrolled spending, abuse, power struggle, lack of consideration, alcohol, drug abuse, or any number of issues. There can be an appearance of many different specific problems, but the real problem is lack of love; not caring to do the right thing for their mate and/or children. Instead of the couple agreeing to compromise, there is often a struggle to gain control. Therefore, if the counselor does not include spiritual healing and establishing a relationship with God, then the sinful, "Adamic" nature, will prevail and reconciliation will only be temporary. The real answer to their problem is to develop a loving attitude; one generated by the Holy Spirit.

As mentioned earlier regarding the internet list of life goals, the things most worldly people desire are self-serving; things to appease themself. Those appetites can only be satisfied to a limited extent through human effort.

Instead, we should want the person to be filled with the fruit of the Spirit. We want them to have new desires, new motivations. We want them to feel inner peace with God. We don't want them to be stressed out by trying to obtain and maintain control of everything.

Therefore, we should pray for them to be convicted by the Holy Spirit and become submissive to His leading. This is the most effective way we can try to help them.

Are We Respectful When We Pray?

Some people believe that praying is a waste of time. God knows what our needs are without us asking, and if He wants to answer our prayers affirmatively, He will, and if He doesn't, then He won't. I think there is an element of truth to this logic; however, God knows it is good for us to specify our request, both mentally and verbally.

We might also wonder, could the reason why God does not answer our prayers is because we do not show enough respect to Him? What is respect, and how do you show it? Are your head and hands pointed up looking towards the heavens? Is your head bowed showing humbleness with hands folded? Should we get on our knees?

Actually, none of these methods indicate respect. True, they show posture, which means something in our society as we observe each other. We look at a person and say, "Yes, I see that the person is humble; they are showing respect to God." But in the Spiritual realm, these things have no value.

To make a point, let's look at Matthew 6, where Jesus warns about how *not* to pray.

> 5 "And when you pray, do not be like the hypocrites, for they love to pray standing in the synagogues and on the street corners to be seen by others. Truly I tell you, they have received their reward in full. 6 But when you pray, go into your room, close the door and pray to your Father, who is unseen. Then your Father, who sees what is done in secret, will reward you. 7 And when you pray, do not keep on babbling like pagans, for they think they will be heard because of their many words. 8 Do not be

So what is the warning? When we pray, we should not make a show to others or think we are making a show to God. God doesn't care whether we are on our knees or back, but He does care about what is in our hearts. Therefore, making a long, flowery request does not impress Him. In fact, it does the opposite. We should not think about our body position or the eloquence of our words. They don't make a difference. Let me say that again! Our physical position or the eloquence of your words does not make a difference. I don't want to imply that it is a bad thing to get on our knees or bow our heads. That is not true either. But I *am* emphasizing that our heart attitude is what God looks at.

For example, let's assume we pray for God to help other believers, but we are not committed to helping them. If this is our attitude, our heart is telling God that our spirit is not in harmony with His. If we do not recognize we are a sinner who needs to be saved, then we are not yet humble. And if we are not humble and recognize our own need, then we will not have true compassion for others. Instead, our prayers will just be bumbling words, without sincerity. Can you imagine what this must sound like to God?

Consider if a friend comes to your house and asks you for help to move his brother. You agree and ask your friend what time to meet him at his brother's house. Your friend responds, "Oh, I'm not going to be there. I have other things I want to do, but I'll tell my brother that you will be there." If we are sincere enough to ask God, then we should have skin in the game also.

The Apostle John tells us in his 1st epistle about insincerity:

The example I provided about not helping someone does not fall in the category of "hate"; nevertheless, it may indicate an attitude of selfishness. It all depends; you may have already had another event planned. The point of my comment is not to make anyone feel guilty. Instead, I am warning about emphasizing posture and the perception of sincerity instead of real, heartfelt sincerity. This is the same problem that the Pharisees had.

We should be able to get along with all other Christians, but in reality, we probably can't because some are "difficult." But if the Spirit leads us, then we should be able to get along with the large majority of them. If we can't, then something is wrong.

Furthermore, our love should go beyond the tolerance of other believers. From the verses of 1John, we should be able to replace the word "hates" with "doesn't care about." If we are indifferent to other believers, then we have essentially the same situation of insincerity. If we claim to be a child of God, yet don't care about fellow brothers and sisters, then we are fooling ourselves. We can't love people and be indifferent to them at the same time. No, either our heart moves us to be helpful to other believers, or it doesn't. We can't claim to be loving and even pray for people yet ignore them on a whim.

It is not our pretend actions that make a difference to God. No, it is what moves our heart, and the real question is, "Where is our heart?" Are we being moved by love and compassion? Do we really care about others? It is our heart that shows our respect to God.

We can repeatedly pray for others, but if it is only in front of others, and if we are not sincere in our hearts, we are not being respectful of God.

In a similar context, let's consider tithing. In Malachi 3, God speaks to the prophet and tells him that his people are robbing him because they don't tithe (give 10%). Does that mean that Gentiles must give 10%? No, the commandment was given to Jews. Jesus tells the religious leaders that they should tithe. Does that mean as Gentiles, we are obligated to give 10%? No, as in Malachi, the commandment was given to Jews only. Besides, tithing is only a number and a general concept. However, if we give 4, 12, or even 16% to our church and we see another believer who desperately needs financial help, not because they wasted money, but because they were laid off unexpectedly, or they had a family emergency, our hearts should tell us that we should help them. We might not be able to help them much, but we should want to help. It is not just our mind that tells us what to do; it should be our heart, for we are judged not by the things we do or don't do, but by how our heart guides us. Our faith should tug at our heartstrings through the influence of the Holy Spirit. We should want to help those in need.

Religious leaders asked Jesus:

> 36 "Teacher, which is the greatest commandment in the Law?"

> 37 Jesus replied: "'Love the Lord your God with all your heart and with all your soul and with all your mind.' 38 This is the first and greatest commandment. 39 And the second is like it: 'Love your neighbor as yourself.' – Matthew 22:36-39

I will admit I don't dwell on these two commandments. However, when someone identifies a legitimate need of someone, the Holy Spirit should be bringing these two desires of God to our minds. If we are not affected, then we should ask ourselves what has happened. "How have I become indifferent to God or others?"

Our country has become greatly polarized over race, religious, and political issues but should we have become so blind and darkened that we ignore the needs of others? If this happens, then truly, the great deceiver has won the battle. We need to fight against the urge to ignore others. We need to continually read our Bibles so that our hearts stay focused on God's grace. He gave us this important book to read; so we can recognize hardness of heart to fight against the evil power of complacency, contentment, and self-aggrandizement.

We spend considerable sums of money on various forms of electronic devices, entertainment, and sporting events. There is nothing wrong with doing so; however, at the same time, believers also need to be mindful of supporting family and helping those who have authentic needs. A failure to do so not only makes us no different than unbelievers; it also causes us to deny God's loving Grace. How can we acknowledge that Jesus gave his life for us without feeling some sense of need to love others through some method? Again, the Holy Spirit should be guiding us in such matters.

Helping others is only one method of showing respect to God. We should also be trying to grow the church. I am not talking specifically about a particular church, but I am talking about spreading the word of God. Even if we don't personally travel abroad, we should be helping missionaries. We should be praying that God opens the eyes of all doubters. We should share our testimony with others. Again, this should be a matter of the heart. We should pray that God opens the door, so we have an opportunity to be his witness(Colossians 4:3). It may not be comfortable if we are not in the habit of doing it; nevertheless, it should be our heart's desire. We don't have to do it well; we should just have the desire and let the Holy Spirit do its work.

It is easy to look back on an a previous conversation and say "Oh I should have been a better witness," or "I should have said this or that." But it doesn't make a difference. The point is that it is a matter of the heart that indicates our love and respect for God.

Paul encourages believers. He says in Philippians:

> 3 I thank my God every time I remember you. 4 In all my prayers for all of you, I always pray with joy 5 because of

your partnership in the gospel from the first day until now, 6 being confident of this, that he who began a good work in you will carry it on to completion until the day of Christ Jesus. – Philippians 1:3-6

Paul is repeatedly praying for the Philippians. He instills confidence in them, telling them how much he appreciates his partnership with him. And he realizes that God will continually work in them so that their faith will grow, and they will continue to profess the love of God through the sacrifice of Jesus. It has been their hearts that were affected. Will they be perfect witnesses? No, but the fact that they continually try to make themselves good witnesses, God will continuously work with them to make them more effective and more powerful as time carries on. And so this is our example. If our heart is dedicated to witnessing to others, God will use us to become more effective. Again, it is not us, but the power of the Holy Spirit in us. It is our respectful heart that pleases God.

Paul said that we are to "be kind to one another, tender-hearted, forgiving each other, just as God in Christ also has forgiven you." (Ephesians 4:32) This is not just a physical act, but it also is an action of the heart. If all we do is put on a facade to put on the appearance of forgiveness, then what have we actually accomplished? Our hearts have not changed; we are not respecting our Creator. No, to truly respect God, our heart must be changed, which is possible only through the power of the Holy Spirit.

16 "I pray that out of his glorious riches he may strengthen you with power through his Spirit in your inner being, 17 so that Christ may dwell in your hearts through faith". - Ephesians 3:16, 17

CHAPTER
26 The Spiritual Life

Several years ago, I had a discussion with friends regarding the event of Adam and Eve in the Garden of Eden. God had promised Adam that if he ate fruit from the Tree of Knowledge, he would die. According to the Bible, Adam ate from the tree, yet he lived to be 930 years old (Genesis 5:5). My question was, "Did God Lie?" It certainly seemed like He did.

One friend said, "No, He didn't lie. Adam did eventually die."

This answer was not very satisfying. "Are you saying that Adam would have lived forever had he not eaten from the tree? It seems like Adam should have died sooner. Given the relationship between God and Adam, i.e., father and son, it seems like God should have been more exacting. Would you tell your son not to jump out of an airplane without a parachute because he would die? Despite your warning, he jumps anyway, and by some miracle, he still lives for another 900 years? That makes no sense."

My question brought a response from one of the other friends.

"There is another way we could look at this interaction between God and Adam. If your teenage son was about to take the car out for the evening and you told him not to drink and drive, or he would die, would this be a lie? In this case, the reason why you told your son what you did was that you wanted him to stay alive. And if he feared what you said might be true, then possibly he would not drink either before or while driving."

He continued, "So perhaps God wasn't lying, but He was just trying to be protective. Maybe the tree contained fruit that was poisonous and deadly if you ate enough of it."

319

This explanation sounded more reasonable, but I was still skeptical. It seems to me that God should have said to Adam instead, "If you eat from the tree of knowledge, then you will likely die."

I never bought into either of the arguments of my friends. In my mind, it seemed like God lied, or at least was not completely truthful. I did not like the idea that God was, perhaps, sneaky.

Several years later, I heard an explanation of the God/Adam conversation by my favorite Bible study teacher, Les Feldick.

His explanation was, "No, God knew what He was saying, and He was not speaking in hyperbole, nor was Adam just lucky that he didn't die. No, he did die, but not physically. Instead, he died spiritually. The explanation was not found in Genesis; instead, it was found in Romans 5:

> Therefore, just as sin entered the world through one man [Adam], and death through sin, and in this way death came to all people, because all sinned— Romans 5:12

What did Paul mean when he said death came to all people because all sinned? Certainly, he was not talking about physical death. No, he was talking about spiritual death, that is, our relationship with God. When Adam sinned, the relationship with God was broken for all people and for all time. We all inherited a sinful nature, and we are all subject to spiritual death.

However, Christ came to give us life, spiritual life; life independent of physical life. He rebuilt our relationship with God.

> 15 For if the many died by the trespass of the one man, how much more did God's grace and the gift that came by the grace of the one man, Jesus Christ, overflow to the many! 16 Nor can the gift of God be compared with the result of one man's sin: The judgment followed one sin and brought condemnation, but the gift followed many

trespasses and brought justification. [17] For if, by the trespass of the one man, death reigned through that one man, how much more will those who receive God's abundant provision of grace and of the gift of righteousness reign in life through the one man, Jesus Christ! - Romans 5:15-17

Therefore, whoever puts their faith in Jesus will have their spiritual life restored. That is, when the Holy Spirit comes to live in us, He both admonishes us of our old lifestyle, and He gives us a new nature and purpose. It is also when He gives us the fruit of the Spirit.

My purpose for relating this conversation with my friends is to show how we all have scotomas. My friends and I had become so fixated on physical life that we couldn't think of the Bible verses in any other realm.

This is often the way life is. We were born with sight, hearing, smelling, tasting, and feeling. These senses make us attuned to the physical world. It is all we know. Consequently, we put great emphasis on the physical aspect. We do not consider the ramifications of spiritual life. How often do we see a young person who tragically dies, and we proclaim, "that person was too young to die." True, it is tragic, and we sometimes experience the event as personal loss. However, the important questions are, "Did the person die spiritually? Are they living eternally with Jesus?"

In the grand scheme of life and the afterlife, our society emphasizes the physical world too much. Mortal life is temporary, but the afterlife is forever. As technology continues to advance, scientists and theorists' generate more discussions about how to extend mortal life. Out of ignorance, they make it sound as if living to 150 or 200 years old would be a panacea.

We believe we can spend time trying to extend physical life while still keeping our mind on spiritual things. We believe this because we consider ourselves multitaskers. After all, "I can walk and chew bubble gum at the same time." Unfortunately, we are not the multitaskers we believe we are. We can do multiple physical activities simultaneously, but that is because it doesn't take any/ much brainpower. But when it comes to actual thinking, we can only focus on one thing at a time. We can only think about physical or spiritual things individually. There needs to be time set aside for both, but we should moderate our time focusing on physical life so that we don't diminish the importance of spiritual life.

My dad believed in the concept of eternal life. After all, he knew the famous verse said by Jesus:

> For God so loved the world that he gave his one and only Son, that whoever believes in him shall not perish but have eternal life. - John 3:16

But I got the impression from him that it was just a concept. I don't know he ever actually believed it. That was a big difference between him and me. I trust all scripture (including that which was written by Paul). He never did. Therefore, he missed out on some of the most encouraging scripture ever written. For example, I don't think he was aware of Paul's letter to the Romans, which includes:

> [38] For I am convinced that neither death nor life, neither angels nor demons, neither the present nor the future, nor any powers, [39] neither height nor depth, nor anything else in all creation, will be able to separate us from the love of God that is in Christ Jesus our Lord. - Romans 8:38, 39

When our prayers for a miracle don't materialize, we get discouraged; maybe we even believe that God doesn't really love us that much. I believe this was my dad's philosophy. "If God really loves us, then he will prove it materially." But the verses just mentioned tell us otherwise. He already proved it; He sacrificed his Son. He loves us even when we may not feel it; it is greater than most people imagine. How unfortunate it is for those who don't believe Paul.

The Natural Body Versus the Spiritual Body

Because my dad never believed Paul, he never understood that there are two important bodies. There is the natural (physical) body and the spiritual (future and eternal) body. Therefore, after my mom passed away, he was uncertain what had happened to her. I don't know if he even believed in spiritual bodies. Oh, how depressing it would be, not knowing if we would ever see or recognize our loved ones again.

My dad is certainly not the only one who ever questioned whether he would have a Spiritual body one day. Many people are unclear about this. What does it mean to have a spiritual body? Does spiritual mean virtual, i.e., just in our mind?

Unfortunately, some people begin asking themselves, "What is so important about Spiritual life? Does it make a difference if we live to be several thousand years old if it is only in the spiritual realm? How fulfilling can life be if we only live spiritually but not physically?"

I remember seeing the movie "Ghost" shortly after its release in 1990. It was about a man and woman in love, and then one day, the husband, portrayed by Patrick Swayze, dies. He still loves his wife, played by Demi Moore. Another man is taking advantage of her, but she doesn't realize it. Patrick Swayze sees the whole scheme unfold because he died, is a ghost, and can see what goes on in the other man's life while not being physically seen. Patrick tries to save his widowed wife but has very little power because he is just a spirit that can't control even the opening or closing of a door. He has virtually no physical power. Could we really enjoy a life like that? No physical person really knows, but I believe it would not be a very fulfilling life. In fact, we might feel very frustrated because we could see tragic events unfolding in front of us, and we couldn't intervene or exert any control. Imagine if we could see how our children were about to make a huge mistake (like drink and drive or take a huge risk) but we couldn't stop them or intervene to warn them. So I wonder how fulfilling it would be to live only as a spirit.

But will we live only as a spiritual body without physical attributes? In 1 Corinthians 15, we don't get a very clear picture. We read from the writing of Paul:

> 35 But someone will ask, "How are the dead raised? With what kind of body will they come?" 36 How foolish! What you sow does not come to life unless it dies. 37 When you sow, you do not plant the body that will be, but just a seed, perhaps of wheat or of something else. 38 But God gives it a body as he has determined, and to each kind of seed he gives its own body. 39 Not all flesh is the same: People have one kind of flesh, animals have another, birds another and fish another. 40 There are also heavenly bodies and there are earthly bodies; but the splendor of the heavenly bodies is one kind, and the splendor of the earthly bodies is another. 41 The sun has one kind of splendor, the moon another and the stars another; and star differs from star in splendor.
>
> 42 So will it be with the resurrection of the dead. The body that is sown is perishable, it is raised imperishable; 43 it is sown in dishonor, it is raised in glory; it is sown in weakness, it is raised in power; 44 it is sown a natural body, it is raised a spiritual body. -1 Corinthians 15:35-44

Ok, we will be raised with power and a spiritual body. It will be different than our physical body; it will be imperishable. But what else does it mean? What will we have the power to do? What does a spiritual body look like? 1 Corinthians isn't very descriptive. But in Philippians, we get a little better glimpse of what our bodies will be like.

All we know is that we will be given a glorious body like Jesus'. After Jesus was raised from the dead, He asked Thomas to put his finger in His wounds. So if His body was nothing but a cloud, then it wouldn't make sense when He asked Thomas to touch His wounds. Likewise, after Jesus' resurrection, He went to a beach and ate fish with the disciples. The fish didn't drop through His body and fall to the ground, but the food stayed inside Him. However, one moment He was in the room with His disciples, and then He would suddenly disappear. We can't explain such phenomena scientifically. All we know is what the Bible tells us. Will we have the same capability? We can't be sure, but scripture implies we will. From the verses in 1 Corinthians 15 and Philippians 3, we are promised a body that will be like Jesus', imperishable, raised in glory, and raised in power. With these wonderful promises, should we be so concerned with our existing physical lives on earth?

When will we get our new body, and where do we go when we first die? Will we be on earth like in the movie Ghost and only get the new body when Christ returns to raise us (1 Thessalonians 4:16)? Like several other verses of scripture, there are many different opinions regarding the correct answer. One well known religious group believe we fall asleep when we die and know nothing until the return of Jesus. Two reasons for their belief is because King Solomon wrote in Ecclesiastes:

If we fall asleep when we die, will we know anything until we awake again?

Their second argument is from the lips of Jesus right before He raised Lazarus from the dead. He compared Lazarus to a sleeping man.

> "Our friend Lazarus has fallen asleep; but I am going there to wake him up." John 11:11

While this is one opinion, I prefer to take my understanding and belief from the words of the Apostle Paul. He wrote in 2 Corinthians 5:

> 8 We are confident, I say, and would prefer to be away from the body and at home with the Lord. - 2 Corinthians 5:8

His writing, which was inspired by the Holy Spirit, implies he expected that being dead in the body was closely associated with being in the presence of Jesus. It may not be simultaneous, but I don't interpret this verse to mean that the two events mentioned would be years apart. If I were to believe as the religious group who teach that we "sleep" until Jesus returns, then the Apostle Paul has been sleeping for 2000 years and still waiting to be with the Lord!

Instead, I interpret the verse to mean that the two events will pretty much coincide and that he would be in heaven with Jesus when he died, not asleep in the grave. Here are some verses from Philippians that provide another example that dying to our natural life provides for the beginning of our Spiritual life:

> 21 For to me, to live is Christ and to die is gain. 22 If I am to go on living in the body, this will mean fruitful labor for me. Yet what shall I choose? I do not know! 23 I am torn between the two: I desire to depart and be with Christ, which is better by far - Philippians 1:21-23

When we die and go to heaven, what will we see? What will life be like? Do we need to be concerned that life will be nothing but a bunch of white clouds or that we will be bored? We read in Revelation 21 of a place far different. The disciple John wrote of a city coming from heaven with a foundation of every kind of precious stone, and the city is pure gold. This image portrays a description that seems more a metaphor than reality. Likewise, we have heard some people say they have had an out of body experience and that heaven is great. These claims sound wonderful, and I want to believe them, but the skepticism in me causes me to not put much faith in their assertions. I am not saying they are not telling the truth; they may very well be honest about their recall. But I just wouldn't bet my future based on their word. Instead, I would rather rely on a memorized Bible verse that I mentioned earlier:

> "What no eye has seen,
>   what no ear has heard,
> and what no human mind has conceived"—
>   the things God has prepared for those who love him—
> 1 Corinthians 2:9

This verse is not specific. We just don't know what our resurrected life will be like, but I trust the promise made in scripture. God sacrificed His Son so that we could have eternal life, and I believe that the next life will be much better than the one we now have. In fact, according to these verses, life will be so good that we can't even imagine or conceive how good it will be! How amazing is that?

Our future rewards are worth contemplating. Relatively speaking, we live on earth for such a short time. The amount of time we spend in heaven will be for a far greater amount of time.

What Should We Be Thinking About?

The Apostle Paul was considered by many in his day as a heretic and insurrectionist; consequently, he was despised, thrown in jail, severely beaten, and executed. If he were alive today, I believe he would still face much opposition, some of which would come from other religions but most from certain Christian denominations. Many people disagree with his gospel message, not that they can prove him wrong, but because he is opposed to being saved by obeying God's laws. His doctrine of God's Grace just doesn't fit into their concept of religion.

However, if he were alive in today's technological world, he would probably post most of his comments on Twitter. He would have his followers and opponents, but his tweets would contain the same words as his letters. He would be arguing with those who claim we are saved by obeying God's laws. He would still be claiming we are saved by God's Grace through the atoning work of His Son. His followers would read:

> 2 *By my gospel you are saved...* For what I received I passed on to you as of first importance: that Christ died for our sins according to the Scriptures, that he was buried, that he was raised on the third day according to the Scriptures – I Corinthians 15:2-3

Despite his great opposition, he would be encouraging his followers to focus on what Christ has done and where the future lies. Do not be concerned about this life but instead be focused on the next life:

> 16 Therefore we do not lose heart. Though outwardly we are wasting away, yet inwardly we are being renewed day by day. 17 For our light and momentary troubles are achieving for us an eternal glory that far outweighs them all. 18 So we fix our eyes not on what is seen, but on what

is unseen, since what is seen is temporary, but what is unseen is eternal. - 2 Corinthians 4:16-18

He would make repeated tweets that would minimize the importance of the natural world and continually iterate where the hope of all believers lies:

If only for this life we have hope in Christ, we are of all people most to be pitied. [20] But Christ has indeed been raised from the dead, the first fruits of those who have fallen asleep. - 1 Corinthians 15;19-20

He would not state how he had been blessed in the physical world because his life would still be difficult as a Christian. Instead, he would tweet how the Holy Spirit has blessed all believers.

… the fruit of the Spirit is love, joy, peace, forbearance, kindness, goodness, faithfulness, gentleness and self-control. - Galatians 5:22-23

He would realize how all people tend to rely on human wisdom, therefore, he would regularly be praying that the Holy Spirit give his followers the wisdom of God:

…We continually ask God to fill you with the knowledge of his will through all the wisdom and understanding that the Spirit gives - Colossians 1:9

Not only would he be praying for believers, but he would also remind them to listen to the Spirit.

So I say, walk by the Spirit, and you will not gratify the desires of the flesh. - Galatians 5:16

For those who struggle with worldly temptations, he would encourage them and remind them of their need to renew their mind:

Do not conform to the pattern of this world, but be transformed by the renewing of your mind. Then you will be able to test and approve what God's will is—his good, pleasing and perfect will. - Romans 12:2

In conjunction with renewing our mind, he would also repeatedly emphasize the importance of keeping our mind on the Spiritual world by tweeting:

[1] Since, then, you have been raised with Christ, set your hearts on things above, where Christ is, seated at the right hand of God. [2] Set your minds on things above, not on earthly things. - Colossians 3:1-2

For those who are weak and sick, he would put the spotlight on how one day all believers will have an eternal, pain-free body like Jesus' after His resurrection.

[44] ...If there is a natural body, there is also a spiritual body. [45] So it is written: "The first man Adam became a living being"; the last Adam, a life-giving spirit. [49] And just as we have borne the image of the earthly man, so shall we bear the image of the heavenly man. - 1 Corinthians 15:44,45,49

For the believers who were testifying their faith in God but unsuccessfully convincing others of God's Grace, Paul would remind them why so many people don't believe. He would be tweeting:

The god of this age has blinded the minds of unbelievers, so that they cannot see the light of the gospel that displays the glory of Christ, who is the image of God. - 2 Corinthians 4:4

And when the unbelievers scoffed at and mistreated true believers, he would tweet the same explanation he gave in 1 Corinthians 2:

The person without the Spirit does not accept the things that come from the Spirit of God but considers them foolishness, and cannot understand them because they are discerned only through the Spirit. - 1 Corinthians 2:14

There are many people in the world, like my dad, who are not sure where to put their faith. What should they believe? Should they only believe in the words of Jesus? If they do, they will miss out on the gospel of Paul and the many other mysteries and encouraging words revealed by him.

It is a tragedy for those who have never come to know about a saving grace. I know in my dad's case, he had great uncertainty and much consternation about his future. I couldn't give him an experiential reason for hope because, obviously, I have not died. I do rely on Bible verses for my inspiration, but he would not read the verses I showed him.

Even though no one really knows what heaven is really like, I believe the Bible verse of 1 Corinthians 2:9, which tells us that we can't even imagine how great heaven will be. This is a tremendous promise, and based on this verse, the best is yet to come!

I pray that when the Holy Spirit comes knocking on the hearts of unbelievers, they open their heart and let him in so that they too can experience new life.

My greatest hope is that someone else will read this book and understand the love with which it was written.

www.ingramcontent.com/pod-product-compliance
Lightning Source LLC
Chambersburg PA
CBHW051545030726
47592CB00001B/143